PROPHECY
AND
PREDICTION

DEWEY M. BEEGLE

Professor of Old Testament
Wesley Theological Seminary

PRYOR PETTENGILL, PUBLISHER
Ann Arbor, Michigan

Library of Congress Catalog Card Number: 78-65891

Grateful acknowledgment is made to the following publishers for permission to quote from copyrighted material:

Basil Blackwell Publisher
 J. Lindblom, *Prophecy in Ancient Israel,* 1962.
Wm. B. Eerdmans Publishing Co.
 F. F. Bruce, *Biblical Exegesis in the Qumran Texts*, 1959.
 Vernard Eller, *The Most Revealing Book in the Bible,* 1974.
 Paul K. Jewett, *The Lord's Day*, 1971.
 Edward J. Young, *The Prophecy of Daniel,* 1949.
Fortress Press
 Paul D. Hanson, *The Dawn of Apocalyptic,* Copyright © 1975 reprinted by permission of Fortress Press.
Harper & Row, Publishers
 J. Gresham Machen, *The Virgin Birth of Christ,* 1930.
 J. Barton Payne, *Encyclopedia of Biblical Prophecy,* 1973.
The Lockman Foundation
 Scripture quotations are from the *New American Standard Bible,* © The Lockman Foundation 1960, 1962, 1963, 1968, 1971, 1972, 1973, 1975.
The Ministry
 Gerhard F. Hasel, "The Seventy Weeks of Daniel 9:24-27," May, 1976.
 T. H. Blincoe *et al.,* "Are There Prophets in the Modern Church?" July, 1977.
National Council of Churches, Division of Christian Education
 The Bible text in this publication is from the Revised Standard Version of the Bible, copyrighted 1946, 1952, © 1971, 1973 by the Division of Christian Education of the National Council of Churches of Christ in the U.S.A., and used by permission.
Oxford University Press
 The Scofield Reference Bible, 1917.
 The New Scofield Reference Bible, 1967.
Presbyterian & Reformed Publishing Co.
 Oswald T. Allis, *Prophecy and the Church,* 1945.
Review and Herald Publishing Association
 Francis D. Nichol, *The Midnight Cry,* 1944. Used by permission.
 H. M. S. Richards, *One World,* 1972. Used by permission.
Vision House Publishers
 There's a New World Coming, by Hal Lindsey, 1973, Vision House Publishers, Santa Ana, California.
Zondervan Corporation
 From *The Late Great Planet Earth* by Hal Lindsey and C. C. Carlson, Copyright © 1970 by Zondervan Publishing House.
 From *Satan Is Alive and Well on Planet Earth* by Hal Lindsey and C. C. Carlson, Copyright © 1973 by the Zondervan Corporation.

In Memory of

Ethel and Edwin Butterworth
who loved me as their own

Table of Contents

Introduction

All Christian groups claim to have the truth and those who are committed express their understanding of that truth by word and action. Obviously, some of these views cannot be true because they contradict other interpretations which can be verified. In such cases sincerity is no assurance of truthfulness.

Either in their formation or development, all Christian systems of doctrine make some claims that cannot stand the test of close examination. *The perennial problem is how to help these traditions become more truthful without undercutting the basic truth of the system.*

After the return from the exile in Babylonia, some of the Jews realized that the written law of Moses did not always apply directly to their own life situations. Therefore, they began to formulate guidelines and rules for living by Moses' law. These interpretations were passed on orally with a few new guidelines being added by each generation.

The Pharisees were the inheritors of this tradition and in order to gain authority for their interpretations they claimed that the guidelines had been given orally to Moses on Mt. Sinai. In other words, the oral law was considered just as binding as the written law.

Jesus was reared in this theological climate, but he felt that some of those teachings were too concerned with externals and not enough in line with the inner motivation and purpose of the law of Moses. What was he to do about this situation? Those who held these interpretations were the orthodox majority of Judaism, and in most instances they were good, sincere people. Would it be worth the risk to try changing their views?

Apparently he decided that the only genuine way of handling the problem was to speak his convictions with love. In warning his followers of the shortcomings of the system taught by the Pharisees, he prefaced examples of their teachings with the statement, "You have heard that it was said to the men of old." Then after the quotation of the oral law he confronted the disciples with the claim, "But I say to you" (Matt. 5:21-22).

Jesus also spoke candidly to the Jewish leaders with the hope that his challenge would result in some revision of teaching and revitalization of life, but they considered him an intolerable threat.

With respect to the struggle of truth with error, Jesus' experience was essentially the same as that of the prophets before him, and he predicted that his followers would be in similar situations (Matt. 10:24-25). And so it has been down through the centuries.

One of the most confusing and debatable areas of Christian teaching has been that of prophecy and prediction. In spite of the claims by various groups, the issues are not clear-cut, even in the Old and New Testaments, let alone when trying to project into the future.

This book is an attempt to meet the need for a thorough discussion of the issues. The aim is to understand what the Bible teaches about prophecy, especially concerning the prediction of events which already have occurred and those which are to come at the end of the age.

On the one hand, the task is very difficult because traditional views about prophecy are often charged with emotion. Constructive criticism is taken as a threat instead of being accepted as an aid to a more accurate comprehension of what Scripture teaches and what to expect. This risk must be taken, however, inasmuch as there seems to be no other road to truth than open, honest discussion of the issues.

On the other hand, there are many Christians who are uneasy about the prophetic systems taught them and they are searching for better alternatives.

Prophecy and Prediction is intended for individual and group study. It is self-contained in that enough Scripture is quoted to present matters clearly, but Bibles will be helpful for more extended study. The *Revised Standard Version* (RSV) has been quoted throughout the book.

January, 1978   Dewey M. Beegle
Washington, D.C.

Chapter 1
"Jesus Is Coming Soon!"

Almost every day of the year the message comes through loud and clear, "Jesus is coming soon!" Articles in religious papers and magazines make the claim as do numerous preachers and evangelists in churches or over radio and TV. The "signs" referred to in Scripture are coming to pass, so they declare; therefore the time of Christ's second coming is near.

"The Lord Is at Hand"

This same air of expectancy runs through the New Testament. Jesus is remembered as saying, "Truly, I say to you, this generation will not pass away till all these things take place" (Matt. 24:34). In another context Jesus says, "Truly, I say to you, there are some standing here who will not taste death before they see the kingdom of God come with power" (Mk. 9:1).

In his earliest letter, the apostle Paul assures the young Christians at Thessalonica that they need not worry about their loved ones who have died. When Christ comes again the dead will be raised first and then "we who are alive . . . shall be caught up together with them in the clouds to meet the Lord in the air" (1 Thess. 4:17). It is implicit that Paul thinks he will still be alive when Jesus returns.

Paul advises the unmarried at Corinth to stay single because of "the impending distress" (1 Cor. 7:26) and notes that "the appointed time has grown very short" (7:29)—"the form of this world is passing away" (7:31). Although while in prison in Rome he hints to the church at Philippi that he may be with Christ before the Lord's return (1:23), yet he encourages them with the assurance, "The Lord is at hand" (4:5).

James commands his readers, "Establish your hearts, for the coming of the Lord is at hand" (James 5:8), and John on Patmos has a revelation of "what must soon take place" (Rev. 1:1).

Only the Father Knows

Running parallel with this note of expectancy is one of caution. Jesus warns his hearers that many false teachers will appear claiming to be Christ and will lead people astray (Matt. 24:5). Moreover, even though the signs of his return will be as clear as new leaves on a fig tree, caution is still required because "of that day and hour no one knows, not even the angels of heaven, nor the Son, but the Father only" (24:36). Inasmuch as "the Lord will come like a thief in the night" (24:43; 1 Thess. 5:2), the only way to balance this tension between the present and the future is to be watchful—"the Son of man is coming at an hour you do not expect" (24:44).

How Soon Is "Soon"?

In 2 Pet. 3:2-4 the readers are encouraged to "remember the predictions of the holy prophets and the commandment of the Lord" because "scoffers will come in the last days . . . saying, 'Where is the promise of his coming?' " The delay is not to be taken as a failure of promise. Rather, as Ps. 90:4 indicates, God's measure of time is different: "one day is as a thousand years, and a thousand years as one day" (3:8). The reason for this delay is that he is patiently waiting "that all should reach repentance" (3:9).

But how soon is "soon"? To explain the delay from God's point of view is not very encouraging when his creatures live only 70-80 years. The ancients realized, as we do, that "hope deferred makes the heart sick" (Prov. 13:12), and so they began to stretch out their expectation by dropping the word "soon." While patiently waiting for the Lord's return they had the assurance of his presence because the Holy Spirit filled their lives and gave them power to carry out Christ's commission to "make disciples of all nations" (Matt. 28:19).

The Church and the Millennium

In general, the church leaders of the 2nd and 3rd centuries A.D. expected Christ to return and set up his reign on earth for 1,000 years, that is, a millennium (Rev. 20:4). With the recognition of Christianity by Constantine (A.D. 288-337) the church entered a period of peace and growth, and so Augustine (A.D. 354-430), Bishop of Hippo in North Africa, interpreted the millennium spiritually. He felt that it began with Jesus' ministry and would close with his second coming. This view started a long period in which there was little expectation of the Lord's return. But as A.D. 1,000 drew near there was great dread and anticipation.

Christ didn't return, however, and so the pangs of frustration and embarrassment resulted in other systems to make possible the postponement of hope. Some considered Constantine's conversion in 312 as the beginning of the millennium, and so 1312 became a new deadline. Again the time came and went; therefore more adjustments had to be made. The 16th-century Reformers equated "the papacy," the hierarchy of the Roman Catholic Church, with Satan. Accordingly, they reasoned that they were living in the period after the millennium when the Devil was released from prison and allowed to carry on his destructive work for a while (Rev. 20:7-8). Others started the millennium in A.D. 800 with the reign of Charlemagne, thus setting up another date for which to prepare.

The Secret Rapture

After this long period of relating the church to the millennium, the pendulum swung back to the old premillennial view that Christ would return before the millennium. The chaos and uncertainty in the aftermath of the Napoleonic Wars resulted in mounting expectation of the Lord's return, both in Great Britain and the United States. A new point of view claimed that the next event on God's agenda was Christ's secret return to take out (rapture) his saints from the earth. Since this secret rapture could occur at any moment there was great concern to be ready.

Hope may spring eternal, but it weakens with a series of disappointments. The prophetic movement waned even further at the end of the 19th century because of internal divisions and loss of credibility among the churches. Aided by two world wars, the movement revived in the 20th century and reached a new peak in the last decade. The chief reasons for this surge were widespread pessimism about the future of the world and renewed confidence that the signs of the Lord's return were evident.

What Is the Answer to the Prophecy Puzzle?

How are we to understand the 1900 years of hopes, frustrations, and revised expectations? What part does prediction play in genuine prophecy? What are we to make of the various points of view clashing with each other and each claiming to have the answer to the prophecy puzzle? These are serious issues and millions of concerned people, in

and out of the church, are looking for some help. But before we can
hope to sort out the issues in this difficult subject we must get
acquainted with the various aspects of prophecy in the Bible.

Chapter 2
Early Prophets of Israel

Our English word "prophet" comes from a Greek word meaning literally "one who speaks for another." This concept is illustrated by Exod. 7:1, one of the earliest uses of the term "prophet" (Hebrew *nabiᵓ*, pronounced *navi*). Moses, as a stammerer, was very reluctant to accept God's call as messenger to the Egyptian king (Exod. 4:10-13). Therefore Yahweh (the personal name for Israel's God) said to him, "See, I make you as God to Pharaoh; and Aaron your brother shall be your prophet." Moses' loquacious brother Aaron would be his mouthpiece while he, functioning as God, would declare the message. In short, Aaron would speak for Moses.

Most scholars think Hebrew *nabiᵓ* stems from an old Semitic root *nabu* "to call, announce." They differ, however, in their interpretation. Some understand the word in the active sense, "an announcer, one who calls out," while others see it as passive, "one who is called." There are biblical passages which indicate that *nabiᵓ* was understood both ways.

The meaning "announcer" is evident in Exod. 7:1 and the idea of "a called one" is clear in Exod. 3:6, 10: "I am the God of your father, the God of Abraham, the God of Isaac, and the God of Jacob. . . . Come, I will send you to Pharaoh that you may bring forth my people, the sons of Israel, out of Egypt." A third aspect is that of "being sent." Moses, the "called one," was "sent" with authority "to announce," through Aaron, God's message to Pharaoh. These three basic features of the prophetic role are summed up in the designation "the messenger of God."

Samuel the Prophet

While Moses, as "a called messenger," exhibited the essential aspects of a prophet, he was a special case, a man "ahead of his times." However, he did not share in some of the characteristics which later prophets exhibit; therefore, it is necessary to move on to the time of Samuel to get a clearer picture of the background from which the classical prophets came.

Samuel began as a leader during the Philistine crisis. The ark had been captured and Shiloh, the religious center of the old tribal league, destroyed. Israel was in despair. In this crucial period Samuel, like Moses, had to wear a number of hats. He functioned as an itinerant priest with a number of sanctuaries on his circuit. During a confrontation between the Israelites and the Philistines at Mizpah, Samuel offered sacrifices and prayed for deliverance. Yahweh answered with a terrific storm which helped the Israelites rout their enemies (1 Sam. 7:7-11). Disputes had to be settled and so he served as a traveling judge as well (7:15-17).

Prophetic Ecstasy

In addition to these other functions, apparently Samuel was the leader of a group of prophets (1 Sam. 19:20). When he anointed Saul as "prince" over Israel, he gave him various "signs" which were to convince him that Yahweh had truly chosen him. One was to occur at "the hill of God," a religious sanctuary near a Philistine fort:

> And there . . . you will meet a band of prophets coming down from the high place with harp, tambourine, flute, and lyre before them, prophesying. Then the spirit of the LORD will come mightily upon you, and you shall prophesy with them and be turned into another man (1 Sam. 10:5-6).

Here "prophesying" has the idea of dancing in a state of ecstasy. Our English word "ecstasy" comes from a Greek word meaning "to stand out, be beside oneself." It is evident that this enthusiastic band of prophets was committed to the old idea of "holy war." Their playing and oracles were intended to stir up the people in the area so that they would drive the Philistines out of the fort nearby.

Samuel's prediction came to pass and while Saul was listening to the captivating music of these prophets he was seized by a powerful emotion which overcame his self-control. He "turned into another man" and danced with frenzy. In a later encounter with Samuel and the band of the prophets, Saul even stripped off his clothes while doing his ecstatic dance. Then exhausted, he "lay naked all that day and all that night" (1 Sam. 19:24).

There is biblical evidence to show that such roving groups of prophets maintained themselves by gifts from persons requesting oracles of them. While there is no indication of what pronouncements Saul made while prophesying, he must have been given some because he was under the control of "the spirit of the LORD." Apparently Saul's startling actions became the focus of the stories rather than the content of his oracles.

Samuel the Seer

Another interesting facet of the talented man Samuel was his ability as a "seer" (Hebrew *ro²eh*). When Saul was ready to give up trying to find his father's lost asses, his servant suggested consulting Samuel, "the man of God," who happened to be in a nearby town that day. "He is a man that is held in honor," the servant remarked, "all that he says comes true" (1 Sam. 9:6).

Samuel was at the town gate because he had received a message from Yahweh that Saul was coming that way. Moreover, although some distance away, he could "see" that the asses had been found and were being taken care of. When Saul approached him he asked, "Where is the house of the seer?" Samuel answered, "I am the seer," and then he set Saul's mind at rest: "As for your asses that were lost three days ago, . . . they have been found" (9:18-20).

Types of Divination

People from earliest times have been concerned about the future, especially in making major national or individual decisions. Knowledge of future events was a tremendous advantage in coping with enemies or other problems of life, and so the supernatural wisdom of the gods and departed spirits was sought by various means. The omens or signs of natural phenomena were studied for clues. Observation of the stars (astrology) became a profession.

Another highly specialized form of divination was minute examination of livers (hepatoscopy) from sacrificial animals. The ancients learned that life was in the blood, and since the liver was considered to be the source of the blood, it was only natural to draw the conclusion that the secrets of life were to be found in the liver. In Mesopotamia, where this practice flourished, a whole class of *baru* priests was trained. The verb *baru* means "to see," and so this group of prophet-priests functioned as seers. No army ever went on a campaign without its chaplain priest. At points where routes forked, for example, the priest sacrificed a sheep and inspected the liver to determine which route to take. If the priest made a mistake or two and the army ran into difficulties, he was likely to be replaced by another priest.

Balaam the Seer

An excellent description of a Mesopotamian seer is found in the biblical story of Balaam. Balak, king of Moab, hired the famous prophet-seer to put a curse on the Israelites. Balaam requested seven altars and animal sacrifices were made on them, but instead of checking them for omens Balaam was seized by "the spirit of God." As a result he pronounced a blessing instead. As an introduction to his oracle the seer describes his experience:

> The oracle of Balaam, the son of Beor,
> the oracle of the man whose eye is opened,
> the oracle of him who hears the words of God,
> who sees the vision of the Almighty,
> falling down, but having his eyes uncovered (Num. 24:3-4).

Although prostrate under the power of God, he hears the words of God and his inner eye comprehends the message.

In *Prophecy in Ancient Israel*, J. Lindblom (p. 94) gives an excellent survey contrasting and comparing the roles of the seer and prophet:

> From a psychological and religio-historical point of view the "seer" can appropriately be described in the following way: Seer is a man or a woman who claims to possess the faculty of knowing things that are concealed from ordinary men. The chief methods used by the seer are dreams, extraordinary perspicacity, clairvoyance, communications from ghosts and spirits, and, finally, external signs and omens. Sometimes the seers also obtain their extraordinary knowledge in a psychic state or trance. Characteristic of the prophets are ecstasies of various kinds, based on a direct contact with the divine world or the divine power ("the spirit of God"), a supernormal state of mind in which divine revelations are communicated in the form of visions and auditions. Being overwhelmed by God the prophet feels himself compelled to proclaim publicly what he has seen or heard. Nevertheless the prophet may occasionally use the methods and do the work of a seer.
> Briefly, one could also say that a seer's general function was, by using different methods, to see things of various kinds on this earth hidden from common men; the main function of a prophet was filled with or

touched by the divinity, to receive revelations from the other world and utter them as oracles to men. The dividing-line between a seer and a prophet can not be drawn sharply. Both could on occasion execute the same functions.

Other Types of Divination

Knowledge of divine wisdom involved the objects and spirits of humans as well: shooting or shaking arrows (belomancy), casting lots (Urim and Thummim in the Bible), consultation of teraphim (idols, household gods), or conversation with the spirits of the dead (necromancy). There is a very interesting biblical passage which pictures the king of Babylon and his army "at the parting of the way, at the head of two ways." To make triply sure that he makes the right decision "he shakes the arrows, he consults the teraphim, he looks at the liver" (Ezek. 21:21). All omens point to Jerusalem. With this graphic description Ezekiel predicts the destruction of the unholy city, the city from which "the glory of the God of Israel had gone up" (Ezek. 9:3). But Ezekiel got his "inside information" by prophetic inspiration from Yahweh, not from the means used by pagan prophets and priests.

Divination and the Word of Yahweh

As we have noted prophetic types of persons were not unique in Israel. Almost every culture in the ancient Near East had some individuals predisposed to having dreams, visions, and audible messages about the future. Many of these claimed to have been called by some deity and in some instances they were given their message directly.

Israel's history was a story of the running battles between two groups with some similar practices and claims. Accordingly, it became necessary to spell out some restrictions: "There shall not be found among you . . . any one who practices divination, a soothsayer, or an augur, or a sorcerer, or a charmer, or a medium, or a wizard, or a necromancer" (Deut. 18:10-11). This is an amazing catalogue of technical terms, both in Hebrew and in English. Most likely each term originally indicated the precise means of divination. Perhaps one method was known by various designations in different periods of history and in different parts of the Near East. In any case, a number of these terms became synonymous.

Saul knew of regulations against divination, but he could get no answer from Yahweh either by dreams, or Urim and Thummim (the sacred dice of the high priest used for casting lots), or by prophets (1 Sam. 28:6). In desperation he disguised himself, went to the medium at Endor, and requested that she bring Samuel up for him (28:8-11). When the medium saw an old man, wrapped in a robe, coming up out of the earth, Saul bowed to the ground. In spite of this act of respect, Samuel wanted to know why he had been disturbed. Saul explained that he was in great distress because of the Philistines and his failure to get any word from God. Then the old prophet informed him, "The LORD has done to you as he spoke by me; for the LORD has torn the kingdom out of your hand, and given it to your neighbor, David" (28:17). While alive, Samuel had given Saul the word of Yahweh, and in death the answer was the same.

In the earlier story about Saul going to Samuel the "seer," a biblical editor inserted an explanation for later readers who did not understand the technical term: "Formerly in Israel, when a man went to inquire of God, he said, 'Come, let us go to the seer'; for he who is now called a prophet was formerly called a seer" (1 Sam. 9:9). The term *nabi* "prophet" took over the meaning of *ro'eh* "seer."

As noted earlier, although some Israelite terms and means of obtaining divine information appeared to be similar to pagan practices, there was a vast difference. Yahweh, the God of Israel, was the only God and only he knew and determined the future. Samuel, as "the man of God," was tuned in to the true source. When just a boy he guarded the ark in the tabernacle at Shiloh. Yahweh called to him and gave him a message for Eli the old priest (1 Sam. 3:10-14). Later on, Yahweh authorized him to anoint Saul as "prince" over Israel (9:16). Samuel's authority as God's prophet was exercised again when he informed Saul that the kingdom had been taken from him (13:13-14).

Court Prophets

After Samuel and his group, the next prophets noted are those associated with David and his rise to power. He received advice from "the prophet Gad" (1 Sam. 22:5) about eluding Saul. After David's census of Israel "the prophet Gad, David's seer" came to him with "the word of the LORD" (2 Sam. 24:11). Here the Hebrew word for "seer" is *hozeh*, not Samuel's title *ro'eh*, but the way these terms are used in the Bible suggests that they are practically synonymous. Both indicate that the persons designated were given insights into the meaning of the historical situations and then authorized, as prophets, to speak the word of warning, judgment, encouragement, etc.

The prophet Nathan, who is consistently called *nabi'*, appears three times. In 2 Sam. 7 David consults him about building a temple. Nathan favors the idea, but that night "the word of the LORD" comes to him in a "vision" rejecting David's proposal. Instead, Yahweh promises David that his house (dynasty) and kingdom will be established forever.

But when David sins by committing adultery with Bathsheba and having her husband killed, Yahweh sends Nathan to trap David with the parable of the ewe lamb (2 Sam. 12). David is indignant and declares that the rich man who took the poor man's lamb ought to die. Then Nathan points his finger at David with accusation, "You are the man."

In the power struggle to determine David's successor, Nathan plays a leading role supporting Bathsheba's claim that David had promised the kingship to her son Solomon (1 Kgs. 1). Then he assists the priest Zadok in anointing Solomon (1:45). These references indicate that Nathan played a number of roles. In addition to being Yahweh's spokesman he played a part in the affairs of the royal chapel and he functioned as a court official. The key point throughout the narrative, however, is that Gad and Nathan were Yahweh's agents to help David live in accordance with the law of Moses and rule with justice.

Ahijah and Shemaiah

The tradition of prophetic activity in politics was carried on by Ahijah, the prophet from Shiloh, and Shemaiah, "the man of God" in Judah. Ahijah was favorable to the old tribal confederation which was centered at Shiloh during Eli's priestly rule; therefore he supported Jeroboam, who had rebelled against Solomon. One day he met Jeroboam in an open field and used a visual aid as a sign of Yahweh's decision to tear most of the kingdom from Rehoboam, Solomon's son. Ahijah tore a new garment into twelve pieces and instructed Jeroboam to take ten (1 Kgs. 11:29-31).

When Israel, the northern tribes, rejected Rehoboam and made Jeroboam king, Rehoboam was ready to fight them. But Shemaiah received "the word of God. . . . You shall not go up or fight against your kinsmen the people of Israel" (1 Kgs. 12:22-24). Jeroboam did not measure up to the conditions of the Mosaic covenant, and so Ahijah turned against him, as Samuel had against Saul, by predicting that God would destroy his family and turn the kingdom over to another (1 Kgs. 14:7-11).

Elijah

About 200 years after Samuel, three more ecstatic prophets appeared on the scene to speak for Yahweh and bring judgment on the debauched conditions in Israel. Elijah, the rustic prophet from Gilead east of the Jordan River, was a zealot for God and he vigorously opposed King Ahab and his Phoenician wife Jezebel. The latter, a zealous worshiper of the Canaanite god Baal, removed the prophets of Yahweh from the royal court of the northern kingdom and replaced them with hundreds of Canaanite prophets (1 Kgs. 18:4, 19).

Elijah's first act was a message to Ahab, predicting that a long drought would occur. This was to let the king know that Yahweh, not Baal, was the one who governed rain and fertility. The famine extended even into Phoenicia, Baal's home turf. To add insult to injury, Elijah went up there and by a series of miracles fed a widow's family and revived her deathly ill son. This victory over Baal was evident to the woman and she confessed, "Now I know that you are a man of God, and that the word of the LORD in your mouth is truth" (1 Kgs. 17:24).

The Contest on Mt. Carmel

Elijah returned to Israel and found Ahab, who accused him of being the "troubler of Israel." He reminded the king that he was the troubler because he had "forsaken the commandments of the LORD" (1 Kgs. 18:18); then he challenged him to a showdown on Mt. Carmel to determine who was really the Lord of creation. The ecstatic prophets of Baal worked themselves up into a frenzy as they did their limping dance around the altar. Elijah mocked them by suggesting that Baal was meditating, or had gone to the bathroom, or was on a journey, or had fallen asleep (18:27). They cut themselves and raved on, pleading for Baal to send down fire and to vindicate them. But, as the narrative so aptly sums up the situation, "there was no voice; no one answered, no one heeded."

Then it was Elijah's turn. He rebuilt the old altar which had been torn down, soaked the wood and sacrificial bull with water, and then made a simple prayer that Yahweh would answer by fire in order to convince the people. Fire fell, consuming the whole sacrifice, and the people shouted, "The LORD, he is God" (18:39). The prophets of Baal were seized and killed. The rains came, and as Ahab rode in his chariot toward the palace, "the hand of the LORD," like "the spirit of the LORD" on Saul, took hold of Elijah. With a remarkable burst of ecstatic energy he ran ahead of Ahab to the palace in Jezreel.

Consolation and Commission on Mt. Horeb

When Jezebel learned what had happened to her prophets she sent a message to Elijah vowing to take his life in exchange for one of Baal's prophets (1 Kgs. 19:2). The normally courageous Elijah must have been psychologically exhausted from his Carmel exploits because he melted in fear when he received Jezebel's threat. This time "the fear of Jezebel," not "the hand of the LORD," spurred him on his flight south. His panic drove him until he came to Beer-sheba, way down in Judah. Here, at last, he would be safe from Jezebel.

After resting and being fed, Elijah continued on down to Horeb (Sinai), the mountain where Yahweh had appeared to Moses. In a cave where he was staying Yahweh appeared to him as well. He didn't chide him for running after the great victory on Carmel. He just asked the simple question "What are you doing here, Elijah?" and then he let the defeated prophet tell his mournful tale (1 Kgs. 19:4-10).

A terrific storm took Elijah's mind off of himself, but "a still small voice," like an echo of Yahweh's instructions to Moses, called him back to his task of defending the faith of Moses in Israel (19:11-12). After letting Elijah talk out his feelings once more, Yahweh commissioned him with three jobs: to anoint Elisha as his successor and to anoint two future kings, Hazael of Syria and Jehu of Israel. Then Yahweh assured Elijah that a remnant of 7,000 faithful would not succumb to Baal worship (19:13-18). On his return to Israel, Elijah consecrated Elisha by putting his mantle on him, and in this act he transferred the anointing of the two kings to his successor.

Naboth's Vineyard

Elijah's work was not over, however, because another immoral situation demanded his attention. King Ahab, wanting more garden space, offered to buy the vineyard of Naboth next to the palace in Jezreel (1 Kgs. 21:1-2). Naboth refused because he took seriously the basic Mosaic claim that the land was Yahweh's. Since the vineyard was part of his family inheritance from the time of Joshua, he had no right to sell it (Lev. 25:23). Ahab was frustrated by the refusal, but ruthless Jezebel took immediate action. She had Naboth framed and stoned to death; then she told Ahab to confiscate the property (21:8-16).

Elijah was alerted to the dastardly act and he confronted Ahab in the stolen field. In the name of Yahweh he predicted that the dogs would lick Ahab's blood in the place where they had licked Naboth's and that his family would be obliterated. Cruel Jezebel would be eaten by the dogs of Jezreel (21:17-24).

Elijah and Elisha

In the narratives about Elijah he is pictured as working on his own, but when Elisha comes into the picture there are prophetic groups called "the sons of the prophets," similar to "the band of prophets" associated with Samuel. There are clusters at Bethel (2 Kgs. 2:3), Jericho (2:5), and Gilgal (4:38). Perhaps Elisha was known to these groups because fifty of the prophets from Jericho accompanied Elijah and Elisha to the bank of the Jordan River.

They watched while the great prophet and his successor crossed to the east side of the river for a farewell tryst. Elisha asked "a hard thing" of Elijah, "I pray you, let me inherit a double share of your spirit" (2 Kgs. 2:9). In Israel the heir received a double portion of the share inherited by the rest of the children. The Elijah-Elisha narratives, which were transmitted orally for many years, interpret the request in another way: Elijah performs seven miracles and Elisha fourteen.

After Elisha's request, the two discussed the matter while they walked. Suddenly they were separated and Elijah was taken up into heaven by a fiery chariot. Elisha exclaimed, "My father, my father! the chariots of Israel and its horsemen" (2:11-12). Apparently Elisha meant that his prophetic father had been more powerful than Israel's army.

When Elisha returned over the Jordan the fifty prophets from Jericho said, "The spirit of Elijah rests on Elisha," and they bowed before him in recognition that he was their leader.

Elisha, Hazael, and Jehu

With Elijah's departure, Elisha still had the two unfinished tasks assigned to him. When he came to Damascus, the Syrian capital, King Benhadad heard that he was there. Since the king was sick he sent Hazael, one of his officers, to find out from "the man of God" whether he would recover or not. As was the custom when seeking information from a prophet, Benhadad sent a little present—40 camel loads of good things (2 Kgs. 8:7-9).

Elisha said that the king would recover from the illness, but Yahweh had shown him that Benhadad would die soon. While staring at Hazael in a prophetic trance Elisha began to weep. When asked why he was weeping, the prophet answered, "Because I know the evil that you will do to the people of Israel; you will set on fire their fortresses, and you will slay their young men with the sword, and dash in pieces their little ones, and rip up their women with child" (8:13). Hazael denied such a thing, but Elisha countered, "the LORD has shown me that you are to be king over Syria."

Hazael told Benhadad that he would recover, but before he could do so Hazael strangled the sick king with a sheet soaked in water. Assyrian records list Hazael as "a son of nobody," meaning that he was a usurper with no royal lineage. Elisha wept because of the awful consequences of authorizing this "son of nobody" to be king. Nevertheless, he carried out Yahweh's difficult order in the conviction that it was God's will to punish sinful Israel.

Syria had gained control of Ramoth-gilead, an Israelite city east of the Jordan River; therefore Joram, king of Israel, tried to take it from Hazael's control. After being injured in one of the battles, Joram put Jehu in charge and then returned to Jezreel to recover. Elisha learned of this and sent "one of the sons of the prophets" with a flask of oil to find Jehu. The prophet took Jehu into a private room, poured the oil on his head, and said, "Thus says the LORD, I anoint you king over Israel" (2 Kgs. 9:1-3). After the prophet fled, the servants asked,

"Why did this mad fellow come to you?" Jehu told them and when the news got around, the army proclaimed, "Jehu is king."

Jehu was a zealot and he determined to obliterate all opposition to his reign. He drove his chariot furiously back to Jezreel where he killed Joram and Ahaziah, king of Judah (9:14-27). He had Jezebel thrown out of a palace window, then horses trampled on her. While he celebrated the death of the evil woman, the dogs of the city ate her flesh (9:30-37). Elijah was right again!

Micaiah and the Court Prophets

One of the most instructive glimpses of genuine prophetic activity is the story of Micaiah. It revolves around Ramoth-gilead also, but a few years earlier than the Joram-Hazael battle. This time Jehoshaphat, king of Judah, conferred with Ahab about reclaiming the Israelite city (1 Kgs. 22:1-4). But before venturing on such a crucial campaign Jehoshaphat requested that they inquire of Yahweh whether or not it was the correct action. Ahab brought in about 400 of his court prophets and asked them for their judgment. With Zedekiah, their leader, bulling his way among them with a pair of iron horns, the prophets worked themselves up into an ecstatic frenzy. "Go up to Ramoth-gilead and triumph," they unanimously replied (22:6, 10-12).

Uneasy with such consensus, Jehoshaphat asked whether there wasn't another prophet to question. Ahab acknowledged that Micaiah, the prophet of Yahweh, was still available, but he added, "I hate him, for he never prophesies good concerning me, but evil" (22:8). Nevertheless he had him summoned. The messenger tried to influence Micaiah by reporting the verdict of the prophets. "As the LORD lives," Micaiah retorted, "what the LORD says to me, that I will speak" (22:14).

But Micaiah startled Ahab by mimicking the yes-men, "Go up and triumph." The king knew that he was being mocked and he shot back, "How many times shall I adjure you that you speak to me nothing but the truth in the name of the LORD?" Then Micaiah revealed his vision: "I saw all Israel scattered upon the mountains, as sheep that have no shepherd" (22:15-17). Not to be outdone, Ahab brushed off the warning with a quip to Jehoshaphat, "Did I not tell you that he would not prophesy good concerning me, but evil?"

To authenticate his vision Micaiah reported to the kings one of the most remarkable scenes in the Old Testament. He saw Yahweh seated on his throne in heaven flanked on both sides with his council of spirits. "Who will entice Ahab," he asked, "that he may go up and fall at Ramoth-gilead?" Finally one of the spirits came forward and volunteered, "I will go forth, and will be a lying spirit in the mouth of the prophets" (22:19-22).

In anger Zedekiah struck Micaiah on the cheek and asked, "How did the spirit of the LORD go from me to speak to you?" Ahab ordered Micaiah put in prison on bread and water until he returned in peace. The prophet laid down the challenge, "If you return in peace, the LORD has not spoken by me." As a final word of warning to those present Micaiah shouted, "Hear, all you peoples!" Then he was shunted off to prison never to be heard from again.

Apparently Ahab realized that he would be a marked man by the Syrians, therefore he disguised himself while ordering Jehoshaphat to wear his robes. The bright colors attracted attention until the Syrians determined that he was not the king of Israel. Then with the stroke of a master the narrator comments, "But a certain man drew his bow at a venture, and struck the king of Israel between the scale armor and the breastplate" (22:34). As the blood ran into the bottom of the chariot, life left the wilful king. Micaiah was right after all!

The stories of Elijah and Micaiah indicate clearly that they were the bridge between the early and the classical prophets. Unlike the vigorous bands of roving prophets, the court prophets became self-serving party liners. They incapacitated themselves for receiving the word of Yahweh, and so individual prophets had to be called out to buck the majority and to speak the hard word.

They confronted the crucial theological, economic, and political issues of their day and made known the relevant word of Yahweh. Moreover, they authenticated their messages by the accuracy of their short-range predictions. Although they suffered for their loyalty and courage, a remnant survived to carry on the interpretation of Yahweh's word.

Chapter 3
Later Prophets

Beginning with Amos (about 750 B.C.) the oracles of the prophets were recorded, and so we have a much more accurate coverage of their thoughts, teachings, and concerns. While groups associated with the earlier prophets cherished their memory and orally passed on stories of special significance, they apparently did not put the oracles down in writing.

At one time scholars tended to make a drastic differentiation between the earlier and later (classical) prophets. Amos was supposedly the first one to have a clear understanding of Yahweh as the only God (monotheism), but it has become increasingly evident that the idea of a practical monotheism goes back to Moses. As John Bright correctly observes, "Amos was no innovator, but a man of the ancient ways. His ethical protest was drawn from a well five hundred years deep" (*The Kingdom of God*, p.65). There are differences between the two groups, of course, but it is essentially a matter of degree, not kind.

Because of the mass of material to be covered, it will be more appropriate to survey the later prophets in a topical fashion rather than individually as in the previous chapter. This approach, moreover, will highlight the distinctive features of classical Israelite prophecy while comparing and contrasting the two groups.

Ecstasy

The most basic bond between the early and later prophets was their prophetic temperament. By genes and chromosomes they received the gift so essential for functioning as a spokesman for God. Yahweh's word to Jeremiah makes this clear: "Before I formed you in the womb I knew you, and before you were born I consecrated you; I appointed you a prophet to the nations" (Jer. 1:5). With respect to ecstasy, Lindblom comments in *Prophecy in Ancient Israel* (pp. 216-17):

> It is true that ecstasy was characteristic of both the earlier and the later prophets. But there is a difference. In the former, orgiastic ecstasy

was more prominent. Besides, in the earlier stages of prophecy ecstasy was in some measure an end in itself, being regarded as the climax of all religious experience and moreover, an experience attained by methodical exercises and deliberate training. This was not the case among the classical prophets. For them ecstasy was only a means of receiving revelations from God. In the books of the great prophets we never hear of training in ecstasy or of artificial methods of producing ecstasy. On the whole, ecstasy in the strict sense is less common in the great prophets than what may be called elevated inspiration. The typical visions were no doubt experienced in a state of ecstasy; but most of the prophetic revelations are not visions, but sermons and proclamations uttered in a state of mental exaltation.

The Call

We know more about the life of Jeremiah than any of the other prophets, but even that is meager. Their contemporaries probably knew much more about them than we do, but apparently they were not concerned to talk about the man. He remained in the shadow of his message. Yahweh's call, however, was an extraordinary experience for most of them; therefore the event is mentioned somewhere among the oracles.

Amos reports in rather low-key fashion, "The LORD took me from following the flock, and the LORD said to me, 'Go, prophesy to my people Israel' " (7:15). Although there are no explicit indications of ecstasy, "took" implies that Yahweh's "hand" or "spirit" took control of his life. The force of the call comes out in an oracle earlier in the book, "The Lord GOD has spoken, who can but prophesy?" (3:8).

Isaiah's Call

The call of Isaiah (6:1-11) is a classic example of an ecstatic vision. When Uzziah, the good, trusted king of Judah, became a leper he had to be quarantined in his own residence away from his family and associates (2 Kgs. 15:5). His son Jotham served as coregent in an executive capacity. But he was not a good leader and he never gained the respect and loyalty of the people. As long as Uzziah was alive there was a sense of security. When death came, a gloomy spirit of uneasiness and fear came over the people.

Apparently young Isaiah went up to the temple to pray about the desperate situation. There he "saw the Lord sitting upon a throne, high and lifted up; and his train filled the temple." Scholars differ widely in trying to explain the various features of the vision, but for our purpose it is only necessary to recognize that Isaiah was aware of his surroundings.

Yahweh was thought to be enthroned over the cherubim in the holy of holies. Whether Isaiah was there on the Day of Atonement and watched the high priest enter the inner sanctuary is difficult to determine. Most likely the ecstatic experience expanded the young prophet's context and understanding so that he "saw" with an "inner eye" a scene similar in some ways to that of Micaiah.

In the bright light of God's holiness he exclaimed, "Woe is me! For I am lost; for I am a man of unclean lips and I dwell in the midst of a people of unclean lips." With the touch of a live coal on his lips his guilt and sin were forgiven. Then he was ready to deal with the problem of his people. When the voice of God asked, "Who will go for us?" Isaiah volunteered eagerly, "Here am I! Send me." His joy was diminished by the demanding orders, "Go, and say to this people: 'Hear and hear, but do not understand; see and see, but do not perceive.' " In response to his anguished question "How long, O Lord?" he got the devastating answer, "Until cities lie waste without inhabitant, and houses without men, and the land is utterly desolate." This jolt certainly helped prepare the young prophet for the long, hard road ahead.

Jeremiah's Call

When Jeremiah was informed that Yahweh had appointed him a prophet before his birth he, like Moses, felt that he was not qualified for the task: "I do not know how to speak, for I am only a youth" (1:6). Yahweh told him not to talk that way and then, touching Jeremiah's mouth with his hand, he said, "Behold, I have put my words in your mouth." The ecstasy of Yahweh's touch was to assure the uneasy youth that he would not have to worry about what to say —the message would be given to him. Unlike Isaiah's call, there was no sense of sin and the need for forgiveness.

"See," Yahweh ordered, "I have set you this day over nations and over kingdoms, to pluck up and to break down, . . . to build and to plant." Like Isaiah, Jeremiah was warned of the difficulties the officials and people would cause him: "I make you this day a fortified city, an iron pillar, and bronze walls, against the whole land, against the kings of Judah, its princes, its priests, and the people of the land. They will fight against you; but they shall not prevail against you" (1:18-19). Many times the prophet felt like quitting, but he could not because there was within him "a burning fire" shut up in his bones (20:9). Here again was the coercive power of Israel's God.

Ezekiel's Call

By far the most ecstatic of the classical prophets was Ezekiel. While in exile in Babylonia "the hand of the LORD was upon him" and he had a vision of God's glory. He "saw" someone like a human being seated on a throne above living creatures with four faces and four wings (1:4-28). The surrealist appearance of the vision makes far more sense in the Babylonian setting. Gates to palaces and throne rooms were guarded by large statues of hybrid creatures, some with human faces, bodies of lions or bulls, and wings of eagles. Apparently Ezekiel had seen some of these creatures or drawings of them. In any case, his vision involved something of his knowledge and experience.

And yet the scene before him was so startling he was overcome and he fell on his face. When a voice told him to get on his feet, the Spirit entered him and helped him up. "Son of man," Yahweh commanded, "I send you to the people of Israel, to a nation of rebels, who have rebelled against me" (2:3). Though the retorts of the rebels would be like briers, thorns, and scorpions, Ezekiel was told, "You shall speak my words to them, whether they hear or refuse to hear" (2:7).

The prophet received Yahweh's word in a very creative way. A scroll written on both sides was offered him and he ate it. Strange as it may seem, the "words of lamentation and mourning and woe" were "as sweet as honey" in his mouth (2:8-3:3). Evidently Ezekiel meant that he accepted God's call even though it involved some bitter messages.

The Council of Yahweh

Associated with the call was a sense of having been taken into Yahweh's council chamber and listening to the decisions and orders issued. There, and there only, was the source of God's authoritative message. Amos had this assurance: "Surely the Lord GOD does nothing without revealing his secret to his servants the prophets" (3:7). The Hebrew word *sod*, translated "secret" here, means what is decided upon after a discussion of an issue.

The term can apply equally well to the group having the discussion. In his running battle with the false prophets, Jeremiah asked, "For who among them has stood in the council of the LORD to perceive and to hear his word or who has given heed to his word and listened" (23:18). A little later he relayed Yahweh's condemnation: "I did not send the prophets, yet they ran; I did not speak to them, yet they prophesied. But if they had stood in my council, then they would have proclaimed my words to my people" (23:21-22).

Variations on the theme of Yahweh's council appear elsewhere. Certainly it is implicit in the creation story when God says, "Let us make man in our image, after our likeness" (Gen. 1:26). The question "Who will go for us?" indicates that Isaiah's call involved the heavenly council. Although a different word than *sod* is used, the idea is quite explicit in Ps. 82:1: "God has taken his place in the divine council; in the midst of the gods he holds judgment." Satan and "the sons of God" represent the council in the story of Job (1:6), and in Micaiah's vision the heavenly spirits flanking Yahweh were involved in plans to thwart Ahab and his court prophets.

The Message of Yahweh

Yahweh's authentic message was commonly referred to by the designations "word," "vision," or "oracle," especially in the editorial introductions to the prophets. Some examples are: "The word of Yahweh that came to Hosea;" "The vision of Isaiah;" and "The oracle of God which Habakkuk the prophet saw."

Because God was often pictured as having human form (anthropomorphic), the terms "voice" and "mouth" also were designations for Yahweh's message. At Mt. Sinai, Yahweh, speaking through Moses, declared, "Now therefore, if you will obey my voice and keep my covenant, you shall be my own possession among all peoples" (Exod. 19:5). Jeremiah felt that what he said was Yahweh's voice. He urged King Zedekiah, "Obey now the voice of the LORD in what I say to you" (38:20). Similarly, he warned his hearers, "Do not listen to the words of the prophets who prophesy to you, filling you with vain hopes; they speak visions of their own minds, not from the mouth of the LORD" (23:16).

A number of times the prophets prefaced their oracles with the command, "Hear the word of the LORD." Often they notarized their messages by prefacing "Thus says the LORD," or concluding with an emphatic "says the LORD." In some instances authentication was by the "name" of Yahweh. Even the false prophets did this, and so Yahweh warned Jeremiah, "The prophets are prophesying lies in my name; I did not send them, nor did I command them or speak to them. They are prophesying to you a lying vision, worthless divination, and the deceit of their own minds" (14:14). Like their earlier counterparts, the prophets from Amos to Malachi had the conviction that their oracles were from Yahweh.

Quite often the prophets referred to God's message from their standpoint as receivers of communication, both hearing and seeing. One of Isaiah's messages, for example, was introduced with the claim, "The LORD of hosts has revealed himself in my ears" (22:14). More often, however, the prophets think in terms of "seeing" the vision or message. This may explain the curious combination in some of the editorial introductions: "The word which Isaiah . . . saw concerning Judah and Jerusalem" (2:1) and "The words of Amos . . . which he saw concerning Israel" (1:1).

True and False Prophets

The most dominant impression the prophets convey is their assurance that they were the recipients of Yahweh's word. Concerning their temperament and state of mind Lindblom comments (*Prophecy in Ancient Israel,* p. 173):

> Typical of the revelatory state of mind is the feeling of being under an influence external to the self, a divine power, the consciousness of hearing words and seeing visions which do not come from the self, but from the invisible divine world, into which, in the moment of revelation, an entrance has been granted.

The prophets resisted vigorously the claim of their contemporaries that they too had received their messages from Yahweh. Jeremiah, as noted above, considered their insights as "visions of their own minds" (23:16) and "a lying vision, worthless divination, and the deceit of their own minds" (14:14). In a letter which he wrote to the exiles in Babylonia he warned, "Do not let your prophets and your diviners who are among you deceive you, and do not listen to the dreams which they dream, for it is a lie which they are prophesying to you in my name; I did not send them, says the LORD" (29:8-9).

Some of the results of this running struggle between the two groups of prophets will be considered in the next chapter.

Preachers and Predictors

Most crucial for our purpose is a clear understanding of the ways Yahweh's message functioned. Traditionally two basic aspects have been considered: "forthtelling," preaching with relevance concerning individual and national issues, and "foretelling," prediction of events or situations, some fairly immediate but others more long-range. Conservative circles have tended to stress the predictive aspect while most liberal scholars have thought of the prophets solely in terms of relevant preaching.

It is unfortunate that the issue developed into such extremes, but as is true with so many other problems, viewpoints tend to polarize. The truth is that both aspects were interwoven through the messages of the prophets. Short-range predictions authenticated the prophet's word, especially in situations where he was confronted by false prophets. Long range statements brought hope to the discouraged and the disillusioned. Since the next two chapters will deal with the predictive side of the issue, it is appropriate to outline some of the main concerns the prophets had about their own generations.

The Broken Covenant

The most pervasive theme of the prophets, both early and late, was Israel's breaking of the covenant with Yahweh. This was considered the greatest sin and from it all other deviations developed.

Yahweh called Amos, an outsider from Judah, to preach at Bethel in the cathedral temple of Jeroboam II. It was a time of great prosperity and the future looked bright, but Amos' perceptive eyes could see the cancer which was eating away beneath surface appearances. Although the people were very religious, "playing temple" was intended to con God and get what they wanted, not to change their life styles.

Accordingly, Amos declared Yahweh's anger, "I hate, I despise your feasts, and I take no delight in your solemn assemblies" (5:21). In a similar situation in Jerusalem, Isaiah delivered Yahweh's condemnation: "When you come to appear before me, who requires of you this trampling of my courts? Bring no more vain offerings; incense is an abomination to me. New moon and sabbath and the calling of assemblies—I cannot endure iniquity and solemn assembly" (1:12-13).

More often than not, the covenant was broken by worshiping the gods of the Canaanites and the nations around Israel. These Gentiles, oddly enough, were faithful to their gods; therefore Jeremiah was dumbfounded that the Israelites were so fickle. Through him, Yahweh asked, "Has a nation changed its gods, even though they are no gods? But my people have changed their glory for that which does not profit. Be appalled, O heavens, at this, be shocked, be utterly desolate" (2:11-12).

With a beautiful metaphor Yahweh highlighted the stupidity of the covenant breakers: "they have forsaken me, the fountain of living waters, and hewed out cisterns for themselves, broken cisterns, that can hold no water" (2:13). The import of this claim is not very impressive in countries with clean water available everywhere in drinking fountains or at faucets. But in the Near East, where every drop of water is precious, the meaning of Jeremiah comes through forcefully. Who in their right mind would exchange a spring of sweet, clean water for rain water stored in a cistern? There was always the possibility, moreover, that after all the hard work of digging the cistern it would not hold the water collected during the rainy season.

Both in Israel and Judah the rich "ripped off" the poor, and officials, even priests and prophets, shared in the spoils. They had come to think that Yahweh's covenant at Sinai had been one of favoritism, therefore Amos tried to shatter their complacency: "You only have I known of all the families of the earth; therefore I will punish you for all your iniquities" (3:2). Israel's election was indeed a privilege of grace, but great responsibility went along with it.

Yahweh's Call to Repentance and Service

Amos' warning did not make a dent in the thinking of Israel because they arrogantly insisted that Yahweh was with them. But he had no other recourse than to counter their illusion with a call to repentance: "Seek good, and not evil, that you may live; and so the LORD, the God of hosts, will be with you, as you have said" (5:14). Then he urged, "Let justice roll down like waters, and righteousness like an ever-flowing stream" (5:24). Evidently Amos' pleas were utterly rejected because the themes of judgment and doom dominate the rest of his oracles.

Isaiah exhorted the people of Jerusalem, "Wash yourselves; make yourselves clean, remove the evil of your doing from before my eyes; cease to do evil, learn to do good; seek justice, correct oppression; defend the fatherless, plead for the widow" (1:16-17). Later on, speaking for sovereign Yahweh, the Holy One of Israel, he made a gracious offer of reconciliation: "In returning and rest you shall be saved; in quietness and trust shall be your strength" (30:15). But they would not return.

The essence of Yahweh's will for his people was beautifully expressed by the question which Micah, Isaiah's contemporary, put to his hearers: "What does the LORD require of you but to do justice, and to love kindness, and to walk humbly with your God" (6:8). A century later, Jeremiah offered Yahweh's call: "Stand by the roads, and look, and ask for the ancient paths, where the good way is; and walk in it, and find rest for your souls" (6:16). But the rebellious people spat back, "We will not walk in it."

The Day of Yahweh

Another evidence of Israel's false optimism was the anticipation of "the day of Yahweh [the LORD]." Some scholars feel that annually there was a day set aside to celebrate Yahweh's vindication of his people. Others claim that the reference was to some future event. In either case the material prosperity during Jeroboam's reign undoubtedly contributed to the idea that they were God's pets. Amos warned them that their expectation was doomed: "Woe to you who desire the day of the LORD! Why would you have the day of the LORD? It is darkness, and not light" (5:18).

Isaiah also believed in a day of reckoning in which Yahweh would judge his own people as well as the nations: "The LORD of hosts has a day against all that is proud and lofty" (2:12). In an oracle against Babylon he warned, "Wail, for the day of the LORD is near; as destruction from the Almighty it will come!" (13:6).

Zephaniah, a contemporary of Jeremiah, gave a frightening description of "doomsday": "The great day of the LORD is near, near and hastening fast; the sound of the day of the LORD is bitter, the mighty man cries aloud there. A day of wrath is that day, a day of distress and anguish, a day of ruin and devastation, a day of darkness and gloom, a day of clouds and thick darkness, a day of trumpet blast and battle cry against the fortified cities and against the lofty battlements" (1:14-16).

Yahweh's Steadfast Love

About the time Amos completed his ministry Hosea, a native northerner, was called to carry on Yahweh's attempt to redeem Israel. In the bitter experiences associated with Gomer, his wayward wife, Hosea realized how Yahweh felt toward his adulterous people. He had taken Israel for his bride at Mt. Sinai and during their honeymoon in the wilderness all went well. But when they came to Canaan they quickly began worshiping the gods of the land. Yahweh's jealousy of his harlotrous people was symbolized by names Hosea gave two of his children. The second child, a daughter, was called "Not Pitied" because Yahweh would "no more have pity on the house of Israel" (1:6). A son born later was named "Not My People" since Yahweh said, "You are not my people and I am not your God" (1:9).

Yet after the infidelity, with all its raging indignation, Hosea could not give up on Gomer. He brought her back, disciplined her, and pledged his love to her (3:1-3; 2:14-23). Yahweh would show the same steadfast (covenant) love for Israel.

The husband-bride analogy was not the only way Hosea understood Yahweh's relation to Israel. The father-son analogy came to have great meaning as well: "When Israel was a child, I loved him, and out of Egypt I called my son" (11:1). While Gomer was whoring around, Hosea probably spent some time caring for the children. As he helped "Not My People" to learn to walk, he sensed again the sorrow that Yahweh must have felt: "Yet it was I who taught Ephraim to walk" (11:3). Since Ephraim was the leading tribe in Israel, the name became a symbol for the northern kingdom.

In one of the greatest passages of Scripture, Hosea expressed Yahweh's surging love and yearning for reconciliation: "How can I give you up, O Ephraim! How can I hand you over, O Israel! . . . My heart recoils within me, my compassion grows warm and tender. I will not execute my fierce anger, I will not again destroy Ephraim; for I am God and not man, the Holy One in your midst, and I will not come to destroy" (11:8-9).

Yahweh's Judgment

Unfortunately Israel did not remain faithful to Yahweh. The people's false hopes and aspirations led to chaos. Instead of trusting Yahweh as their king, contending groups coveted the throne. Israel had three kings within a year of Jeroboam's death and Hosea couldn't help comment on the struggle: "On the day of our king the princes became sick with the heat of wine; . . . for like an oven their hearts burn with intrigue. . . . All of them are hot as an oven, and they devour their rulers. All their kings have fallen; and none of them calls upon me" (7:5, 6, 7).

In the futile attempt to gain support for their cause, they got into the game of international power politics. Hosea had something to say about this situation too: "Ephraim is like a dove, silly and without sense, calling to Egypt, going to Assyria" (7:11). The stupidity of this vacillation led finally to Israel's destruction by the Assyrians. One day when Amos was looking at a basket of summer fruit (Hebrew *qayits*), Yahweh flashed the message, "The end (*qets*) has come upon my people Israel" (8:1-2). And so it did!

The Remnant

Elijah had been promised a remnant of 7,000 faithful in Israel, but because of the hope of a genuine reconciliation Hosea never dealt seriously with the concept of a remnant. It was Isaiah in Judah who finally came to a clear understanding of the remnant idea. He found, as Yahweh had warned him at his call, that most of the people were impervious to his message. However, even if the worst should come, a period of captivity such as Israel was suffering, Yahweh would not utterly destroy. In judgment he would redeem a faithful remnant to carry on as God's light to the nations. Confident of this fact, Isaiah named his first son *Shear-jashub* "A Remnant Shall Return."

Later on, in an oracle of doom, destruction was decreed with only a remnant returning. But the confidence remained that "the remnant of Israel and the survivors of the house of Judah" would "lean upon the LORD, the Holy One of Israel, in truth" (10:20-22).

The Irrationality of Sin

Amos, Hosea, Isaiah, and Micah experienced the awful callousness of their people and described in various ways their spiritual sickness. Isaiah, for example, said of Judah, "The whole head is sick, and the whole heart is faint. From the sole of the foot even to the head, there is no soundness in it, but bruises and sores and bleeding wounds" (1:5-6).

But these 8th-century prophets did not attempt to explain the apparent perversity. It was Jeremiah, facing the same hardness of heart a century later, who confessed, "The heart is deceitful above all things, and desperately corrupt; who can understand it?" (17:9). "The sin of Judah," he asserted, "is written with a pen of iron; with a point of diamond it is engraved on the tablet of their heart" (17:1).

A New Covenant and A New Heart

Deut. 6:6 had instructed that the commandments should be on the hearts of the people. Jeremiah realized that this would be impossible as long as sin was inscribed there. The answer was a new covenant: "Behold, the days are coming, says the LORD, when I will make a new covenant with the house of Israel and the house of Judah, . . . I will put my law within them, and I will write it upon their hearts" (31:31, 33).

Ezekiel had another explanation for the hardheartedness of the people—they had "a stony heart" and the only cure was a heart transplant, which Yahweh promised to perform: "I will give them one (or a new) heart, and put a new spirit within them; I will take the stony heart out of their flesh and give them a heart of flesh" (11:19).

Yahweh's Love For All People

The messages of the early prophets seldom moved beyond the concerns of Israel as God's people, and some of the later prophets never got beyond this narrow outlook.

With Amos, however, the horizon moved out to include other nations in the Near East. While not denying for a minute Yahweh's unique covenant with Israel, yet he believed that God had been involved in bringing other peoples into existence as well. " 'Are you not like the Ethiopians to me, O people of Israel?' says the LORD. 'Did I not bring up Israel from the land of Egypt, and the Philistines from Caphtor and the Syrians from Kir?' " (9:7).

Isaiah and Micah looked forward to a time when the nations of the world would say, "Come, let us go up to the mountain of the LORD, to the house of the God of Jacob; that he may teach us his ways and that we may walk in his paths" (Is. 2:3 and Micah 4:2).

But the full implications of Yahweh's love for the nations was not clearly understood until the Apostle Paul. By revelation he came to the insight of "the mystery of Christ, which was not made known to the sons of men in other generations . . . how the Gentiles are fellow heirs, members of the same body, and partakers of the promise in Christ Jesus through the gospel" (Eph. 3:4-6).

In summary, we have seen that true prophecy spoke to the needs of people and nations; therefore its major emphasis was with the present. Yet the ultimate answers to life's questions and concerns involved the future. This was true for the people of God in the Old Testament and it is just as true for the church of Jesus Christ.

Chapter 4
Short-range Predictions

Whenever a prophet proclaimed an oracle in the name of Yahweh [the LORD] the hearers had a problem: "How may we know the word which the LORD has not spoken?" (Deut. 18:21). Since the name of Yahweh was used by well meaning, but deluded, prophets it was necessary to have other tests for checking out the accuracy of an oracle.

The basic rule of thumb was:

> When a prophet speaks in the name of the LORD, if the word does not come to pass or come true, that is a word which the LORD has not spoken; the prophet has spoken it presumptuously, you need not be afraid of him (Deut. 18:22).

But even this test was not foolproof because false prophets had some ability to predict accurately. Thus, another guideline had to be spelled out:

> If a prophet arises among you, or a dreamer of dreams, and gives you a sign or a wonder, and the sign or wonder which he tells you comes to pass, and if he says, "Let us go after other gods," which you have not known, "and let us serve them," you shall not listen to the words of that prophet or to that dreamer of dreams; for the LORD your God is testing you, to know whether you love the LORD your God with all your heart and with all your soul (Deut. 13:1-3).

The penalty for the traitorous prophet was death because he "taught rebellion against the LORD" (Deut. 13:5). How often this law was implemented is hard to say, but it was probably rare. It was just as true of ancient law codes as it is of ours that a law on the books is no true indication of how well it is carried out.

While the theological criterion was fundamental for maintaining true Mosaic faith, it was not very helpful when two religiously valid, but contradictory, oracles were given by contemporary prophets. The most foolproof check in such a showdown was still the accuracy of the prediction. A most dramatic example is the contest between Jeremiah and Hananiah.

The Sign of the Yoke

Late in 595 and early in 594 B.C. there was a serious revolt in the army of Nebuchadnezzar, king of Babylon. The Jewish exiles had been in Babylonia for almost four years and the rebellion raised hopes, both in Babylonia and Judah, of a return home. Two of the exiles, Ahab and Zedekiah, fanned the flames of hope by predicting an early return. Nebuchadnezzar got word of their seditious activities and had them put to death (Jer. 29:22).

Zedekiah, king of Judah, encouraged by the revolt, hosted a summit conference in Jerusalem to discuss strategy for the area. Envoys from Edom, Moab, Tyre, and Sidon attended. In 605, Nebuchadnezzar's first year as king, Jeremiah had predicted by the word of Yahweh that Judah and the surrounding nations would go into captivity for 70 years (Jer. 25:11). Yahweh had not changed his mind and so he ordered Jeremiah to attend the conference wearing yoke bars strapped around his neck (27:2). The visual aid was to dramatize the simple message for Zedekiah and the envoys: they had better put their necks "under the yoke of the king of Babylon" or they would be in trouble (27:8).

The Iron Yoke

Not long after the conference Jeremiah appeared in the outer courtyard of the temple wearing his wooden yoke. A crowd of priests and people were there waiting to see what would happen. Suddenly Hananiah, a prophet from Gibeon, confronted Jeremiah with an oracle: "Thus says the LORD of hosts, the God of Israel: I have broken the yoke of the king of Babylon" (28:2). Then he predicted that within two years King Jehoiachin (Jeconiah) would return from captivity with the exiles and the temple vessels which had been taken in 597 B.C. (28:3-4). Apparently Hananiah believed that the captives would have about six years of punishment and then be brought home for the sabbatical year.

Jeremiah wished that the prophecy were true and so he said, "Amen! May the LORD do so," but then he countered the wishful oracle with a warning to use the basic test of true prophecy:

> The prophets who preceded you and me from ancient times prophesied war, famine, and pestilence against many countries and great kingdoms.

As for the prophet who prophesies peace, when the word of that prophet comes to pass, then it will be known that the LORD has truly sent the prophet (28:8-9).

Hananiah was so angry he took the yoke bars from Jeremiah's neck and broke them. The people watched in amazement and then heard Hananiah prophesy in Yahweh's name, "Even so will I break the yoke of Nebuchadnezzar king of Babylon from the neck of all the nations within two years" (28:11). The audacity of making such a prediction in the name of Yahweh left Jeremiah speechless. No word of rebuttal came from Yahweh and so he left the temple. The people probably thought that Hananiah was the true prophet.

But later on, the word of Yahweh did come: "Go, tell Hananiah, 'Thus says the LORD: You have broken wooden bars, but I will make in their place bars of iron' " (28:13). When Jeremiah found Hananiah he shouted out, "Listen, Hananiah, the LORD has not sent you, and you have made this people trust in a lie." Then as a clincher in the dispute Jeremiah passed on Yahweh's prediction: "Behold, I will remove you from the face of the earth. This very year you shall die, because you have uttered rebellion against the LORD" (28:15-16).

Two months later Hananiah was dead!

The Syria-Israel Coalition

A most instructive illustration of short-range prediction is Isaiah's attempt to authenticate his message to King Ahaz, who reigned about 735-715 B.C.

During the reign of Tiglath-pileser III (745-727 B.C.) the Assyrians regained control of Mesopotamia and moved out to threaten the regions west of the Euphrates River. The first to realize the danger was Rezin, king of Syria, whose capital was at Damascus. Pekah, king of Israel, was next in line and so he and Rezin decided to form a coalition of the smaller countries in order to resist the Assyrian threat.

There was a precedent for this. When Shalmaneser III (859-825 B.C.), one of Tiglath-pileser's predecessors, was threatening the west, the fearful kings banded together. One of them was Ahab, king of Israel, who supplied 10,000 foot soldiers and 2,000 chariots. The test of the coalition occurred in 853 at Qarqar, in Syria. Shalmaneser boasted of victory, but the fact that he didn't come west again for a number of years indicates that the western kings were successful.

Neither the battle of Qarqar nor Ahab's part in the coalition is mentioned in the Bible, but most certainly Rezin and Pekah knew about it. They invited Jotham, king of Judah, to join them against Tiglath-pileser, but the offer was refused because he wanted to remain neutral. Apparently this was not drastic enough action for the strong pro-Assyrian faction in the government; therefore they retired Jotham and put his 16-yr.-old son Ahaz on the throne. This young king had just begun his rule when Rezin and Pekah decided to force his cooperation. They had the Edomites attack Judah from the south while they came south and put Jerusalem under siege.

Isaiah and Ahaz

In this crucial situation Yahweh told Isaiah to take his son *Shear-jashub* "A Remnant Shall Return" and help calm the young king. Since water was the urgent need in a siege, Ahaz was out checking the water system and supply. His heart was shaking like "the trees of the forest shake before the wind" (Is. 7:2). "Take heed, be quiet, do not fear," Isaiah comforted him, "and do not let your heart be faint because of these two smoldering stumps of firebrands" (7:4).

The prophet's words of assurance didn't have much effect on Ahaz. Evidently the frightened young king had determined to send for Tiglath-pileser to help him. The future of Judah was at stake, and so Isaiah kept interacting with Ahaz. "If you will not believe," the prophet warned, "surely you shall not be established" (7:9). By using a play on two words derived from the same Hebrew verb Isaiah made a powerful point: trust in Yahweh, not the Assyrians, was the best way to maintain his independence and that of his people.

In addition to Isaiah's words of advice, little *Shear-jashub* must have jogged Ahaz. "A Remnant Shall Return," the strange name of the preacher's kid, had a double-edged thrust. It was an assurance that some of the people would come back, but more basically it was a warning to Ahaz that Judah would go into exile if it failed to live by the covenant of Yahweh.

The Sign for Ahaz

Apparently all the warnings were ignored by Ahaz because, on another occasion soon afterward, Isaiah visited the king again. He hoped that some special act of Yahweh would convince Ahaz to change his mind, and so he boldly urged, "Ask a sign of the LORD your God, let it be as deep as Sheol or high as heaven" (7:11). Ahaz did not want any sign, however, because he had already sent a present to Tiglath-pileser with the request, "I am your servant and your son. Come up, and rescue me from the hand of the king of Syria and from the hand of the king of Israel, who are attacking me" (2 Kgs. 16:7).

Because of the murmurings in the wilderness and their awful consequences it became a tradition among pious Israelites never to question Yahweh by demanding that he prove himself. In a very pious fashion Ahaz replied, "I will not ask, and I will not put the LORD to the test" (Is. 7:12).

Isaiah was incensed at the king's false use of tradition to cover up his faithless intentions:

> Therefore the Lord himself will give you a sign. Behold, a young woman shall conceive and bear a son, and shall call his name Immanuel. He shall eat curds and honey when he knows how to refuse the evil and choose the good. For before the child knows how to refuse the evil and choose the good, the land before whose two kings you are in dread will be deserted (7:14-16).

In Jewish tradition today a boy is considered a responsible individual when he is thirteen. A very special service initiates him as a *Bar Mitzvah* "A son of the commandment" into the religious community devoted to Torah, the Law. The age of accountability was very much the same in ancient Israel, and so the time span of the sign was probably thirteen years after the birth of Immanuel. Since Isaiah gave the sign in 735 B.C., the child would have been born in 734 and the land of Syria and Israel deserted by 721.

In the years 734-732 Tiglath-pileser captured Syria and the northern part of Israel, including the territory in Transjordan. Rezin was executed by Tiglath-pileser and Pekah was assassinated by Hoshea, who then became a vassal of the Assyrians. When he rebelled against his overlord a siege was put on Samaria, the Israelite capital, and by 721 the northern kingdom was in captivity.

Isaiah's prediction had come true!

The Hebrew Word *ᶜAlmah*

The woman in Is. 7:14 is called an *ᶜalmah*; the meaning of the feminine noun is crucial for interpreting the passage. The word occurs nine times in the Hebrew Bible but in two places it is used as a technical musical term. There are only seven passages, therefore, where the context might help to explain the precise meaning of the term. Since Is. 7:14 is our basic problem, there are six verses left.

The basic Hebrew word meaning "virgin" is *bethulah*. In Gen. 24:16 Rebekah, the future wife of Isaac, is described as a *bethulah* "whom no man had known." Later on in the story she is called an *ᶜalmah* (24:43). In the Septuagint (LXX), the Greek translation of the Old Testament, the translator of Genesis did not bother to distinguish between the two terms. Since both referred to the same young woman and she was explicitly called a "virgin," the translator used *parthenos,* the normal Greek term for "virgin," in both places. Thus Gen. 24 is no help, either in Hebrew or Greek, for defining *ᶜalmah*.

The remaining five passages (Exod. 2:8; Ps. 68:25; Prov. 30:19; and Song of Solomon 1:3 and 6:8) are ambiguous in meaning, but in each case the Septuagint has a Greek term meaning "young woman." Some conservatives have argued strenuously that the women in the five verses are virgins, but this is far from certain. Moses' sister was probably still a girl when she walked along the Nile watching the floating basket with her baby brother. She was undoubtedly a virgin, but the real issue is whether the biblical writer had this connotation in mind when he described her as an *ᶜalmah*.

The Meaning of *ᶜAlmah*

Tradition has derived *ᶜalmah* from the Hebrew verb *ᶜalam*, which occurs 26 times in the Old Testament with the meaning "to hide, cover, conceal." A "covered" girl or young woman was "obviously" one who had not been uncovered (known) by a man, therefore a "virgin."

The problem is that there is not a particle of truth in the whole argument. The Semitic alphabet was originally fairly large, but some of the letters fell together in the Hebrew alphabet. Since this is true, each Hebrew letter which has a double significance must be checked to determine which one was originally meant. The Hebrew letter *ᶜayin*, the first letter (ᶜ) in *ᶜalmah*, is one of these troublesome symbols. Fortunately Arabic, where the two letters are still distinguished, has preserved the verb with the other letter. It means "to be young, vigorous," the time of special sexual urge and drive. Thus, *ᶜalmah* means "young woman."

When we refer to a "young woman" in English the idea of whether she is a virgin or not is simply not involved, and the same is true of Hebrew ᶜalmah. The masculine form of the same noun is ᶜelem. It occurs in 1 Sam. 17:56, where Saul asks Abner about David's identity, and also in 1 Sam. 20:22, when Jonathan tells David about a plan involving a youth collecting arrows. The major translations have "stripling, youth, lad, boy, or young man." None of them, no matter how conservative, has the idea of virginity associated with the word. In fact, such a connotation is absurd in either context.

It is certain, therefore, that when Isaiah used the word ᶜalmah he was thinking of "a young woman," not "a virgin." This conclusion is supported further by the fact that Isaiah did *not* use *bethulah*, the basic Hebrew word for "virgin." He certainly knew the word because he used it in 23:4 and 12. Some traditionalists have tried to get around the problem by assuming that originally Isaiah used *bethulah*, but then ᶜalmah was substituted later on. This dreamy explanation is challenged by the Isaiah Scroll found near the Dead Sea. This copy, dating from about 100 B.C., has ᶜalmah in Is. 7:14, and it is virtually certain that that is the word Isaiah used in talking to Ahaz.

The Meaning of "Sign"

In support of the traditional belief that the "sign" to Ahaz referred to Jesus, some conservatives claim that it had to be such a marvelous event because the limits offered by Isaiah ranged from Sheol, under the earth, up to heaven. Once it is assumed that the sign would involve a miracle then it is an easy step to believe that Isaiah made a prediction over 700 years before its fulfillment.

Yet this understanding of "sign" fails to recognize that Isaiah uses the same Hebrew word (ᵓoth) in 8:18, where he notes: "I and the children whom the LORD has given me are signs and portents in Israel." The signs were their names. *Isaiah* means "Yahweh is Salvation," or "Yahweh Saves." We have noted that Isaiah's first son was named *Shear-jashub* "A Remnant Shall Return." His second son was given the tongue twisting name *Maher-shalal-hash-baz* "The Spoil Speeds, the Prey Hastes." Thus, Isaiah and his sons were walking sermons. Most certainly the names of the sons were conversation pieces. Wherever they went people were curious about the meaning of their names and this gave them or Isaiah an opportunity to speak a

word of explanation and warning. The same would be true of the boy
Immanuel "God Is With Us." He would be a constant reminder that
God was with them and ready to protect them if they were obedient to
the covenant.

Yahweh and Ahaz

The most crucial fact in coming to a mature, balanced
understanding of Is. 7:14 is to recognize that Yahweh was trying to get
Ahaz to be faithful to the covenant. This was the primary purpose in
sending Isaiah. If the "sign" were to be effective at all it had to draw
the attention of the young king. The *Revised Standard Version*,
quoted earlier, reads "a young woman shall conceive." The meaning of
the Hebrew text is made absolutely clear by the *Good News Bible*: "a
young woman who is pregnant will have a son and will name him
'Immanuel.' "

In other words, Yahweh had informed Isaiah that the young wife
of Ahaz was already pregnant. That is why the Hebrew text has
ha^calmah "the young woman." It was a specific reference to "the"
person in Ahaz' life. The fact that the prophet knew the family secret
must have startled the king. To take advantage of his shock, Isaiah
went on to tell Ahaz what would happen before the boy reached the
age of responsibility. If God was primarily thinking about Jesus when
he gave Isaiah the sign, then he was playing games with Ahaz and the
prophet.

The only thing missing is a specific statement about the birth of
Immanuel. His presence is implied, however, in two of Isaiah's oracles
later on. In 8:7-8 he likens the Assyrians to the mighty Euphrates
River in flood. As it flows into Judah, Isaiah comments, "its outspread
wings will fill the breadth of your land, O Immanuel." When the
nations plot against God's people, the prophet warns, "Take counsel
together, but it will come to nought; speak a word, but it will not
stand, for God is with us (Hebrew *^cimmanuel*)" (8:10).

Matthew's Method of Interpretation

Matthew relates the story of Jesus' early life in 1:18-2:23. He is
not content to let the narrative go on its own merits. He feels that he
must support the units of material with a quotation or inference from
the Old Testament. The authority of the Hebrew Bible was so

pervasive in the thinking of various Jewish groups and Christians, they felt compelled to authenticate their identity and mission by quoting from Scripture. This was especially true of the Essenes and the Christians. This way of thinking was as much a part of them as the air they breathed.

The method was applied in a wide range of ways, however. Some writers like Paul were more careful to take into account the historical setting of the passage quoted. Others simply seized on the specific words in which they were interested and ignored the original context completely.

The headings in Matthew's quotations read as follows:

All this took place to fulfill what the Lord had
spoken by the prophet (1:22);

For so it is written by the prophet (2:5);

This was to fulfill what the Lord had spoken by
the prophet (2:15);

Then was fulfilled what was spoken by the
prophet Jeremiah (2:17);

That what was spoken by the prophets might
be fulfilled (2:23).

There is a strong purposive sense in the Greek text and this comes through in the English translation. Matthew seems to be saying that there is a cause-effect relation between the Old Testament passages and the life of Jesus. In other words, he is implying that the quoted verses were given by God to the prophets as prewritten history of what would happen in the life of Christ. His purpose in doing this is to convince his Jewish readers that Jesus was indeed the Christ, the Messiah "Anointed One," for whom they had been looking.

And yet when we check the historical contexts of Matthew's quotations we see that in some of them there is practically nothing which points forward in a real way to Jesus. After relating how Joseph took Mary and Jesus to Egypt until the death of Herod, Matthew claims that this event fulfilled Hosea 11:1: "Out of Egypt have I called my son" (2:15). But in Hosea the passage is not a prophecy. It is a reference to the Exodus under Moses.

For this reason some scholars interpret Matthew to mean that he is simply quoting the passages as illustrations. In his extensive *Encyclopedia of Biblical Prophecy* (1973), p. 77, J. Barton Payne, for example, notes that the expression "that it might be fulfilled" may also "denote a loose relationship of illustration to elucidate some principle, or of similarity in words or ideas to an OT affirmation that may not in itself have been predictive at all."

Matthew's Use of Is. 7:14

How, then, are we to understand Matthew's use of Is. 7:14? In the narrative the angel allays Joseph's fears about Mary and then he notes, "she will bear a son, and you shall call his name Jesus, for he will save his people from their sins" (1:21). The name "Jesus" is the Greek form of the Hebrew name "Joshua," meaning "Yahweh is salvation," or "Yahweh saves." His name, therefore, was a sign of his mission. Then Matthew comments:

All this took place to fulfil what the Lord had spoken by the prophet:
"Behold, a virgin shall conceive and bear a son,
and his name shall be called Emman'u-el"
(which means, God with us).

The explanation of the name is Matthew's addition and by noting it he seems to imply that Jesus was "God with us." If this was the primary purpose for quoting the verse, as some interpreters claim, it would have helped his readers to have an explicit statement something like, "The boy Emmanuel was a symbol that God was with his people, but Jesus was truly 'God with us.' " In fact, one wonders why the angel didn't have Jesus named Immanuel instead if Is. 7:14 was to apply literally.

The Meaning of Parthenos

Without denying that Matthew saw some significance in the name Immanuel, it appears that his main concern was the catchword *parthenos* because his quotation is from the Septuagint, not the Hebrew. It is the basic Greek word for "virgin," but it was used sometimes for "a young woman." This is true in Gen. 34:3, where Dinah is referred to twice as a *parthenos* after she has been raped by Shechem.

It is equally clear that the Septuagint translator had this more general meaning in mind when he used *parthenos* in Is. 7:14. There is no evidence anywhere that Jews expected the Messiah to be born of a virgin, and so there is no basis for reading that idea into the Septuagint. After discussing the evidence about *parthenos*, the conservative scholar J. Gresham Machen concludes that any attempt to find a virgin birth in the Septuagint "is surely venturesome in the extreme" (*The Virgin Birth of Christ*, p. 297).

The Meaning of Matthew's Quotation

The crux of the whole problem is then the ambiguous word *parthenos*. It meant "young woman" in Is. 7:14 of the Septuagint, but with the story about Jesus' virgin birth foremost in Matthew's mind *parthenos* leaped off the scroll with the meaning "virgin." Thus the Old Testament passage was transformed at that moment into a prooftext to support the narrative about Jesus' remarkable birth. Matthew's idea was so overwhelming there was no recognition of the original meaning of the verse.

The Validity of Matthew's Method

The most pressing issue is the evaluation of Matthew's method. It was a meaningful method to convince people in the 1st century A.D., but is it imperative that 20th-century Christians follow the same logic? Matt. 1:18-21 and Luke 1:26-34 clearly claim that Jesus was born of a virgin. Why do we need a prooftext?

Some conservatives feel that we must accept the New Testament method of interpretation because Jesus did the same thing. When he read Is. 61:1-2 in his home synagogue in Nazareth he claimed, "Today this scripture has been fulfilled in your hearing" (Luke 4:21). There is no doubt that Jesus came to his sense of mission by reading the Old Testament and that he was filling to the full those hopes which the prophets had expressed centuries before. But our faith in Jesus rests on his whole life and death. We believe him because of what he was and what he did, not his method of trying to authenticate himself to his contemporaries.

In other words, the method used by Jesus and all the New Testament writers was perfectly valid for its day and served its purpose, but we in the 20th century do not reason that way. It is no more appropriate for us than tunics and sandals would be for our basic clothing.

The Problems of Accepting Matthew's Method

Notwithstanding all the evidence to the contrary, many conservative, dedicated Christians feel that Matthew was an infallible interpreter and that they must follow his lead. This places a great burden on them. Once they accept the interpretation that the genuine fulfillment of Is. 7:14 was Jesus Christ then the problem is what to do with the history of God's activity with Isaiah and Ahaz. This necessitates all kinds of mental wheelspinning and jumping through hoops.

One of the standard explanations is that Isaiah saw the promise of Immanuel so clearly, like viewing a distant mountain on a clear day, he thought the event was going to happen soon. Therefore, he predicted that the land of the two kings would be deserted before the boy came to the age of accountability. This view tries to solve the problem by admitting that Isaiah misunderstood the timing of what he saw and so the child was not actually born then. But this does not do justice to Isaiah and his time.

Another explanation is that of Machen:

> It may be held that the prophet has before him in vision the birth of the child Immanuel, and that irrespective of the ultimate fulfillment the vision itself is present. "I see a wonderful child," the prophet on this interpretation would say, "a wonderful child whose birth shall bring salvation to his people; and before such a period of time shall elapse as would lie between the conception of the child in his mother's womb and his coming to years of discretion, the land of Israel and of Syria shall be forsaken."

Machen recognized the difficulties of this view when he added, "This interpretation, we think, is by no means impossible. It is difficult, indeed, to set it forth adequately in our bald modern speech; but the objections to it largely fall away when one reads the exalted language of the prophet as the language of prophetic vision ought really to be read (*The Virgin Birth of Christ*, p. 292). This is an uneasy, subjective argument which says in essence that one will not really understand the mystery of the passage until one accepts Machen's view of prophecy. For all its wordiness this interpretation does not deal seriously with the vital struggle in which Isaiah and Ahaz were involved.

The logical outcome of accepting Matthew's interpretation is the necessity of translating "virgin" in Is. 7:14. Payne comments:

But when one recognizes that Matthew's contextual stress rests upon the virgin birth of Christ, as conceived in the womb of Mary by the Holy Spirit (vv. 18, 20), then the fact of "correspondence in phraseology" requires the presence of the term "virgin" in Isaiah as well (*Encyclopedia of Biblical Prophecy*, p. 78, note 83).

"Since no one pretends," Payne continues, "that any such virgin birth actually occurred in the prophet's own time . . . , then the reference must indeed be Messianic."

The recent Roman Catholic translation *The New American Bible* (1970) has "the virgin shall be with child." Some of the translation committee did not agree with this translation, but they were compelled to follow it because it was the official teaching of the church. A footnote comments, "The church has always followed St. Matthew in seeing the transcendent fulfillment of this verse in Christ and his virgin Mother."

The Living Bible (1971) reads, "a child shall be born to a virgin." A footnote acknowledges that the immediate fulfillment was in Isaiah's time and that it was not a virgin birth. Then the note explains, "However, the Gospel of Matthew (1:23) tells us that there was a further fulfillment of this prophecy, in that a virgin (Mary) conceived and bore a son, Immanuel, the Christ. We have therefore properly used this high meaning, "virgin," in verse 14, as otherwise the Matthew account loses its significance." But this is precisely what cannot be done and still be true to Isaiah's prediction of Immanuel from "a young woman."

Both the *New American Standard Bible* (1971) and the *New International Version* translation of *Isaiah* (1975) have "a virgin will be with child." There are no footnotes of explanation.

Let Matthew Speak for His Generation

It should be very apparent by now that Matthew has created a serious problem for Christians. The facts tell us that God was working seriously in both periods of history. Isaiah was given a genuine, short-range prophecy as an impressive "sign" for the doubting Ahaz. Although the king did not believe, the prophet was authenticated by the events leading up to the fall of Israel.

Some conservatives fully accept this understanding of Is. 7:14-16, but prefer to think of another fulfillment of the Immanuel sign in Jesus. This dual-fulfillment approach attempts to follow Matthew's reasoning as well. The question comes down to the definition of "fulfillment."

The mother of Immanuel was the young wife of Ahaz, while Jesus' mother became pregnant during the betrothal period before Joseph had sexual relations with her. A virgin birth cannot be a fulfillment of a normal birth. Moreover, the mother named Immanuel while Joseph named Jesus. The two boys had different names and their mission was different as well. After making a comparison of the two situations, it is evident that there is very little that can literally be called fulfillment. The most meaningful tie between the two events is the name Immanuel, and yet it is one of contrast. The son of Ahaz was a walking sign that God was with his people, but Jesus was actually "God with us."

God was certainly working out his purpose in Jesus, but it is far better to understand his life as the fulfillment of the Messianic hopes of the prophets, not a promise understood to predict the virgin birth of Jesus. It is not necessary to pit one period against the other or to try to explain one by the other. If we let Matthew speak for his generation, then we are free to read the Old Testament with openness for what it actually says. It is an incomplete book and when its aspirations flow over into the future then we can follow them with integrity.

Chapter 5
Were the Prophets Inerrant?

We have noted some examples of accurate short-range prediction by the prophets, both early and later, but these are only a fraction of the total. On the other hand, there are some oracles which pose problems and it is necessary to check them.

Micah and Jerusalem

The introduction to the oracles of Micah notes that he prophesied against Samaria and Jerusalem during the reigns of Jotham, Ahaz and Hezekiah. While none of his messages is dated, it is certain that he was a younger contemporary of Isaiah. He was reared in Moresheth, a town in the western foothills of Palestine with a magnificent view of the coastal plain. This was the highway over which the great armies of Egypt and Assyria had marched and in 711 B.C. Micah had a ringside seat to watch Sargon, king of Assyria, capture Ashdod. While the country preacher watched history taking place in his very sight he felt that the same thing would happen to Judah and Jerusalem if the people did not repent.

Rural people have always been sensitive to the evil and corruption of the cities. Micah got reports about the big city in Judah and in his eyes Jerusalem was "Sin City." He accused the leaders of building "Zion with blood and Jerusalem with wrong" (3:10). Then he got specific: "Its heads give judgment for a bribe, its priests teach for hire, its prophets divine for money." To make matters worse, they had the gall to claim, "Is not the LORD in the midst of us? No evil shall come upon us" (3:11). Yahweh, the covenant God, would not tolerate this situation very long, therefore Micah predicted: "Zion shall be plowed as a field; Jerusalem shall become a heap of ruins" (3:12).

Isaiah and Jerusalem

Isaiah was reared in Jerusalem and he saw the hardness and sins of the people firsthand. Yahweh was angry with his people because they had "rejected the law of the LORD" and had "despised the word of the Holy One of Israel" (5:24). Therefore, "He will raise a signal for a nation afar off, and whistle for it from the ends of the earth; and lo, swiftly, speedily it comes!" (5:26). Thus he and Micah were saying essentially the same thing.

Yet in 701 B.C., when the Assyrian army of Sennacherib surrounded Jerusalem, Isaiah received a different word from Yahweh. The army would move on before it could set up a siege and enter the city. "I will defend this city to save it," said Yahweh, "for my own sake and for the sake of my servant David" (Is. 37:35). A plague devastated the army and Sennacherib returned home.

Micah's Problem

Imagine Micah's astonishment when he learned that Isaiah's revised prediction had come true! He and his followers had been convinced that Jerusalem would be leveled. King Hezekiah and some others were penitent, but in general the city had not really repented and yet Yahweh had spared it. How could the covenant God, who demanded justice, do such a thing? We know that Micah was eventually right twice (587/6 B.C. and A.D. 70), but these events did not do him and his generation much good. The trouble with an "armchair" approach to the Bible is that it fails to get involved with real-life situations back there.

Undoubtedly some of the people figured that Micah was wrong, and yet so much of what he had to say was meaningful and helpful his followers passed on his oracles, including the one prediction which had missed the mark.

The religious authorities didn't have Micah put to death as a false prophet either. In fact, a century later some of the elders of Judah defended Jeremiah by noting that Micah had prophesied the destruction of Jerusalem and yet King Hezekiah and Judah had not put him to death (Jer. 26:16-19). The defense of Jeremiah occurred in 609 B.C. after his temple sermon. Jerusalem was still an active city, but if the people did not repent then Yahweh would destroy it and the temple like he had at Shiloh in the days of Samuel (26:4-6). In short, Micah had come back in the form of Jeremiah.

Ezekiel and Jerusalem

As a young man Ezekiel was taken captive to Babylon. There God called him (593 B.C.) as his messenger to the exiles. As a visual aid to emphasize his prediction he took a mud brick and portrayed Jerusalem on it with siege equipment all around the city (4:1-3). This was "a sign for the house of Israel" that the city would fall. In January 588 B.C. he received Yahweh's word: "Son of man, write down the name of this day, this very day. The king of Babylon has laid siege to Jerusalem this very day" (24:2).

Ezekiel was correct right down the line until the destruction of Jerusalem. His oracles generated great interest among the people. They used to talk together in the streets and at the doors of their homes and when they learned that the prophet had another message they encouraged each other, "Come, and hear what the word is that comes from the LORD" (33:30). But they were more interested in him and his visual aids than in the content of his messages. Although they showed much love, their heart was greedy. Ezekiel may have sung some of his oracles because God informed him, "You are to them like one who sings love songs with a beautiful voice and plays well on an instrument, for they hear what you say, but they will not do it" (33:32). Then he received the assurance that when his words come true the people will "know that a prophet has been among them."

Ezekiel and Tyre

Tyre was one of the great commercial centers of the ancient world. While the main city was an island half a mile off the coast of Lebanon, there were "daughter" towns on the mainland. Its merchant fleet sailed all over the Mediterranean Sea with its famous royal purple dye and cloth. Wealth and fame led to arrogance, however, and Ezekiel felt that Yahweh would destroy Tyre as he had Jerusalem. He predicted that Nebuchadnezzar, king of Babylon, would slaughter Tyre's "daughters" on the mainland and then destroy the main city itself (26:7-13). "I will make you a bare rock; you shall be a place for the spreading of nets; you shall never be rebuilt; for I the LORD have spoken, says the Lord GOD" (26:14).

Not long after Nebuchadnezzar sacked Jerusalem he besieged Tyre (about 586 B.C.). But he found that the fortified island was no pushover. After thirteen years of siege the stubborn city remained unconquered. Apparently the weary city and army came to a compromise: the city would not be destroyed if it would recognize the sovereignty of Nebuchadnezzar. Records indicate that later on Babylonian officials were stationed in the city.

Ezekiel didn't say, "Sorry, folks, I made a mistake." In a very interesting oracle, dated 571, he simply issued a revised prediction in the name of Yahweh:

Son of man, Nebuchadnezzar king of Babylon made his army labor hard against Tyre; every head was made bald and every shoulder was rubbed bare; yet neither he nor his army got anything from Tyre to pay for the labor that he had performed against it. Therefore thus says the Lord GOD: Behold, I will give the land of Egypt to Nebuchadnezzar king of Babylon; and he shall carry off its wealth and despoil it and plunder it; and it shall be the wages for his army. I have given him the land of Egypt as his recompense for which he labored, because they worked for me, says the Lord GOD (29:18-20).

Tyre wasn't conquered until 332 B.C., over 250 years after Ezekiel's prophecy. Alexander the Great accomplished the difficult feat by having his army build a causeway out to the island. Moreover, the city was *rebuilt* under the Seleucid kings because the site was too important to leave in ruins. In the light of this historical background it is a futile effort to claim that Ezekiel's original prediction finally came true. Every major city of the ancient world was destroyed sooner or later. The fact that Tyre was rebuilt nullified the prophecy for any future time.

The essential point is that during Ezekiel's lifetime the prediction did not come true. The revised prediction was not completely fulfilled either because Egypt never became a part of the Babylonian empire. The fact that Ezekiel himself changed his point of view should warn us against trying to make him inerrant. Apparently his followers accepted this shift because they included his oracles just as they were given. Ezekiel's batting average was so good he was considered a genuine prophet even though he overshot the mark sometimes.

Ezekiel and Judah's Return

After the destruction of Jerusalem and the temple, Ezekiel's message shifted from an emphasis on wrath and judgment to one of comfort and hope for the exiles. For the sake of his holy name, Yahweh would bring them back to their own land (36:22-24). One of David's descendants would be a "prince" among them. He would not be a lordly king, but a shepherd feeding his flock (34:23-24). In other words, David's heir would maintain law and order and supply the physical necessities of life.

But Ezekiel, who was a *priest* or a son of a priest (1:3) as well as a prophet, had a vision in which most of restored Jerusalem was a holy district controlled by Levites and Zadokite priests. The center of power and influence was the temple, not the palace. As he had seen "the glory of the God of Israel" rise from the old temple and hover over the Mt. of Olives, now he saw the glory of God's presence return from the east and fill the temple (43:2-5). In short, Ezekiel felt that in restored Jerusalem the high priest and the prince would share leadership responsibilities and work together harmoniously.

Isaiah and Judah's Return

The book of Isaiah had encouragement for the exiles too:

Comfort, comfort my people,
    says your God.
Speak tenderly to Jerusalem,
    and cry to her
that her warfare is ended,
    that her iniquity is pardoned,
and that she has received from the LORD's hand
    double for all her sins (40:1-2).

The return to Jerusalem, like a second Exodus, would begin soon: "I bring near my deliverance, it is not far off, and my salvation will not tarry" (46:13).

The return journey would be blessed because God would guide the released prisoners:

They shall feed along the ways,
    on all bare heights shall be their pasture;
They shall not hunger or thirst,
    neither scorching wind nor sun shall smite them,
for he who has pity on them will lead them,
    and by springs of water will guide them.
And I will make all my mountains a way,
    and my highways will be raised up (49:9b-11).

Even nature would rejoice as God's people passed by on their way home:

For you shall go out in joy,
    and be led forth in peace;
the mountains and the hills before you

shall break forth into singing
and all the trees of the field shall clap their hands (55:12).

The Return to Jerusalem

Cyrus the Persian conquered Babylon in 539 B.C. and the next year he issued an order releasing all the exiles whom the Babylonians had taken. He even offered to help rebuild the temple in Jerusalem (Ezra 1:1-4). Then "everyone whose spirit God had stirred to go up to rebuild the house of the LORD" prepared to leave. The first group included leaders from the family groups Judah and Benjamin as well as some priests and Levites (1:5). The person in charge was Sheshbazzar, "the prince of Judah," one of the sons born to King Jehoiachin when he was in captivity. His name appears as "Shenazzar" in 1 Chron. 3:18. As another pledge of his intentions Cyrus turned over to him the gold and silver bowls which had been taken from the temple as spoils of war (Ezra 1:8-10).

With the thrilling words of Ezekiel and Isaiah ringing in their ears, their departure from Babylonia must have been an ecstatic experience. At last they were going home to rebuild and live in peace! The anticipation must have put a spring in their step. But the return journey (following along the Euphrates River and then south through Syria) was over 800 miles and took months to complete. The enthusiasm must have waned somewhat as the hot days wore on and the dangers of attack became evident.

They made it, however, and started building the foundations of the temple (Ezra 5:16). Yet the idyllic scenes pictured by Isaiah failed to materialize. The Edomites had moved into southern Judah after the fall of Jerusalem and they were not happy to see the exiles return. Neither were the Ammonites on the east, the Samaritans on the north, and the Philistines on the west. Accordingly, the building program bogged down.

The Return of Joshua and Zerubbabel

The biblical narrative of the years after the return is very confusing. Sheshbazzar disappears completely and without clear-cut indications of when they arrived, Joshua (Jeshua), the legitimate Zadokite high priest, and Zerubbabel, the son of Shealtiel, have joint leadership (Ezra 3:2). Since Shealtiel was the eldest son of Jehoiachin

(1 Chron. 3:17), Zerubbabel was the legitimate heir to the throne of David. The story implies that they came up with the first group, but there are many indications that they started out later on as the leaders of a second group of exiles.

The first thing they did was to build an altar "for fear was upon them because of the peoples of the lands, and they offered burnt offerings to the LORD . . . morning and evening" (Ezra 3:3). Work on the foundations was resumed. When they were completed, the priests and Levites conducted a service of praise and thanks to Yahweh. The young people shouted with joy, but the old timers, who had seen the earlier temple, wept out loud. This little temple was not what they had expected!

The Samaritans offered to help build the temple, but Zerubbabel gave them a curt reply, "You have nothing to do with us in building a house to our God; but we alone will build to the LORD . . . as Cyrus the king of Persia has commanded us" (4:3). But threats from the Samaritans and others made the people afraid and they stopped work on the temple.

Haggai and Zechariah

The prophets Haggai and Zechariah appeared on the scene in the second year of King Darius (520 B.C.). They urged Zerubbabel and Joshua to resume work in the temple and they encouraged the people to help them (5:1-2). The prophets were successful and work began in September 520 (Hag.1:14-15).

Revolt in the Persian Empire

Cyrus was a remarkably humane ruler for his time and he did all he could to satisfy the peoples under his control. Unfortunately his reign was cut short when he lost his life (530 B.C.) fighting some nomadic peoples at the northeastern corner of his empire. Cambyses, his eldest son, assumed control. He enlarged the empire by conquering Egypt in 525. In 522, while in Palestine en route home from Egypt, he received news that a rebel named Gaumata had gotten the support of the eastern provinces of the empire and usurped the throne. The staggering news drove Cambyses to commit suicide.

Darius, one of Cambyses' officers and a member of the royal family, took command and with the support of the army captured

Gaumata, who was then executed. But this was just the beginning of Darius' problems because news of Gaumata's rebellion and Cambyses' death had sparked revolts all over the massive empire.

It appeared that the huge juggernaut was falling to pieces and hopes of freedom soared among the conquered peoples. Little Judah, just a drop in the Persian bucket, got caught up in nationalistic fervor too. Haggai and Zechariah were convinced that Yahweh was intervening among the nations and would restore the old kingdom with a new David and a new Zadok.

Haggai's Promises

In October 520, while Darius was fighting to regain control of the empire, Haggai received Yahweh's word of encouragement for Zerubbabel and Joshua:

> Who is left among you that saw this house in its former glory? How do you see it now? Is it not in your sight as nothing? Yet now take courage, O Zerubbabel, says the LORD; take courage, O Joshua, . . . the high priest; take courage, all you people of the land, says the LORD; work, for I am with you, says the LORD of hosts, according to the promise that I made you when you came out of Egypt. My Spirit abides among you; fear not (2:3-5).

Then Yahweh promised:

> Once again, in a little while, I will shake the heavens and the earth and the sea and the dry land; and I will shake all the nations, so that the treasures of all nations shall come in, and I will fill this house with splendor, says the LORD of hosts. The silver is mine, and the gold is mine, says the LORD of hosts. The latter splendor of this house shall be greater than the former (2:6-9).

Haggai was exhorting the leaders and the people not to be discouraged about small beginnings. At the Sinai covenant Yahweh shook the heavens and the mountain with thunders and lightning (Exod. 19:16-18) and soon he would shake the heavens and the earth again. In the process the nations would be shaken so that their wealth would pour into Jerusalem. The temple would be expanded and decorated until it would have greater splendor than Solomon's. This promise stirred the imagination of the people and they went to work with anticipation.

In December 520 Haggai received another exhilarating promise:

> Speak to Zerubbabel, governor of Judah, saying, I am about to shake the heavens and the earth, and to overthrow the throne of nations; I am about to destroy the strength of the kingdoms of the nations, and overthrow the chariots and their riders; and the horses and their riders shall go down, every one by the sword of his fellow. On that day, says the LORD of hosts, I will take you, O Zerubbabel my servant, the son of Shealtiel, says the LORD, and make you like a signet ring; for I have chosen you, says the LORD of hosts (2:20-23).

A signet ring was the stamp used by a king to authenticate his official orders and papers, therefore Haggai's oracle predicted that Yahweh was going to promote Zerubbabel from governor to king.

Zechariah's Promises

Zechariah began prophesying in October 520, but most of his oracles came in the form of eight visions which an angel of Yahweh interpreted for him in February 519. Joshua was cleansed for his role by stripping off his filthy (sinful) garments and putting on new garments and a new turban (3:3-5). After the angel charged Joshua concerning his duties, he added, "Hear now, O Joshua the high priest, you and your friends who sit before you, for they are men of good omen: behold, I will bring my servant the Branch" (3:8).

The idea of a "branch" as a symbol or name for the Davidic heir goes back to Is. 4:2 and 11:1. It is certain that Zechariah was referring to Zerubbabel because the next vision refers to his role:

> The hands of Zerubbabel have laid the foundation of this house; his hands shall also complete it. Then you will know that the LORD of hosts has sent me to you. For whoever has despised the day of small things shall rejoice, and shall see the plummet in the hand of Zerubbabel (4:9-10).

The Joint Rule of Joshua and Zerubbabel

Zechariah saw an olive tree on each side of a golden lampstand. When he inquired about the identity of the trees the angel answered, "These are the two anointed who stand by the Lord of the whole earth" (4:13). Almost certainly the reference was to Joshua and Zerubbabel because both priests and kings were anointed in preparation for their service.

The same theme appears again in 6:9-14, although the present Hebrew text has some difficulties and scholars disagree on the precise understanding of the passage. Zechariah was told to take silver and gold from the exiles, make "crowns," and place them on the head of Joshua. It was not the custom to crown a priest, let alone with two crowns. Some scholars think that the original oracle mentioned just one crown and that Zerubbabel's name appeared instead of Joshua's. On the other hand, if Joshua and Zerubbabel were considered corulers both of them could have been named and each crowned on coronation day.

Whether named or not, Zerubbabel was clearly portrayed in the oracle:

> Behold, the man whose name is the Branch: for he shall grow up in his place, and he shall build the temple of the LORD. It is he who shall build the temple of the LORD, and shall bear royal honor, and shall sit and rule upon his throne. And there shall be a priest by his throne, and peaceful understanding shall be between them both (6:12-13).

The Disappearance of Zerubbabel

The marvelous promises of Haggai and Zechariah spread like wildfire among the people. Apparently they were so sure of the outcome they expressed their joy openly and the news reached unfriendly ears among Judah's enemies. In his battle to control the empire, Darius set up an extensive spy system to pick up any warnings of new revolts. To the Persian authorities in the province west of the Euphrates River, the oracles of Haggai and Zechariah would have been alarming.

There is no indication in either the Persian records or the Bible what happened to Zerubbabel. It is unlikely that he was killed, but at least he was removed from Judah. The last we hear of him is in the 519 visions of Zechariah. He was supposed to complete the temple, but Ezra 6:14-15 notes that "the elders of the Jews" finished the building in March 515 B.C. Zerubbabel is not named, and the simplest explanation is that he was not there.

Haggai and Zechariah had meant well and they were certain that Yahweh was going to intervene. But Darius was not overthrown and Zerubbabel did not become king. It was ironic that oracles in the name of Yahweh resulted in the removal of David's heir. Nevertheless, the messages of Haggai and Zechariah were preserved, even those which had led to false hopes, because they were instrumental in getting the temple built. Even though the dreams of a kingdom under a new David were dashed, Judah continued under the theocratic rule of Joshua and his son (Neh. 12:26). Yet despair overcame many of the Jews and they quit dreaming. A cloud came over Judah and we hear nothing about the struggling community for 55-60 years. Not until the time of Ezra and Malachi was there another word from Yahweh.

Traditional Interpretations

The thought that Haggai and Zechariah might have been wrong has been too painful for most conservatives to entertain. The assumption that the prophets were inerrant in their predictions has resulted in some very interesting maneuvering. The most recent, thorough, and typical example of conservative scholarship about prophecy is J. Barton Payne's *Encyclopedia of Biblical Prophecy*; therefore rather than quote a number of sources it will be helpful to see how he handles Haggai (pp. 444-46) and Zechariah (pp. 454-55).

Concerning "in a little while" (Hag. 2:6), Payne comments with a quotation, "The future, as often in prophecy, is foreshortened." He believes, in other words, that the shaking of the heavens and the earth had nothing to do with the shaking of the Persian empire. The fulfillment, according to Payne, will be "the passing away of the present universe." The real question is how such an understanding would have been of any encouragement to Zerubbabel, Joshua, and the people.

It seems to satisfy those who have an "armchair" approach to the Scripture, but if we put ourselves in the 520 B.C. context and listen with Zerubbabel and his friends, there is no chance in the world that we would interpret Haggai to mean God's act at the end of time. Isaiah had talked about God's "new thing" and Haggai shared the expectation that Yahweh was bringing it to pass.

In connection with the statement "I will shake all nations" (Hag. 2:7), Payne quotes Karl F. Keil, a conservative 19th-century German scholar, "What is here predicted was . . . the overthrow of the might of all the kindoms of the heathen, and therefore could not take place in Zerubbabel's lifetime." The Hebrew text says nothing about "the might of all the kingdoms of the heathen." This is found in 2:22, where

Yahweh promises "to overthrow the throne of kingdoms." Verses 6-7 are similar to 21-22 and both are statements which describe with figurative overtones the anticipated collapse of the Persian empire. Payne accepts Keil's interpretation, however, and goes on to claim that the fulfillment will be during the final judgment when, according to his interpretation of Ezek. 38:19-21, Yahweh will shake Gog as he and his army try to conquer Israel. This kind of an explanation would have been mysterious doubletalk in the context of the tottering Persian giant.

With respect to "the treasures (precious things) of all nations shall come in," Payne notes that it might be interpreted as referring to the end-time because the previous context looks that far into the future. He prefers, however, to understand the fulfillment as the silver and gold coming from the various countries of the Persian empire "for the completion and beautification of the second temple." In this instance Payne is correct.

Temple Splendor

After Haggai noted that the latter splendor (glory) of the temple would be greater than the former, he added Yahweh's promise, "and in this place I will give peace" (2:9). The term "peace" (Hebrew *shalom*) has the basic meaning of "being whole, complete" and so it can refer to all aspects of human existence: physical health and prosperity, psychological peace, and spiritual peace and salvation. Since the context is talking about silver and gold coming in to complete and beautify the temple, the RSV translates "prosperity."

But Payne understands the spiritual aspect of *shalom*, thus he thinks in terms of "spiritual glory" within the temple. Inasmuch as Herod's temple was actually an elaborate rebuilding of the small temple completed in 515 B.C., Payne claims that the prophecy was fulfilled when Jesus, with all his glory, taught in the temple.

There is no doubt that Jesus' presence gave the temple an aura of God's glory which it had not had before, especially when he cleansed it, but again the question is whether God intended this understanding of the oracle when it was given. If he did, then we cannot help wondering why he gave it 550 years before the event. Surely it was playing games with Haggai and his contemporaries to use their despair as the occasion for giving a promise which people of God 2,500 years later could marvel at and point to as proof of God's predictive accuracy. God does not need that kind of adulation.

All the evidence indicates that Haggai thought his oracle would be fulfilled literally in his time by expanding and decorating the temple with the wealth which would come in from other nations after the Persian downfall. *The fact that it did not come true does not give us the right to push it into the future.* If Payne is correct one would think that Jesus would have referred to the passage in his attempt to authenticate his mission. Neither he nor the New Testament writers quote Hag. 2:9 as being fulfilled by Jesus, and there is no good reason why we should either.

Haggai and Zerubbabel

Payne notes two traditional interpretations of the promise about Zerubbabel being a signet ring. Keil, for example, was more consistent by understanding the fulfillment to be in Jesus. In order to get this meaning, however, he had to say of Zerubbabel, "The promise did not apply to his own particular person, but rather to the official post he held."

Since Payne takes 2:21 to refer to the final judgment after the millennium and 2:22 to the final overthrow of the heathen, he is forced to see the fulfillment in a resurrected Zerubbabel receiving "high standing, close to God, in the New Jerusalem." Had Keil's and Payne's interpretations of Haggai been explained to Zerubbabel it would have been so much "Mumbo Jumbo."

Zechariah and Joshua

The "crowns" of Zech. 6:11 mean, according to Payne, "two circlets" combining to produce one crown. Since priests were not crowned, Joshua has to be a "type" for an "antitype" in the future, and so Payne translates the latter part of 6:13 as follows:

> He . . . shall sit and rule upon His throne; and He shall be a priest upon his throne; and the counsel of peace . . . shall be between them both.

In order to make sense out of this translation Payne explains that "between them both" has to be understood as "between the two offices united in Him." Then he comments that the fulfillment was "Christ's possession of the crowns both of priesthood and of kingship, though they rest upon His head as priest."

To arrive at this interpretation Payne has had to make an awkward translation of the Hebrew. The text reads literally, "And he shall sit and rule upon his throne, and a priest shall be upon his throne." In other words, there are two persons involved, whereas Payne's translation has only one person. Had the Hebrew meant to say what Payne thinks it does, it would have read, "And he shall sit and rule and be a priest on his throne." Then the second "upon his throne" would have been dropped. The fact that it is there means that the "priest" is the subject of the verb, not the predicate.

But since the Hebrew word meaning "upon" can also mean "against, by" it is perfectly legitimate to translate as the RSV does, "and there shall be a priest by his throne." While Payne admits that this is "grammatically possible" (*Encyclopedia of Biblical Prophecy*, p. 454, note 33) he thinks the RSV is inconsistent in translating "upon his throne" in two ways. His reason for thinking so is that the meaning derived "is opposed to the total context of the passage." The RSV indicates very clearly the actual situation in 520 B.C. Joshua and Zerubbabel were to be corulers with equal authority, working peacefully together in establishing the new kingdom. It is Payne's *interpretation of the context*, not the actual context, which is opposed by the RSV translation.

The only remaining problem is whether there were two thrones or just one. Taken literally the Hebrew text seems to say that the Branch had his throne and the priest had his. This would have been a unique situation indeed, but with two corulers and two crowns it is possible that each had a throne for the anticipated coronation service.

As noted earlier, however, the original Hebrew text probably had Zerubbabel being crowned, but when he was removed and the leadership fell on Joshua the oracle was revised by substituting Joshua for Zerubbabel.

Conservatism and Liberalism

In connection with the interpretation of Zerubbabel as a signet ring, Payne comments in a footnote, "liberalism here sees an abortive attempt to crown Zerubbabel as the Messiah" (*Encyclopedia of Biblical Prophecy*, p. 446). The implication is that because "liberalism" holds such a view it cannot possibly be right and so there is no point in giving it any more space.

During the last 150 years there have been literally millions of study-hours spent on critical examination of the Bible. Almost without exception insights of the liberal scholars have been rejected by right-wing conservatives.

There have been, and still are, some very destructive higher critics, but they cannot be used as examples of liberal scholarship as a whole. Biblical criticism has included some very devout, intelligent, objective scholars who have sought above all else to know the truth about Scripture and its message. Moderate and mediating scholars like S. R. Driver, George Adam Smith, and James Orr are good examples.

Conservative Rigidity

There is a reason for the rigidity of conservative biblical scholars. It is a kind of "supernaturalism" which is rooted in the doctrine of inerrancy. The usual claim is that God through his Spirit kept all the biblical writers from making any errors. This was true in spite of the fact that they were human beings and lived in cultures which were not concerned with precise details such as we are. This "supernatural" control resulted in a perfect book, when properly understood.

Each bit of biblical information is considered, as it were, as one piece of a giant jigsaw puzzle. When all the pieces are put together in the proper way, one can see the complete picture of God's activity in history and his plans for the future. But already we have had enough clear-cut examples to show us that there are pieces from a number of puzzles and that they cannot be forced into one picture.

Conservative Methodology

The results of the "single-puzzle" approach to the Bible are well illustrated by Payne's interpretation of the Zerubbabel-Joshua oracles in Haggai and Zechariah. He finds a few fulfillments in the Persian period, but only those items which do not force him to admit that the prophets were wrong.

The pieces which cannot be fitted into the Persian part of the jigsaw puzzle are tried in other parts. He finds that some pieces fit in the time of Christ. Some seem to belong to the Messianic kingdom during the millennium. Still others are appropriate to the time of the final judgment. The "signet ring" piece fits, according to his judgment, at the end of the puzzle, therefore Zerubbabel will have to wait until the New Jerusalem to benefit from the oracle addressed to him.

Most conservatives reject "literary criticism" because it splits up biblical material into different sources, sometimes even two or three in a single verse. Undoubtedly some literary critics have pushed their theories to absurdity, but here is Payne with his kind of "prophetic criticism" splitting verses into two or three units of material whose fulfillment is separated by hundreds or thousands of years.

This kind of "supernaturalism" borders on the magical. It always has to be right, and so in its encounter with liberal scholarship it takes the attitude "Heads, I win; tails, you lose." In this way it can continue to reject all liberal insights as untruthful. It simply is not possible that a variety of critical scholars working diligently for 150 years have been 99.44% wrong! Any objective person with a knowledge of mathematical probability should know that the percentage of accuracy is much higher.

Prisoners of a System

Conservatives have not been able to accept the correct insights of liberal scholarship because they have been locked into their system. When some new idea or bit of information comes within their range, they do not ask first "Is it true?" Rather, they inquire "Does it fit into my system?" If it doesn't, then the idea is rejected. The assumption is that the system is perfect and contains all the truth.

But there are no perfect systems as far as human beings are concerned. All of us have acquired at home, church, or school some ideas which need to be revised or discarded. The tragedy is that so many sincere conservatives, utterly committed to honesty and the search for truth, become prisoners of systems which prevent them from carrying out their noble intentions. Where our inadequate views are maintained with emotion, the task of making the revision is difficult. The only way is to be willing to test our views and systems. This means an honesty with respect to new data which challenges our old points of view. If the new insights are allowed to accumulate, then in time there may be enough evidence to warrant a change.

Sooner or later all of us will have to face up to ultimate reality. The time to prepare for that day is the present. Each of us should be as open as possible to the truth in Scripture and around us. If this attitude is put into practice then it becomes a way of life. But even with the greatest sincerity and diligence some blind spots will remain. Thus all of us are in for some surprises, but those who have not kept up in their search for truth will find revelation day absolutely shocking. Unless God "brainwashes" them of their misguided notions they will hardly be able to tolerate their new environment. It seems that it would be much wiser to begin the brainwashing process now and on our own.

Chapter 6
Long-range Predictions

We have noted that the basic test for determining a true prophet was the accuracy of short-range predictions. The fact that certain prophets were accepted into the canon of Scripture is evidence that they passed the scrutiny of their contemporaries. While they missed the mark sometimes, their overall average was so high they were judged as true spokesmen for Yahweh.

When we come to long-range predictions we face some different problems. The test of accuracy was not applicable as far as their hearers were concerned, but in some instances it is for us. Moreover, we will need to determine in some cases whether the predictions are what is claimed for them.

The Prophecy Against Bethel

In Chapter 2 we described how Ahijah, the prophet from Shiloh, was instrumental in having Jeroboam I (922-901 B.C.) made king of Israel, the northern kingdom. When Israel rebelled against Judah it cut itself off from worshipping at the temple in Jerusalem. Rather than have the official northern sanctuary at Shechem, which was rebuilt as the first capital, Jeroboam designated two national shrines. One was at Bethel, the holy place associated with Jacob, which was as close to Jerusalem as possible. The other was at Dan, near the northern boundary. Altars were built and sacrifices offered.

Jeroboam had a gold bull set up in each shrine, apparently as a pedestal for God's presence just as Yahweh was thought to be enthroned over the cherubim in Jerusalem. But since the bull was the symbol of Baal, the Canaanite god, some of the conservatives considered Jeroboam's innovation as actual worship of the bull. The king instituted a joyous fall festival of ingathering like the Feast of Booths in Judah, except that he held it on the 15th of the 8th month, a month after the time specified by the old calendar. It was apparently innovations of this sort which finally turned Ahijah against Jeroboam. The king even got opposition from the southern kingdom. Yahweh sent "a man of God" from Judah to put a curse on the Bethel shrine.

At the sanctuary he found Jeroboam at the altar ready to burn incense. The worship service was interrupted by the word of Yahweh:

> O altar, altar, thus says the LORD: "Behold, a son shall be born to the house of David, Josiah by name; and he shall sacrifice upon you the priests of the high places who burn incense upon you, and men's bones shall be burned upon you" (1 Kgs. 13:2).

As a sign of the predictive curse he added, "Behold, the altar shall be torn down, and the ashes that are upon it shall be poured out" (13:3).

The Prediction about Josiah

It is quite understandable how a follower of Yahweh in Judah would be concerned about the quality of worship in Israel. He felt called of Yahweh, just as Amos would about 170 years later, to go to Bethel. It is easy to see why he felt that a king of Judah, an heir of David, would be the one to stop the worship. The problem is whether the original prophecy had the specific words "Josiah by name."

Josiah reigned 640-609 B.C. After the scroll was found in the temple in 621, he launched a major religious reform. Since the Assyrian empire was in its death throes and very weak, Josiah moved into the Samaritan province to the north, desecrated the sanctuary at Bethel, destroyed the local shrines on the high places, and killed the priests who functioned there. The fulfillment of the prophecy is described in 2 Kgs. 23:15-16, where it notes that Josiah pulled down the altar and crushed the stones to dust. Then he took the bones from local tombs and burned them on the site of the altar, thus defiling it "according to the word of the LORD which the man of God proclaimed."

Josiah's zealous crusade into Samaria is not dated, but it probably occurred 620-615 B.C., almost exactly 300 years after the prophecy. Tradition has accepted the prediction as it appears and exclaimed, "Isn't that marvelous!" But if we get out of the armchair and put ourselves in the sanctuary at Bethel we are simply puzzled by the name Josiah and wonder how long it will be before he comes to reign.

In the narrative of 1 Kgs. 13 there is a reference to "the cities of Samaria" (vs. 32). Before the fall of the northern kingdom in 721 B.C. the area was known as "Israel" or "Ephraim." After the Assyrians took the Israelites captive and brought in other captive peoples to take their place, the Assyrian province was called "Samaria," the name of the Israelite capital, and the new inhabitants were called "Samaritans." It is quite certain, therefore, that a Judean scribe edited the old story. The fact that Josiah had fulfilled the prophecy of the man of God from Judah led the scribe to include the name of Josiah in the original prediction.

The Man of God from Judah

There is more to the story about the man of God from Judah. Although the incident is not related specifically to long-range prediction, it sheds additional light on the problem of how to determine the authentic word of Yahweh.

Jeroboam was angry with the intruder from Judah and pointed at him with the instructions, "Lay hold of him." Simultaneously his arm withered in the outstretched position. Then he begged the man of God to pray for him and when he did, the arm functioned normally. In gratitude Jeroboam asked the man of God to come home with him, refresh himself, and get a reward. He rejected the invitation flatly because Yahweh had instructed him, "You shall neither eat bread, nor drink water, nor return by the way that you came" (13:9). To accept the hospitality of anyone up north would have implied sharing in their theological views and practices.

The Old Prophet from Bethel

While he was on his way home by another route, an old prophet from Bethel caught up with him and invited him to come to his home for a meal (13:15). He refused and then explained why. The old prophet answered, "I also am a prophet as you are, and an angel spoke to me by the word of the Lord, saying, 'Bring him back with you into your house that he may eat bread and drink water'" (13:18). The contradiction of claims was quickly resolved by the narrator when he added, "But he lied to him."

Evidently the man of God figured that Yahweh had changed his instructions and so he accompanied the old prophet home. As they were eating, the word of Yahweh came to the prophet, "Because you have disobeyed the word of the Lord . . . your body shall not come to the tomb of your fathers" (13:21-22). A lion killed the man of God on his way home. When the prophet heard of it he placed the body in his own grave and mourned, "Alas, my brother!" Then he commanded his sons, "When I die, bury me in the grave in which the man of God is buried; lay my bones beside his bones" (13:30-31).

This is certainly a strange story. The narrator's judgment that the prophet lied implies that he intended tricking the man of God because he had cursed the Bethel shrine. The affection displayed at the burial could be taken as remorse for his deed, but it appears very sincere. Most likely the invitation of the prophet was genuine. It came, however, as Yahweh's test of his servant from Judah.

The clear lesson of the story, and probably the reason it was preserved, is that the man of God should never have doubted Yahweh's prohibition. Had Yahweh changed his mind he would have notified him personally rather than through the prophet. This is what happened in the case of Isaiah.

The Prediction of Cyrus

Similar to the Josiah problem is Isaiah's prediction of Cyrus, the king of Persia. In Is. 44:28 Yahweh is described as the one "who says of Cyrus, 'He is my shepherd, and he shall fulfill all my purpose.' " Then Yahweh spoke "to his anointed, to Cyrus" and informed him, "For the sake of my servant Jacob, and Israel my chosen, I call you by your name, I surname you, though you do not know me" (45:1, 4).

These oracles refer to the historical situation not long before the capture of Babylon in 539 B.C. If they are authentic predictions of Isaiah then they were given 150 years or more before the event. Again, the question is why did Yahweh reveal such precise information so far ahead of time? It would have meant nothing to the prophet and his contemporaries. Furthermore, in 605 B.C. Jeremiah predicted that exiles would serve the king of Babylon 70 years after which Yahweh would punish the Babylonian king and his people (Jer. 25:11-12). The conqueror is not mentioned, however, either by name or country. If there had been a tradition from Isaiah about Cyrus conquering Babylonia, it is strange that Jeremiah did not mention it in his prediction.

We have already noted that Is. 40-55 has numerous prophecies about the return to Palestine. If these are genuine oracles of Isaiah, we have the unique situation of a series of double predictions: in addition to looking forward to the Babylonian exile, the prophet then stands in that new context and anticipates the return home. It is theoretically and theologically possible that God could have done such a thing, but there seems to be no purpose except that generations centuries and millennia later could marvel at the accuracy.

The Book of Isaiah

The first unit of Isaiah consists of chapters 1-35, largely in poetry. The prophet is named six times and some of the oracles are dated by actual references to historical situations. Although there are some questions about some of the oracles, chapters 1-35 are essentially the work of Isaiah, the 8th-century prophet.

The next distinctive unit is the historical narrative in chapters 36-39. Except for two variations it is the same story as found in 2 Kgs. 18:13-20:19.

The third unit is the collection of poetic oracles in 40-66. Isaiah is never named in this section and none of the oracles is dated.

Tradition has claimed that the unit 40-66 represents oracles which came to Isaiah later in life and thus there would be no reason to mention his name. Conservative scholars go to great pains to show how many similar words, expressions, and ideas there are between the two poetic sections.

But this argument from style, word usage, and ideas is a slippery one which can work both ways. It is just as easy to reason that a young man who cherished the message of Isaiah was called by Yahweh to speak his word to the exiles. In drinking deeply from the spiritual pool of Isaiah the basic insights and wording became so much a part of him, Yahweh's word to the exiles continued the same theme with many of the same expressions. Moreover, it is easier to explain the genuine differences between the two units as due to two different persons than to two periods in the life of Isaiah.

Exilic Isaiah

Since we do not know the name of the prophet, scholars have referred to him as the great unknown prophet and designated him "Second Isaiah" (Deutero-Isaiah). A more fitting title would be "Exilic Isaiah." The loss of his identity is probably due to the necessity of being anonymous. We must remember that he was prophesying right

in the heart of the Babylonian empire and so he had to be cautious
about identifying himself.

We know that Cyrus came to power in 550 B.C. and that by 546
he had reached western Asia Minor, where he captured Croesus, the
rich king of Lydia. News of his activities leaked back into Babylonia
and the young prophet was convinced that Yahweh was preparing
Cyrus to deliver his people from exile. He is referred to in Is. 41:2
where Yahweh asks, "Who stirred up one from the east whom victory
meets at every step?" Yahweh, of course! Although Cyrus did not
know it, Yahweh had chosen him as "his anointed" (45:1).

But such seditious messages could not be delivered openly
without running the risk of death by the king of Babylon. Therefore,
the oracles of Exilic Isaiah were written down and collected by his
followers. Since the narrative in 2 Kgs. 18:13-20:19 was a transition
section between Assyria and the rise of Babylonia, it was copied out
and used as a fitting bond between the old prophet Isaiah and his
counterpart in exile. God was continually calling his prophets in time
of need and, just as Isaiah and Micah worked at the same time, it is
natural to find him calling Exilic Isaiah to work along with Ezekiel
during the difficult years of the exile.

There are two rock-bottom reasons why most conservatives reject
the theory of two Isaiahs. One is that it eliminates the mention of
Cyrus as a long-range prediction. But it certainly adds a number of
precise short-range predictions. The other objection is that deception
is involved. Yet if the young prophet got many of his ideas and much
of his vocabulary from Isaiah there is a definite continuity between the
two. Who is to say that God could not work through two devoted
persons as well as he could between two different periods in the life of
the same person?

The followers of Exilic Isaiah felt that the proper place for his
oracles was as an addition to the old prophet. It was hardly intended
to deceive anyone. The exiles knew the extent of Isaiah's prophecies.
The addition was made during the exile and so the combined book
was part of the postexilic canon. That the Isaiah Scroll from Cave 1
near Qumran begins chapter 40 on the last line of a column is no
proof of the unity of Isaiah, as some conservatives like to think,
because it dates from about 100 B.C., 400 years after the compilation
of the book.

Zechariah 9-14 and Malachi 1-4

This process of combination was continued after the exile. Excellent examples are Zech. 9-14 and Mal. 1-4. The genuine oracles of Zechariah are in chapters 1-8. They are all in prose form, they date from Oct. 520 to Nov. 518 B.C., and Zechariah is named four times in them as well as implied a number of times. The rest of the book consists of two sections with the heading "An Oracle." The first (9-11) is largely poetry, and the second (12-14) is largely prose. None of the oracles is dated and the name of Zechariah appears nowhere in the six chapters. The differences between 9-14 and 1-8 are far greater than those between the two sections in Isaiah, and it is wishful thinking to attribute both units to Zechariah.

Although most translations do not indicate it, the book of Malachi has the heading "An Oracle." In 3:1 God states, "Behold, I send my messenger to prepare the way before me." In Hebrew the expression "my messenger" is *malachi*. Thus, "Malachi" is probably a general title and not the precise name of the prophet who produced the four chapters. In reality, then, the collection we call the Minor Prophets closes with three anonymous units each with the simple heading "An Oracle."

Chapter 7
The Messiah and the Suffering Servant

Two of the major prophetic themes are the Messiah and the Suffering Servant. While the prophets spoke to conditions in their time and generally expected Yahweh to carry out his promises in the not too distant future, their expectations were often delayed, and so these two themes move over into the category of long-range expectations. The question to be considered is whether these hopes remain as valid predictions.

The Land of Zebulun and Naphtali

In our discussion of Is. 7:14-16 we noted that Tiglath-pileser III conquered Syria and executed Rezin. From Damascus he followed the main route past the Sea of Galilee and captured northern Israel, which included the territory of the old tribes Zebulun and Naphtali. In contrast to the gloom and anguish of that humiliation Isaiah looked forward to a day of glory for that region:

> In the former time he brought into contempt the land of Zebulun and the land of Naphtali, but in the latter time he will make glorious the way of the sea, the land beyond the Jordan, Galilee of the nations (9:1).

Immediately following this transitional verse in prose comes Isaiah's poetic hope for the future:

> The people who walked in darkness
>   have seen a great light;
> those who dwelt in a land of deep darkness,
>   on them has light shined.
> Thou hast multiplied the nation,
>   thou hast increased its joy;
> they rejoice before thee
>   as with joy at the harvest,
>   as men rejoice when they divide the spoil.
> For the yoke of his burden,
>   and the staff for his shoulder,
>   the rod of his oppressor,
>   thou hast broken as on the day of Midian.

For every boot of the tramping warrior in battle tumult
and every garment rolled in blood
will be burned as fuel for the fire (9:2-5).

The Prince of Peace

Then Isaiah makes clear the basis for his hope:

For to us a child is born,
to us a son is given;
and the government will be upon his shoulder,
and his name will be called
"Wonderful Counselor, Mighty God,
Everlasting Father, Prince of Peace."
Of the increase of his government and of peace
there will be no end,
upon the throne of David, and over his kingdom,
to establish it, and to uphold it
with justice and with righteousness
from this time forth and for evermore.
The zeal of the LORD of hosts will do this (9:6-7).

The context of this glorious vision seems to be about 731-730, just after Tiglath-pileser's devastation of northern Israel. Isaiah despaired of the character and leadership of King Ahaz, and he longed for a king who would embody the ideals of God's will. Some scholars think that Isaiah had Hezekiah, Ahaz's older son, in mind but he would have been a young boy.

Since the vision follows chapters 7-8, where Immanuel appears, it seems that the "child-son" the prophet had in mind was the promised "sign," then 3-4 years old. The new David would break the "yoke" of the Assyrian oppressor in the Galilee region and form a united kingdom again as it was in the golden days of David. He would be called "Prince of Peace." But the Messianic kingdom did not come in Isaiah's time. The promise was preserved, however, with the hope that Yahweh would fulfill his word in his own time.

Eschatology

The Greek word *eschaton* "the end, last thing" has been used by scholars to designate various biblical hopes about the end of one age and the beginning of a new era. The coined word "eschatology" is the study of things pertaining to end times. The major end-time (eschatological) hope of the preexilic prophets was that Yahweh would send the Messiah, renew the earth, and set up his kingdom of peace.

This hope, postponed generation after generation, was very much alive in the first century A.D., and some features of it were considered fulfilled by Jesus. Yet other aspects did not occur and to this day they have not come true. This latter issue will be discussed many times in future chapters; therefore we need not consider it here.

Is. 9:1-2 and Jesus

Matthew relates how Jesus came to Capernaum "by the sea, in the territory of Zebulun and Naphtali," to begin his ministry (4:13). As proof of this event he quotes a condensed form of Is. 9:1-2. It is interesting that Jesus and most of his disciples came from the region overrun by Tiglath-pileser, but Matthew has to do some fudging to make the situations match.

After the conquest of Canaan under Joshua, the tribe of Zebulun settled a number of miles west of the Sea of Galilee. Zebulun was mentioned in Is. 9:1 because it was part of the area conquered by Tiglath-pileser. Both Capernaum and the Sea of Galilee were in Naphtali, but Matthew put them "in the territory of Zebulun and Naphtali" to agree with the quotation. The people of the area were in darkness because of the arrest of John the Baptist and the threat of his death. They saw a "great light" when Jesus came into their area.

It is clear again that Matthew was prooftexting by giving the "catchwords" different meanings from those intended by Isaiah. Is. 9:6, the heart of Isaiah's vision, is more appropriately related to Jesus, but Matthew never quoted the passage. Apparently he did not find a catchword suitable to his purposes.

The Branch from Jesse

Another part of Isaiah's messianic vision appears in 11:1: "There shall come forth a shoot from the stump of Jesse, and a branch shall grow out of his roots." As a Jerusalemite, Isaiah believed strongly in the covenant Yahweh made with David, and yet he knew all too well the checkered history of David's successors.

It is very interesting that Isaiah spoke of Jesse, not David. When Yahweh informed Samuel that Saul's successor was to be found among the sons of Jesse, he went to Bethlehem to inspect them (1 Sam. 16:1-13). Jesse brought in seven and paraded them in front of Samuel, but none suited him. "Are all your sons here?" Samuel asked. No, the youngest was tending his flock. David was the one and Samuel anointed him. In Is. 11:1 it seems that Isaiah, like Samuel, is asking, "Jesse, don't you have any more sons from which to choose?"

After noting that Jesus came to live in Nazareth, Matthew comments, "that what was spoken by the prophets might be fulfilled, 'He shall be called a Nazarene' " (2:23). None of the prophets says this explicitly, so Matthew must have been playing with words again. It is quite possible that his source was Is. 11:1, where the Hebrew word *netser* "branch" appears. The similarity to Nazareth may have triggered the idea. Wherever Matthew got his idea, his creativity does not prove his point for us.

The Shepherd King

Whether Isaiah had a modified view of the Davidic covenant or not, it is quite clear that Micah did. His theology was based on the Mosaic covenant. The leaders in Jerusalem had broken Yahweh's word and so they would have to be punished and the city leveled. The only hope, according to Yahweh's word to Micah, was a ruler from Bethlehem:

> But you, O Bethlehem Ephrathah,
>   who are little to be among the clans of Judah,
> from you shall come forth for me
>   one who is to be ruler in Israel,
> whose origin is from of old,
>   from ancient days (5:2).

The new ruler would "stand and feed his flock in the strength of the LORD" (5:4).

The true shepherd king could not possibly be born in Jerusalem. In that sinful city the leaders mauled the sheep instead of protecting them. Yahweh's chosen one would come from Jesse's small town where life was simple and the people genuine. His roots would go back over 300 years to the time when David was anointed.

Matthew and Micah 5:2

When Herod heard that the wise men had come to worship the "king of the Jews," he was worried and asked the "chief priests and scribes" where the Christ (Messiah) was to be born. "In Bethlehem of Judea," they reported, "for so it is written by the prophets" (Matt. 2:5). Then they quoted Mic. 5:2.

Because the quotation is in the story and introduced by the priests and scribes it does not have Matthew's usual introduction, but it is safe to say that Matthew believed that Jesus was born in Bethlehem in order that Mic. 5:2 might be fulfilled. Most conservatives concur and think of Micah's statement as one of the most marvelous predictions in the Old Testament. But granting Micah's love for small towns and his knowledge of the anointing of Jesse's son David, Bethlehem had to be the home of the shepherd king. The remarkable part about the whole episode was that Mary was in Bethlehem when Jesus was born. Jesus would still have been the Christ had he been born in Nazareth, where he was conceived.

The Ideal King

The "branch" from the roots of Jesse (Is. 11:1) is described as an ideal king:

> And the Spirit of the LORD shall rest upon him,
>   the spirit of wisdom and understanding,
>   the spirit of counsel and might,
>   the spirit of knowledge and the fear of the LORD.
> And his delight shall be in the fear of the LORD (11:2-3a).

This son of Jesse will "not judge by what his eyes see, or decide by what his ears hear; but with righteousness he shall judge the poor, and decide with equity for the meek of the earth. . . . Righteousness shall be the girdle of his waist, and faithfulness the girdle of his loins" (11:3b-5).

The Ideal Kingdom

Associated with the idea of an ideal king was the dream of an ideal kingdom:

> It shall come to pass in the latter days
>   that the mountain of the house of the LORD
> shall be established as the highest of the mountains,
>   and shall be raised above the hills;

and all the nations shall flow to it,
    and many peoples shall come, and say:
"Come, let us go up to the mountain of the LORD,
    to the house of the God of Jacob;
that he may teach us his ways
    and that we may walk in his paths."
For out of Zion shall go forth the law,
    and the word of the LORD from Jerusalem.
He shall judge between the nations
    and decide for many peoples;
and they shall beat their swords into plowshares,
    and their spears into pruning hooks;
nation shall not lift up sword against nation,
    neither shall they learn war any more (Is. 2:2-4).

In the new age, Zion will be exalted and the nations will come to learn of Yahweh's will. With this knowledge they will honor Yahweh's verdict when he hears disputes between the nations and they will convert their weapons to productive tools. Never again will human beings harm each other. What a marvelous prospect!

It is a curious fact that the same passage appears in Mic. 4:1-3. The explanation of this repetition is not certain because we do not have enough information. It seems unlikely that either prophet borrowed from the other, since they were quite independent and claimed to get their messages directly from Yahweh. It is possible, of course, that a compiler of one collection copied it from the other. Perhaps the vision came from an earlier time and each prophet took it as Yahweh's word to him. In any case, Micah adds the following comment about the ideal kingdom:

They shall sit every man under his vine and under his fig tree, and none shall make them afraid (4:4).

The New Eden

Yet Isaiah took the dream of an ideal kingdom one step further. In addition to solving the human problem, God would renew the animal kingdom as well:

The wolf shall dwell with the lamb,
    and the leopard shall lie down with the kid,
and the calf and the lion and the fatling together,
    and a little child shall lead them.

The cow and the bear shall feed;
   their young shall lie down together;
   and the lion shall eat straw like the ox.
The sucking child shall play over the hole of the asp,
   and the weaned child shall put his hand on the adder's den.
They shall not hurt or destroy
   in all my holy mountain;
for the earth shall be full of the knowledge of the LORD
   as the waters cover the sea (11:6-9).

The idea certainly goes back to the peaceable kingdom in the Garden of Eden (Gen. 2:8-3:24). Isaiah took the story as literal fact. If paradise was lost because of sin, then Yahweh would restore it when the problem of human sin was remedied.

But aside from the biblical story and other ancient concepts about a paradise, there is no evidence anywhere that such ideal conditions ever existed in the natural world. The whole balance of nature depends on the carnivorous cycles of larger creatures feeding on smaller ones. To have an Eden would demand a complete miracle in which animal instincts would be changed radically, additional means of sustenance provided, and limits of reproduction imposed.

The question remains, then, whether this vision is an authentic prediction of what Yahweh plans to accomplish or whether it represents the fond hope of Isaiah. Christians are divided in their answers. Some claim that its appearance in the Bible guarantees it as an authentic prediction, but others doubt that it comes within the purpose of God.

The Messiah

The term "Messiah" (Hebrew *mashiah*) means "Anointed One." In Greek it became *christos*, from which came our word "Christ." It was a custom to anoint kings and priests with fragrant oil when they began their service. Although there is no indication that Moses and Elijah were anointed to serve as prophets, there are indications within the prophetic tradition that anointing was necessary to consecrate a prophet for his task. Elijah was told to anoint Elisha as his successor (1 Kgs. 19:16). Ps. 105:15 states, "Touch not my anointed ones, do my prophets no harm."

In Is. 61:1 the prophet states, "The Spirit of the Lord GOD is upon me, because the LORD has anointed me to bring good tidings to the afflicted." Apparently the presence of the Spirit was considered as valid an anointing as with oil. In this sense the expectation of the return of Elijah (Mal. 4:5-6) was looking for a Messiah. The Essenes at Qumran near the Dead Sea looked for two Messiahs: the priestly one from Aaron and the political one from Israel.

There is no doubt, however, that the dominant expectation in Israel was for a kingly Messiah from the line of David. Basic to this hope was the covenant which Yahweh had made with David. In addition to the examples noted earlier, there are a number of other oracles expecting a kingly Messiah.

The Problem of the Davidic Covenant

Yet there is a problem with this tradition. Samuel was basically right when he resisted the people's demand for a king. He knew the evils of a monarchy and warned them what would happen, but still they insisted. When Samuel prayed about the problem Yahweh told him, "Hearken to the voice of the people in all that they say to you; for they have not rejected you, but they have rejected me from being king over them" (1 Sam. 8:7).

The story of the monarchy in both the unified and divided kingdoms is one of the saddest aspects of Israel's history. At first it gave some physical security to the people and as long as David was true to Yahweh's will and served as his regent on earth the result was favorable. But even before David's reign was completed, the spiritual aspects of the Mosaic covenant were being pushed aside. As far as God's purpose for his people was concerned, Solomon's reign was a travesty.

Yet in spite of the sordid history of the monarchy and many of David's successors the dream of a greater David persisted. It is probably more accurate to say, as we have indicated with the dreams of Isaiah and Micah, that the awful spiritual conditions increased the urgency for a new David who would be God's true son.

The Son of David

Since Matthew was written to convince Jews that Jesus was their promised Messiah, the author places more stress on the Davidic covenant and genealogy than any other gospel writer. He wastes no time in making his point. In 1:1, the introduction to the genealogy, Jesus is called "the son of David." He is given this title eight more times in the gospel. The genealogy starts with Abraham, runs through David, and then continues with Solomon and the kings of Judah (1:6-11). In short, Matthew is concerned to show that Jesus was the royal son of David, the legitimate heir to the kingdom of heaven (God).

While Luke traces the genealogy down to David, he makes a drastic change by following the collateral line of Nathan (3:31), another son of David (2 Sam. 5:14). There is no way to reconcile the differences; therefore one has to make a choice between the two lists. The probability is that Luke's genealogy is more accurate overall.

Matthew has a further problem because his genealogy comes down to Joseph. Inasmuch as he believes in the virgin birth of Jesus, he has to explain: "Joseph the husband of Mary, of whom Jesus was born, who is called Christ" (1:6). In other words, Matthew's list does not deal with Jesus' physical lineage. It is only in the legal sense, as the adopted son of Joseph, that Jesus is "the son of David."

Jesus the Messiah (Christ)

It is important to note this fact because Jesus played down the idea of a royal, kingly Messiah. Concerning the beginning of his ministry Matthew comments, "Jesus began to preach, saying, 'Repent, for the kingdom of heaven is at hand' " (4:17). Mark quotes Jesus as declaring, "The time is fulfilled, and the kingdom of God is at hand; repent, and believe in the gospel" (1:15). The kingdom, therefore was not physical, but spiritual. One could enter it only by penitence. Brute force and violence would have no place in his kingdom; therefore he had no desire to associate his ministry with the zealots' desire to break the Roman yoke.

When Peter stated openly that Jesus was the Messiah (Christ), he and the rest of the disciples were commanded not to tell anyone (Matt. 16:16-20; Mk. 8:29-30; Lk. 9:20-21). In Mark's gospel the fact that Jesus was the Christ is kept secret until Peter's confession. Jesus' idea of God's Messiah was different. From beginning to end Jesus understood his earthly role more like "the Suffering Servant." To use the title Messiah was sure to raise expectations contrary to his purpose.

Only after his resurrection and ascension did the lordly aspects of Jesus become dominant. Because of his obedience on earth the Father gave him new power. His authority came from God, the king of all creation. To trace it through the Davidic covenant is a prooftexting approach.

Yahweh's Servant

A decidedly different view of God's chosen one is the description of the servant in four songs of Exilic Isaiah (42:1-4; 49:1-6; 50:4-11; 52:13-53:12). Yahweh says:

Behold my servant whom I uphold,
   my chosen in whom my soul delights;
I have put my Spirit upon him,
   he will bring forth justice to the nations.
He will not cry or lift up his voice,
   or make it heard in the street;
a bruised reed he will not break,
   and a dimly burning wick he will not quench;
   he will faithfully bring forth justice.
He will not fail or be discouraged
   till he has established justice in the earth;
   and the coastlands wait for his law (42:1-4).

Yahweh's servant will be gentle and patient in his mission of spreading knowledge of Yahweh's teaching or law (Hebrew *torah*) and of establishing justice throughout the nations of the Near East. This servant is clearly different from Cyrus, Yahweh's anointed one, even though he was a kind king, but his identity is not indicated. One thing is certain, however: Exilic Isaiah had in mind some group or person from his time. If his messages were to have any meaning for his audience they had to tie in with that historical situation.

Although most scholars do not include 42:5-9 as part of the first song, the passage has a definite bearing on our understanding of the servant. Yahweh, who created the heavens and earth and gave breath to the people on it, says:

I am the LORD, I have called you in righteousness,
   I have taken you by the hand and kept you;
I have given you as a covenant to the people,
   a light to the nations,
   to open the eyes that are blind,

to bring out the prisoners from the dungeon,
from the prison those who sit in darkness.
I am the LORD, that is my name;
my glory I give to no other,
nor my praise to graven images.
Behold, the former things have come to pass,
and new things I now declare;
before they spring forth
I tell you of them (42:6-9).

Because the phrase "a light to the nations" is missing from one of the important manuscripts of the Septuagint, some scholars remove it and interpret the servant's task as delivering the exiles from their dungeon in Babylonia. But unique as it may be, the idea of Yahweh's servant being a light to the peoples ignorant of Yahweh's law certainly fits in with 42:4. This will be possible because Yahweh will soon bring about his "new thing," the establishment of his reign of justice and peace.

Who Was the Servant?

In the second song the servant addresses peoples afar off:

The LORD called me from the womb,
from the body of my mother he named my name.
He made my mouth like a sharp sword,
in the shadow of his hand he hid me;
he made me a polished arrow,
in his quiver he hid me away.
And he said to me, "You are my servant,
Israel, in whom I will be glorified" (49:1-3).

And yet in 49:5 the servant's mission is "to bring Jacob back to him (Yahweh), and that Israel might be gathered to him." In other words, the servant seems to be a remnant or a person within captive Israel.

The interpretation of the second song hinges on the word "Israel" in 49:3. Was it originally in the song, or did an editor add it later on? Those commentators who favor the view that the servant was a collective group retain the word, but those who think in terms of an individual prefer to remove it. There are some good reasons for accepting either interpretation.

In his book *The Suffering Servant in Deutero-Isaiah* (1950), Christopher R. North discusses the wide range of views which have been proposed concerning the identity of the Servant. In spite of tremendous effort there is no completely convincing answer. The collective or corporate possibilities suggested have been Israel as a whole, ideal Israel, the remnant of Israel, the prophets, or the priests. Some examples of historical individuals proposed are Moses, Hezekiah, Isaiah, Jeremiah, Ezekiel, or Zerubbabel.

While some conservatives have interpreted the songs as predictive prophecy about Jesus as the Messiah, others have recognized the fact of different descriptions of the servant. Some of this mediating group of scholars have illustrated their composite view by a pyramid: Israel, as the base, had certain functions to perform; the remnant or spiritual Israel, the smaller group at the middle, had more specific tasks to accomplish; and finally the Messiah, at the summit, was to have the role of Redeemer.

Others have used the analogy of two concentric circles around a common center: Israel was the outer circle; Jeshurun "Upright One," spiritual Israel, was the inner circle; and Christ the center. One interpreter described the servant of Yahweh as a complex person: Messiah and his people or Christ as the head of the church.

The Difficult Mission

Exilic Isaiah seems to have thought of the servant in various ways. After noting the servant's role to Israel, Yahweh broadens his mission: "It is too light a thing that you should be my servant to raise up the tribes of Jacob and to restore the preserved of Israel; I will give you as a light to the nations, that my salvation may reach to the end of the earth" (49:6).

But before he gets to that phase of his work, he encounters great difficulty with his own people. The third song relates how he tried to sustain the weary exiles with words of comfort, but they considered his messages as lies and reacted violently. Because of his utter confidence that Yahweh would vindicate him ultimately he accepted willingly the abuse of his audience:

> I gave my back to the smiters,
>   and my cheeks to those who pulled out the beard;
> I hid not my face
>   from shame and spitting.
> For the Lord GOD helps me;
>   therefore I have not been confounded;

therefore I have set my face like a flint,
and I know that I shall not be put to shame;
he who vindicates me is near (50:6-8a).

It is possible that in the description of the servant we are seeing some
of the bitter experiences of Exilic Isaiah.

The Suffering Servant

The fourth servant song is Is. 52:13-53:12. There are a number of
difficulties in the Hebrew text, one of which is the variation in tenses
of the verbs. Overall, however, the actions of the servant are described
in the past and present tenses, while the rewards for his labor are in
the future. Conservatives have tended to interpret the past (or, perfect)
verb forms as "prophetic perfects": that is, the prophet was so certain
that the events would occur he put them in the past tense even though
they were still in the future. This is true in some instances, but when
the servant songs are viewed as a whole there are too many indications
that the prophet had in mind some group or person of his generation
or earlier.

The fourth song is in five units or strophes. In the first one
Yahweh tells us that the servant, disfigured by brutal attacks, will be
exalted:

Behold, my servant shall prosper,
he shall be exalted and lifted up,
and shall be very high.
As many were astonished at him—
his appearance was so marred, beyond human semblance,
and his form beyond that of the sons of men—
so shall he startle many nations;
kings shall shut their mouths because of him;
for that which has not been told them they shall see,
and that which they have not heard they shall understand (52:13-15).

Apparently the beaten servant is beginning his international ministry,
and as he does so the startled rulers of the nations are dumbfounded
by the gruesome sight of Yahweh's messenger.

The Confession of the Kings and Their People

In the second strophe the astonished kings express to their people
the difficulty of believing what they have seen and heard:

Who has believed what we have heard?
And to whom has the arm of the LORD been revealed:
For he grew up before him like a young plant,
    and like a root out of dry ground;
he had no form or comeliness that we should look at him,
    and no beauty that we should desire him.
He was despised and rejected by men;
    a man of sorrows, and acquainted with grief;
and as one from whom men hide their faces
    he was despised, and we esteemed him not (53:1-3).

The message of the servant, "the arm of the LORD," seemed incredible. His environment was so unpromising and as he grew up before Yahweh he had no beauty or personality that would attract people. This "man of sorrows" was so pathetic, people looked the other way.

But as the kings meditate on what they have seen and heard they begin to understand what the wounded servant was doing:

Surely he has borne our griefs
    and carried our sorrows;
yet we esteemed him stricken,
    smitten by God, and afflicted.
But he was wounded for our transgressions,
    he was bruised for our iniquities;
upon him was the chastisement that made us whole,
    and with his stripes we are healed.
All we like sheep have gone astray;
    we have turned every one to his own way;
and the LORD has laid on him
    the iniquity of us all (53:4-6).

The servant was suffering in their place for their sins, not his own. Then the kings and their people acknowledge that, like straying sheep, they were sinners, but now they are forgiven because the LORD laid their iniquity on his servant.

In the fourth strophe the kings and people marvel at the inner fortitude of the servant.

He was oppressed, and he was afflicted,
    yet he opened not his mouth;
like a lamb that is led to the slaughter,
    and like a sheep that before its shearers is dumb,
    so he opened not his mouth.

By oppression and judgment he was taken away;
  and as for his generation who considered
that he was cut off out of the land of the living,
  stricken for the transgression of my people?
And they made his grave with the wicked
  and with a rich man in his death,
although he had done no violence,
  and there was no deceit in his mouth (53:7-9).

Evidently the servant was brought to trial and unjustly treated, but unlike Job and Jeremiah he did not open his mouth. Although he was innocent of any violent acts or words he was condemned, executed, and buried with the wicked.

The Purpose of Yahweh

The fifth and final strophe of the fourth song is Yahweh's explanation of what happened and what would result from the servant's suffering:

Yet it was the will of the LORD to bruise him;
  he has put him to grief;
when he makes himself an offering for sin,
  he shall see his offspring, he shall prolong his days;
the will of the LORD shall prosper in his hand;
  he shall see the fruit of the travail of his soul and be satisfied;
by his knowledge shall the righteous one, my servant,
    make many to be accounted righteous;
    and he shall bear their iniquities.
Therefore I will divide him a portion with the great,
  and he shall divide the spoil with the strong;
because he poured out his soul to death,
  and was numbered with the transgressors;
yet he bore the sin of many,
  and made intercession for the transgressors (53:10-12).

The servant's suffering and death were the will of Yahweh to show his judgment of sin and his mercy for sinners. In spite of the grief, the servant will be glad that he was obedient. He will be satisfied because of the many who will come to righteousness and of the reward which Yahweh will give him.

Vicarious Sacrifice

The idea of vicarious sacrifice (suffering in the place of others) was common in the ancient world and it was accepted by the Israelites. Animals took on the burden of their donor's sins and they were slain or driven out into the wilderness (Lev. 16:5-10, 20-22). But the concept was raised to a new level by Exilic Isaiah's insight that the sin problem would be solved with a human sacrifice. The remarkable fourth song is one of the greatest passages in all of Scripture. It has no parallel in the Old Testament and it stands supremely above any of the insights of other nations in the ancient world.

Some of those who take the collective interpretation understand the servant as Israel in the exile. God's people suffer unjustly and the nations witnessing the humiliation in Babylonia are astonished and do not know what to make of it. Then they realize that their own salvation and future rests with the servant people. They watch them perish, but as in Ezekiel's "valley of dry bones" the "whole house of Israel" comes to life (Ezek. 37:1-14). When they return home they do not regret their experience because many have come to the knowledge of Yahweh by means of their witness. Moreover, Yahweh will bless them and make them great because of their obedience.

There is an element of truth in this point of view, and perhaps Exilic Isaiah thought in such terms at times while receiving the vision, but it seems that during his revelatory experience the prophet came to understand the servant as an individual. It is rather difficult to interpret some of the details of the vision as figurative language for Israel. While the suffering servant vision had some basis in the historical context of the prophet, it exceeded his own understanding and schedule. Its deepest meaning was not filled to the full in his day, yet it was a valid vision because it anticipated what Yahweh was going to do in a more distant future through one of Israel's sons.

Jesus, the Suffering Servant

Eight of the fifteen verses in the fourth servant song are quoted in part or as a whole in the New Testament. There are allusions to the song in other places, but it is amazing that so little use was made of its most important aspects.

Paul took the last part of Is. 52:15 as his guideline for preaching the gospel where others had not gone (Rom. 15:20-21). He (Rom. 10:16) and John (12:37-38) quote 53:1 as an explanation why the gospel and Jesus' signs were rejected. Matthew (8:16-17) thinks the first part of 53:4 foretold how Jesus would cast out demons and heal the sick.

The Ethiopian eunuch was puzzled by 53:7-8 until Philip explained the verses as "the good news of Jesus" (Acts 8:30-35). 1 Pet. 2:21-25 describes Jesus as an example of patient suffering for God's will. Peter is clearly basing his illustration on 53:5-12. He cites two verses (5,9) and uses language similar to other parts of the passage.

The only explicit indication that Jesus saw himself in the fourth song is Lk 22:37: "For I tell you that this scripture must be fulfilled in me, 'And he was reckoned with transgressors' " (53:12). And yet it seems that the model for his ministry was influenced by "the Suffering Servant."

Chapter 8
The Book of Daniel

The book of Daniel is one of the most basic prophetic books in the Bible. In a sense it is a "key" book because proper understanding of it "unlocks" a number of mysteries connected with predictive prophecy.

It is one of the most puzzling books to interpret, moreover, because it swarms with ambiguous symbols and statements. This difficulty led to some marginal comments later on by persons trying to be helpful. These in turn were copied into the text, thereby complicating even more the task of trying to make sense out of the book.

While most conservative scholars have tried to defend every little detail of Daniel, radical critics have discounted much of the book. The truth is somewhere between these extremes.

There are two distinctive units in Daniel: chapters 1-6 and 7-12. The first unit has six stories:

1. Daniel and three friends in the Babylonian court (1:1-21);
2. Daniel interprets Nebuchadnezzar's dream (2:1-49);
3. Daniel's three friends in the fiery furnace (3:1-30);
4. Nebuchadnezzar's madness (4:1-37);
5. Belshazzar's feast (5:1-31);
6. Daniel in the lions' den (6:1-28).

The second unit has four dream-visions of Daniel:

1. The four beasts (7:1-28);
2. The ram and the he-goat (8:1-27);
3. The seventy weeks (9:1-27);
4. The survey of history and the last days (10:1-12:13).

Early Eschatology

We noted earlier that "eschatology" was a technical term dealing with end times and last things. Prior to the exile the prophets held in tension (1) the vision of God's will for the future and (2) the fact of realities here on earth. God's covenant with Israel would be worked out in the stream of human history. The ultimate, as expressed by Isaiah, was the ideal kingdom of justice and peace here on this planet.

But after years of appealing to the people to repent, Jeremiah realized that the human heart was etched with sin and desperately wicked. The only hope was for God to make a new covenant in which the will of God would be written on the hearts of his people. Yet that future was to be on this earth. Ezekiel explained the same stubbornness as the petrification of the heart. Yahweh would perform a transplant by substituting a "heart of flesh" for the "heart of stone." Although Ezekiel's visions have some cosmic, other-worldly elements, still he looked forward to the rebuilding of the temple in Jerusalem after the exile. The prophet was still keeping the heavenly and the earthly in tension.

For many of the exiles the capture and destruction of Jerusalem was traumatic. They had cut their teeth on the theory that God's presence was in the temple and that he would protect that building and the city of Jerusalem because it was his palace. This idea that God was a prisoner in Zion, David's city, was smashed by Nebuchadnezzar. The only explanation for those who held this point of view was that Marduk, the god of Babylon, was the truly powerful, sovereign god. Exilic Isaiah saved the situation by raising the narrow, parochial view which Judah had prior to the exile to a new level. Yahweh was the cosmic God: "It is he who sits above the circle of the earth, and its inhabitants are like grasshoppers; who stretches out the heavens like a curtain, and spreads them like a tent to dwell in; who brings princes to naught, and makes the rulers of the earth as nothing" (Is. 40:22-23).

It was actually Yahweh, Exilic Isaiah claimed, who brought Nebuchadnezzar to destroy Jerusalem and to take his covenant people into exile. The power and sovereignty of Yahweh had been exerted to punish his disobedient people. Marduk and Nebuchadnezzar were simply tools in the hands of Yahweh. The cosmic God of Israel was still involved with human history, however, and so Exilic Isaiah looked forward to the return to Jerusalem and Judah.

Apocalyptic Eschatology

In the postexilic period, on the other hand, the disillusionment and suffering of some Jewish groups led to such deep despair they gave up on history. There was no justice and no progress toward it;

therefore God could not work out the salvation of his people in this earthly stream of activity. He would have to pull out his righteous ones and close the age with a catastrophic destruction of the world.

And yet in this whole process God had a timetable. His plans were made known to the prophets of despair in visions with bizarre symbolism. Most of the time the meaning of the message was revealed to the prophet, but sometimes even he groped in darkness. These secrets of God were shared with the righteous elect of their own group, but not with outsiders.

This was a drastic shift from the regular prophets. Their primary call, as we have seen, was to be God's messengers. The revelations of God burned within them so that they had to share their truths with their own people anywhere. Moreover, the classical prophets tied God's activities to events in human history. In the later type of revelation there was no concern or attempt to be relevant to what was going around them. Those who shared this view had their eyes fixed on God's cosmic timetable while they watched for their deliverance from the misery and sorrow of this life. Their "secret" was what gave them hope.

This kind of outlook and the literature produced by it have been labeled "apocalyptic." This technical term comes from the Greek word *apokalypsis* meaning "unveiling, revelation." From it, via Latin, came our word "apocalypse." As we have noted, this apocalyptic point of view had its roots in prophecy, but classical prophecy came to an end in the postexilic period when the apocalyptic seers began their rise to authority. Some scholars have labeled preexilic prophecy as "eschatology," while reserving "apocalyptic" for the later development in Judah. Others prefer to use "eschatology" in the general sense of anything pertaining to end times, and so they designate this later phase as "apocalyptic eschatology."

The book of Daniel, especially chapters 7-12, was a product of the apocalyptic point of view. This perspective did not stop there, however, because the early Christians were influenced by it. It is no surprise, therefore, to find an apocalypse as the final book of the New Testament. In fact, the book of Revelation is described as the "revelation (*apokalypsis*) of Jesus Christ."

The Date of Daniel

The book informs us that Daniel was one of the exiles captured by Nebuchadnezzar in 605 B.C. and brought back to Babylonia "the land of Shinar" (1:1-4). He and three of his young Jewish friends were chosen because of their attractiveness and wisdom to be trained for service in the court of Nebuchadnezzar. His last vision is dated in the third year of Cyrus, that is, 535 B.C. If Daniel were only fifteen when he was taken captive he would have been 85 when he received his last revelation. This is theoretically possible but there is no indication that any of the other prophets lived that long, let alone were active at that advanced age.

Tradition has found further evidence for the historicity of a 6th-century Daniel in the references to a certain Daniel in Ezekiel. In a warning to some of the disobedient exiles, Ezekiel told them that they could not hope for salvation in the day of Yahweh's judgment. Even if "Noah, Daniel, and Job" were there "they would deliver but their own lives by their righteousness" (14:14, 20). Noah and Job were patriarchs from ancient times. It is certainly strange to find a contemporary of Ezekiel sandwiched in between them.

The Identity of Ezekiel's "Dan²el"

There is a further problem because the name in Ezekiel is spelled *Dan²el* instead of *Daniel*. The Bible reader doesn't know this since most of the translations have considered it only a different spelling and so they have retained the usual form of the name. It is interesting that one of the Canaanite epics discovered in Syria tells of a just old man by the name of *Dan²el*, the same spelling as in Ezekiel. The late Edward J. Young, a staunch defender of the literal accuracy of the book of Daniel, recognized the similarity of names, but he rejected the idea that Ezekiel was referring to the Canaanite *Dan²el* because the epic did not describe him as being righteous.

In an oracle against the prince of Tyre, that infamous Phoenician (Canaanite) port, Ezekiel refers to his arrogant claim: "I am a god, I sit in the seat of the gods, in the heart of the seas" (28:2). Although Ezekiel reminds him that he is "a man, not god," yet the prophet does grant that the prince is "indeed wiser than Daniel" (28:3). The name is *Dan²el* again and he seems to be an ancient wise man known among the Canaanites.

Thus far we have learned that this patriarch was a just and wise person. It is likely that a person of this caliber was righteous as well, and perhaps Ezekiel knew this from stories which have not come to our knowledge. Yet in spite of all the evidence which points the other way, Young insists that Ezekiel "deliberately" placed Daniel "between the two devout men of antiquity for the purpose of glorifying him" (*The Prophecy of Daniel*, p. 275). This is another case of a presupposition determining the answer to a problem in the face of valid contrary evidence.

Historical Accuracy of Daniel

In addition to the almost magical forms of miracle which characterize the stories of Daniel, there are a number of details which have led scholars to doubt the historical accuracy of the book. We must not get sidetracked from our purpose of dealing with prophecy and prediction, but it will help us to evaluate the book of Daniel by considering two of these problems.

One occurs in the very first verse: "In the third year of the reign of Jehoiakim king of Judah, Nebuchadnezzar king of Babylon came to Jerusalem and besieged it" (1:1). Jehoiakim reigned 609-598 B.C. According to one system of reckoning a king's reign the third year would be 606, while another would have 605. A verse in Jeremiah helps clarify the issue: "The word that came to Jeremiah concerning all the people of Judah, in the fourth year of Jehoiakim the son of Josiah, king of Judah (that was the first year of Nebuchadrezzar king of Babylon)" (25:1). Nebuchadrezzar is a more original spelling of Nebuchadnezzar and so the verses are referring to the same person.

There is no evidence anywhere that Nebuchadnezzar got as far south as Judah in 606 B.C.; therefore conservatives have argued that the third year of Jehoiakim in Daniel is the same as the fourth year in Jeremiah, that is, both verses are referring to 605 B.C. This may well be the situation.

The Siege of Jerusalem

But the real problem in the verse is the claim that Nebuchadnezzar "besieged" Jerusalem. Our knowledge of the Babylonian kings was greatly enriched in 1956 when Donald J. Wiseman published records of their activities preserved on clay tablets in the British

Museum. Because King Nabopolassar stayed in Babylon during the summer of 605 B.C. his son Nebuchadnezzar assumed command of the army and routed the last of the Assyrians and their Egyptian allies at Carchemish.

In August, while chasing the Egyptians down through Syria-Palestine, he learned of his father's death. He returned to Babylon immediately and ascended the throne on Sept. 7. Evidently he felt very secure because he returned west in October and stayed out there until February 604. No doubt he was consolidating his hold on Syria-Palestine by making sure that the Egyptians stayed home and also by having the small kings of the area recognize his sovereignty.

Jerusalem is located in the central hill country over 2,500 feet above sea level. From the coastal plain it was a long, uphill march for an army to reach the city. Since Nebuchadnezzar was chasing the Egyptians along the coastal plain he had no interest then in bothering the people in the hill country.

2 Kgs. 24:7 makes a general statement: "And the king of Egypt did not come again out of his land, for the king of Babylon had taken all that belonged to the king of Egypt from the brook of Egypt to the river Euphrates." Inasmuch as the king of Egypt did not control Judah, it is implicit that Nebuchadnezzar did not overrun the area either. Josephus, the 1st-century A.D. Jewish historian, makes this explicit: "So the king of Babylon passed over Euphrates, and took all of Syria, as far as Pelusium, excepting Judea" (*Antiquities of the Jews*, Book X, Chap. VI, paragraph 1). Pelusium was the eastern area of Egypt; therefore 2 Kgs. 24:7 and Josephus are saying the same thing.

2 Kgs. 24:1 states, "In his days Nebuchadnezzar king of Babylon came up, and Jehoiakim became his servant three years, then he turned and rebelled against him." Jehoiakim's recognition of Nebuchadnezzar probably happened in the October-February campaign after his coronation. He led his army through the west accepting acknowledgment from various small kings that they would be his servants and pay tribute to him. Those that resisted got special attention from the army. This is clearly what happened in the case of Jehoiakim. At first he recognized Nebuchadnezzar's sovereignty and paid his taxes for three years, but when he missed the next April 15th deadline the Babylonians got after him.

It was in 605 after Nebuchadnezzar's victory at Carchemish that Jeremiah warned the people of Judah that because of their disobedience they would go into exile for seventy years (Jer. 25:3-11). Nowhere does Jeremiah mention a siege of Jerusalem. He was very active in the years 605 and 604 and had there been a siege he would have issued warnings and exhortations as he did later on during the 598 and 587 invasions.

All the evidence indicates that the Babylonian king did not lay siege to Jerusalem in 605. The verb used in Dan. 1:1 is one commonly employed to describe a siege. If the writer meant it that way then he was wrong. Some conservatives admit there is a real problem but they tend to understand the verb more in the sense of Nebuchadnezzar putting psychological pressure on Jehoiakim to become his servant. If this was the intent of the writer it was a strange way to express it. On the other hand, if the verb "besieged" has to be reinterpreted to make the detail fit our present knowledge of the historical context, what assurance is there that the book is using language in a normal way?

Nebuchadnezzar and Belshazzar

The narrative of Daniel shifts from Nebuchadnezzar in chap. 4 to Belshazzar in chap. 5. Although there is no transition between the two kings, it seems that one story flows out from the other. Four times Nebuchadnezzar is referred to as the father of Belshazzar (5:2, 11, 13, 18) and once Belshazzar is called the son of Nebuchadnezzar (5:22).

To most readers today the "father-son" relationship between the kings is assumed, but the actual list of Babylonian kings indicates otherwise:

> Nabopolassar (626-605), succeeded by his son
> Nebuchadnezzar (605-562), succeeded by his son
> Amel-marduk (562-560), succeeded by his brother-in-law
> Neriglissar (560-556), succeeded by his son
> Labashi-marduk (a few months in 556), overthrown by
> Nabonidus (556-539), a member of a leading family whose son
> Belshazzar was coregent (554-539) while his father was away
> from Babylon.

Not only were there four rulers between Nebuchadnezzar and Belshazzar, there was no direct relationship between them because the bloodline was broken twice, first by a brother-in-law and then by a usurper.

Robert Dick Wilson notes seven different ways "father" was used in antiquity and then he lists twelve uses of "son" (*Studies in the Book of Daniel*, Vol. I, pp. 117-18). It is true that the ancients used the two terms with many meanings, but when Wilson argues that Daniel may have meant that Nebuchadnezzar was the "predecessor" or "great-grandfather" of Belshazzar, the solution does not increase our confidence in the precision of the story.

A fragmentary text found at Qumran seems to provide a better answer to the problem. It describes the madness of a king named Nabonidus. If the story of Dan. 4 applied to him, then the father-son relationship is accurate. But this means that the less-known name Nabonidus in the original story was replaced by the better-known Nebuchadnezzar. Thus the apparent solution raises a problem about the accuracy of the Daniel text which we have.

Conservatives like Edward J. Young and J. Barton Payne, building on the work of Robert Dick Wilson and Ernst Wilhelm Hengstenberg (1802-1869), the patriarch of conservatism, claim that the book of Daniel is innocent of any historical errors until proven guilty. Yet when the contrary evidence is brought to bear, their zeal and imagination create solutions which seem plausible to them.

The whole point of this discussion about historical accuracy is to indicate that one has an uneasy feeling when a number of times the credibility of Daniel has to be supported by subjective, strained explanations.

Historical Prediction in Daniel

The most positive clue for determining a date for Daniel is the historical survey in chap. 11. An angel "having the appearance of a man" comforted Daniel (10:18-11:1) and then revealed to him the history down to end-times. Dan. 11:2-4 covers the rest of the Persian empire and the kingdom of Alexander the Great and his successors. Then begins a rather detailed summary (11:5-20) of the conflicts between "the king of the south," the series of Ptolemaic kings ruling in Egypt, and "the king of the north," the Seleucid kings in Syria.

The most detailed description (11:21-45) is given concerning Antiochus Epiphanes, the Syrian king who ruled 175-163 B.C. The survey is accurate down through verse 39, but nothing in 40-45 fits the later history of this king. Although some conservatives think the activities of Antiochus cease at verse 35, there is practically unanimous agreement between conservative and liberal scholars that the historical survey is talking about Antiochus. What the conservatives do is to take either verses 36-45 or 40-45 and project them into the future as a description of what will happen at the end-time.

What is the basis for separating by thousands of years the two sections of the summary? It is the presupposition that the angel and Daniel cannot be wrong. As long as the survey coincides with known history the conservatives follow it, but the material which disagrees is assumed to be prophecy for some future time. Again it is a case of "Heads I win; tails, you lose."

The events in the section 11:36-39, where history breaks off, occurred about 166 B.C. If Daniel received this information in 535, then he had precise historical knowledge 369 years ahead of time. If this be so, then it is the longest, most detailed prophecy in all of the Old Testament. God could have done it, but again we canot help asking, "Why?" The periods of history covered are very interesting and the section about Antiochus is a crucial period in Jewish history, but why in the light of God's total purpose for humankind would he divulge to a person in exile prewritten history centuries ahead of time?

As painful as the answer may be to conservatives, the strong probability is that the writer was one of the Jews suffering under the atrocities of Antiochus and he was summarizing previous history as a prelude to his word of assurance that God would deliver them.

Two Daniels

Most critical scholars would say that the entire book of Daniel was written about 167 or 166 B.C. But there seem to be some distinctive differences between the two halves:

1-6	7-12
1. Stories about Daniel	1. Dream-visions of Daniel
2. Babylonian atmosphere	2. Little Babylonian atmosphere
3. Angels mentioned (3:28; 6:22) but not named	3. Developed angelology with Gabriel (8:16; 9:21) and Michael (10:13, 21; 12:1)

The first section appears to have been written in Babylonia. The stories repeat the theme of God's protection of those who have the courage to maintain their convictions in the face of persecution and suffering.

These stories spoke to the *Hasidim*, "Pious, Faithful" Jews who were threatened by Antiochus "the contemptible person" (11:21). When thwarted by the Romans from conquering Egypt he returned to Palestine where he took out his anger on the Jews by stopping the burnt offerings and erecting a pagan altar in the temple. This was "the abomination that makes desolate" (11:30-31).

In his attempt to force conversion of the Jews to the Greek faith and culture, Antiochus instructed his officers to invite Jews to pork barbecues and then order them to eat or be killed. Many of the faithful "wise" ones died or suffered torture (11:33). The "little help" in 11:34 was the revolt started by the priest Mattathias and carried on by his son Judas Maccabeus. It was during this period that one of the *Hasidim* received revelations of what God was going to do. He wrote down chapters 7-12 to encourage his fellow sufferers and to inform them what God's plans were.

An interesting feature of Daniel is that about half of the book is in Aramaic, a Semitic language closely related to Hebrew. It became the official language for the Assyrian, Babylonian, and Persian empires, and eventually it replaced Hebrew as the common language in Palestine. Daniel shifts to Aramaic in 2:4 where the Chaldeans say to King Nebuchadnezzar "O king, live for ever!" and it continues through 7:28. Scholars have been puzzled by this odd situation and a number of theories have been proposed to explain it. Some consider the two units of the book to be 1-7 and 8-12, but it is more likely that when Maccabean Daniel attached his unit 7-12 he translated the first chapter into Aramaic as a natural bond with the stories about Daniel.

Pseudonymity

The fact that a writer about 166 B.C. would put his revelations in the framework of the early Persian empire and attach his message to an earlier book causes great difficulty to the conservative mind. "It makes the book's record of itself a deception" Payne declares, "and it necessarily involves Jesus Christ—who believed that 'Daniel the prophet' did predict Roman imperialism (Matt. 24:15)—in a falsehood based on His presumed ignorance of Scripture" (*Encyclopedia of Biblical Prophecy*, pp. 372-73).

The whole issue hinges on the definition of "deception." Jewish tradition felt that Malachi was the last of the prophets. With him the spirit of prophecy disappeared. In essence Judaism closed the prophetic canon because they expected no more books. But the apocalyptic seers were convinced that God was speaking to them, therefore they wrote down their visions and shared them with their own groups. Later when the apocalyptic point of view became more dominant some of these writings were attached to earlier books. Zech. 9-14 is a case in point.

An alternative method of gaining authority and a hearing for one's message was to put it in the mouth of some patriarch or famous person from earlier times. The use of a pseudonym or "pen name" was true of most of the apocalypses which are outside the Hebrew canon, and it seems to be the case with Daniel. These writers were not liars as such. They were good people convinced that they had God's word and they used this means to get a hearing. This "means to an end" must not be judged in the light of the Christian standard of honesty.

The Integrity of Jesus

The claim that belief in a Maccabean Daniel involves Jesus in a falsehood is itself a false, emotional argument. Matt. 24:15 reads: "So when you see the desolating sacrilege spoken of by the prophet Daniel, standing in the holy place (let the reader understand), then let those who are in Judea flee to the mountains." The parallel passage in Mk. 13:14 has: "But when you see the desolating sacrilege set up where it ought not to be (let the reader understand), then let those who are in Judea flee to the mountains." There is no reference to the prophet Daniel in Mark. The probability is that the words "spoken of by the prophet Daniel" were added by Matthew and not a part of Jesus' original statement.

Jesus *was predicting* that in the light of the way the Jews were acting the Romans would desecrate the temple, as Antiochus had, and then destroy the city. Jesus attended the Feast of Dedication (Hanukkah) in Jerusalem (John 10:22) in which the cleansing of the temple by Judas was celebrated. He had heard the story about Antiochus and he knew that Daniel's prophecy had been fulfilled in the Maccabean period. In his warning Jesus *was predicting* that history was going to repeat itself—there would be another "desolating sacrilege." Thus, when Payne claims that Jesus believed that Daniel predicted the Roman destruction of Jerusalem he is actually reading his own interpretation into what Jesus said. As we shall see in the next chapter Daniel predicted the cleansing of the temple by Judas and he was right. Jesus predicted another desecration of the temple and he was right too.

The same fallacious argument is made when it is claimed by conservatives that we make Jesus a liar if we do not believe that the story of Jonah is completely literal, historical fact. Jesus referred to Jonah simply to illustrate a point from a book which his audience knew. His statement says nothing about his thoughts concerning the historicity, authorship, and date of the book. We simply do not know how much he knew about the critical issues related to Scripture. Even if he did have some insight into these matters it would not have served his purpose to discuss them. In such situations it is the conservatives' rigid views which are at stake, not the integrity of Jesus.

Chapter 9
The Visions of Daniel

Now that we have discussed the background of the book of Daniel and the critical issues associated with its composition, we are ready to consider the meaning of the apocalyptic visions described there.

The Ram and the He-goat

The most explicit vision is in chap. 8, where the text returns to the Hebrew language. In the third year of King Belshazzar (552 B.C.) Maccabean Daniel was taken in vision to Susa, the winter capital of the Persians. This experience was similar to Ezekiel's being taken by the spirit to Jerusalem.

There by the river Ulai (Eulaeus) he saw a ram standing on the bank of the river. "It had two horns; and both were high, but one was higher than the other, and the higher one came up last. I saw the ram charging westward and northward and southward; no beast could stand before him, and there was no one who could rescue from his power; he did as he pleased and magnified himself" (8:3-4). In 8:20 the horns are identified as "the kings of Media and Persia." The Medes came to power first but they soon lost their sovereignty to Cyrus the Persian. Thus the ram was the Medo-Persian empire.

While he was watching the ram strut around, a he-goat came from the west. He "had a conspicuous horn between his eyes" (8:5), like the fabled unicorn. The angry goat struck the ram, broke his two horns, and trampled on him. The goat is identified in 8:21 as the Greek empire and the big horn as the first king, that is, Alexander the Great. "Then the he-goat magnified himself exceedingly; but when he was strong, the great horn was broken, and instead of it there came up four conspicuous horns toward the four winds of heaven" (8:8).

Alexander extended his empire as far as India, but on his return through Babylonia in 323 B.C. he died at the young age of 33. The empire was divided among his generals: Cassander in the west controlled Greece; Lysimachus in the north governed Asia Minor and Thrace; Seleucus ruled Babylonia and Syria on the east; and in the south Ptolemy was king of Egypt.

The Little Horn

One of the four horns produced "a little horn, which grew exceedingly great" (8:9). "It magnified itself, even up to the Prince of the host; and the continual burnt offering was taken away from him, and the place of his sanctuary was overthrown" (8:11). Practically every interpreter, whether conservative or liberal, recognizes the little horn as the Seleucid king Antiochus Epiphanes. A constant refrain of these visions about the earthly kingdoms is that they "magnified" themselves. This arrogance will be judged when God's kingdom comes.

The "Prince" was probably the high priest Onias III, who was ordered slain in 171 B.C. by Menelaus the wicked priest appointed by Antiochus. The "host" was the Jews, the people of God. On the 15th of Kislev (about Dec.1) 168 B.C., burnt offerings were stopped and the temple desecrated by an altar of Zeus, the Greek God worshipped by Antiochus, erected over the Jewish altar.

When a "holy one" inquired as to the duration of the desecration, Daniel heard "another holy one" reply, "For 2,300 evenings and mornings; then the sanctuary shall be restored to its rightful state" (8:13-14). The text is not clear whether "evenings and mornings" are to be considered as units of "one day," or to be counted as two separate items. Tradition tends to take the former view and claims that the writer meant 2,300 days; about 6 years, 4 months. Payne, for example, begins the period in mid-171 when the brother of Menelaus, the corrupt priest, stole sacred vessels from the temple, and ends it with the cleansing of the temple by Judas on Kislev 25, 165 (*Encyclopedia of Biblical Prophecy*, p. 382).

But burnt offerings were not stopped until 168; therefore the liberals have contended that the reference is to the evening and morning sacrifices which used to be offered in the temple. Accordingly, the answer to the question "How long will the desecration last?" was 2,300 sacrifices, that is, 1,150 days.

We know that Judas cleansed the temple 3 years and 10 days after the desecration by Antiochus. That was 1,090 or 1,102 days later, depending on which calendar was used. Since Maccabean Daniel was writing during the period of desecration, his prediction came true even though his projection was a little long.

Daniel's Perplexity and Fear

We have noted the interpretation as we went along, but of course it was not given to Daniel until after the vision was complete. While he pondered over its meaning the angel Gabriel was instructed to give him the answer. Daniel was frightened and bowed to the ground. "Understand, O son of man," Gabriel said, "that the vision is for the time of the end" (8:17). This is a clear indication that Daniel thought the Messianic kingdom would follow the terrible reign of Antiochus. After interpreting part of the vision Gabriel offered more description about Antiochus:

> His power shall be great, and he shall cause fearful destruction, and shall succeed in what he does, and destroy mighty men and the people of the saints. By his cunning he shall make deceit prosper under his hand, and in his own mind he shall magnify himself. Without warning he shall destroy many; and he shall even rise up against the Prince of princes; but, by no human hand, he shall be broken (8:24-25).

Then Gabriel instructed Daniel to "seal up the vision, for it pertains to many days hence" (8:26). The experience overcame Daniel and he was sick for days. He finally recovered enough to get back to work, but he "was appalled by the vision and did not understand it" (8:27). No doubt the "little horn" puzzled him because it had been described but not identified.

The Great Image

Chapter 2 in Daniel tells of Nebuchadnezzar's dream about a great image. "The head of the image was fine gold, its breast and arms of silver, its belly and thighs of bronze, its legs of iron, its feet partly of iron and partly of clay" (2:32-33). Then a stone "cut out by no human hand" struck the image and shattered it until nothing was left. "But the stone that struck the image became a great mountain and filled the earth" (2:34-35).

When the king's wise men could not solve the riddle, Daniel did. "You are the head of gold," he informed Nebuchadnezzar, "after you shall arise another kindom inferior to you, and yet a third kingdom of bronze, which shall rule over all the earth. And there shall be a fourth kingdom, strong as iron" (2:38-40). Then Daniel added, "And as you saw the feet and toes partly of potter's clay and partly of iron, it shall be a divided kingdom; . . . As you saw the iron mixed with miry clay, so they will mix with one another in marriage (*literally*, by the seed of men), but they will not hold together, just as iron does not mix with clay" (2:41, 43).

God's Kingdom

Finally Daniel explained the stone which smashed the image: "And in the days of those kings the God of heaven will set up a kingdom which shall never be destroyed, nor shall its sovereignty be left to another people. It shall break in pieces all these kingdoms and bring them to an end, and it shall stand for ever" (2:44). The reference is clearly to the universal Messianic kingdom for which the Jews longed.

Yet Daniel's answer indicates the difficulty of trying to interpret the details of these dream-visions literally. There is no problem in a stone crushing the image, but when the parts are interpreted as successive kingdoms over centuries, what does it mean to say that the kingdom will be set up "in the days of those kings" and it will "break in pieces all these kingdoms and bring them to an end"? If the series of kingdoms is considered as one composite Gentile power, like the image, then it is implied that God's kingdom will come at the last and crush the feet of the fourth kingdom.

The Four Kingdoms

The problem comes in determining what the other three kingdoms were. Tradition has maintained one list whereas liberal scholarship has proposed another:

Kingdom	Tradition	Liberals
Gold head	Babylonian	Babylonian
Silver breast and arms	Medo-Persian	Median
Bronze belly and thighs	Grecian	Persian
Iron legs	Roman	Grecian
Iron and clay feet	?	Seleucids and Ptolemies

Both groups have difficulty in squaring their lists with all the details of the vision. It comes down to weighing the evidence and comparing it with data from the other visions. But obviously presuppositions tend to determine which items will have the most weight.

We noted that in 8:17 the vision ending with Antiochus referred to "the time of the end" and that the writer thought God's kingdom was coming after Antiochus. "This phrase is very difficult," Edward J. Young admits, "but the key to its interpretation is to be found in the phrase *in the latter part of the indignation* (vs. 19). Thus, it refers to the end of time when afflictions or indignation are to be permitted upon Israel. It is the end of the OT period and the ushering in of the New" (*The Prophecy of Daniel*, p. 176). Young wants to make all the visions refer in one way or another to Jesus Christ, and so to get around the very difficult phrase he reads his whole presupposition into the text.

The Fourth Kingdom

The plain meaning of 8:17 is one of the reasons liberals have argued that the fourth kingdom in chapter 2 must be the Grecian empire. Then the idea of the iron and clay mixing with one another "by the seed of men" would refer to the treaty marriages that were attempted between the Seleucid and Ptolemaic kingdoms. Furthermore, Antiochus would be part of the feet of iron and clay struck by God's new kingdom. But to do this they have to make Media the second empire and Persia the third. And yet 8:20 claims that the kings of Media and Persia were the two horns of the ram. This would imply that the writer thought in terms of one empire, the Medo-Persian. This, of course, is precisely what the conservatives claim.

The liberals stress 8:3 instead, where it notes that one of the ram's horns came up and then "the higher one came up last." They contend also that the writer thought in terms of a separate Median kingdom because at the death of Belshazzar "Darius the Mede received his kingdom" (5:31). Conservatives counter that the kingdom is not described as being Median. Rather, Darius received Belshazzar's kingdom.

Young devotes many pages to the problem. He notes that Cyrus captured the Median empire *before* he conquered Babylon; therefore there never was a Median kingdom between the Babylonian and Persian empires. He goes over the data about Darius and Cyrus with a finetooth comb and shows logically that the writer could not have thought in terms of two separate kingdoms. Yet details of apocalyptic visions are not logically put together. We know that he should not have thought in terms of a separate Median kingdom, but that does not prove that he did not think so. It is more probable that Maccabean Daniel understood the fourth kingdom as Alexander's empire.

Iron and Clay Feet

It should be noted that the identification of the iron and clay feet was a question mark in the traditional list. Here there is no traditional answer. Most conservatives are convinced that the fourth kingdom was the Roman empire because that permits them to understand Jesus as the stone not cut by human hands. But what does one do with the mixed feet and divided kingdom? During the life of Jesus the Roman Emperors Caesar Augustus (44 B.C.-A.D. 14) and Tiberius (A.D. 14-37) ruled supremely.

Some conservatives suggest the eastern and western sections of the Roman empire, but the split came centuries after Jesus lived. Young solves the whole problem by translating "the kingdom will be composite or diverse" (*The Prophecy of Daniel*, p. 77). Here is a scholar who spends pages straining out grammatical and linguistic gnats trying to prove his point and then when caught in a difficulty he swallows a camel without batting an eyelash. Everywhere in Aramaic and Hebrew the verb means "to divide, split."

Enough has been said to indicate that trying to solve the apocalyptic puzzles is like trying to catch a greased pig. You think you have the answer and then you don't. As far as the understanding of Maccabean Daniel and the Jews who lived then are concerned, the evidence is in favor of Greece as being the fourth empire. But when the Messianic kingdom did not come, then of course the Jews began to reinterpret the fourth kingdom as the Roman empire.

The Four Beasts

In the first year of Belshazzar (554 B.C.) Daniel had a dream and in good apocalyptic style he wrote the vision down immediately after the revelation (7:1). In it four great beasts come up out of the sea (7:3) and they represent four kingdoms. Although using different symbols, there is a definite parallelism between this vision and the great image in chapter 2. The problems are much the same, except that there is more information concerning the fourth kingdom.

The first beast "was like a lion and had eagles' wings," then "its wings were plucked off, and it was lifted up from the ground and made to stand upon two feet like a man; and the mind of a man was given to it" (7:4). Statues of lions with eagles' wings were common at the palaces of the Assyrian and Babylonian kings; therefore the first beast is undoubtedly the Babylonian empire. What the rest of the verse means is still a puzzle and all attempts to solve it are guesses at best. Since the identity of the beast is certain most commentators are cautious about pressing the details.

The second beast, "like a bear . . . was raised up on one side; it had three ribs in its mouth between its teeth; and it was told 'Arise, devour much flesh' " (7:5). Tradition has claimed that this was the Medo-Persian empire. Liberals interpret the bear as Media. The bear was considered less powerful than the lion, just as the silver kingdom "was inferior" to the gold kingdom of Nebuchadnezzar. This is a strong argument because the Persian empire was bigger and stronger than the Babylonian kingdom.

The three ribs in the bear's mouth "point to the ravenous nature of the beast," according to R. H. Charles, "an idea suggested by those passages of the prophets in which the Medes are summoned to ravage Babylon (Isa. 13^{17}, Jer. $51^{11,28}$)" (*A Critical and Exegetical Commentary on the Book of Daniel*, p. 178). Cyrus was the most humane of ancient kings. He could hardly be characterized as a bloodthirsty tyrant like some of his predecessors.

The third beast was "like a leopard, with four wings of a bird on its back; and the beast had four heads; and dominion was given to it" (7:6). Tradition takes the leopard to be Alexander's empire while the liberals identify it with the Persian kingdom. The main characteristics of the third beast can be applied to either kingdom; therefore no strong case can be made for one or the other.

As Daniel lay in bed dreaming, the vision of the fourth beast startled him. It was "terrible and dreadful and exceeding strong; and it had great iron teeth; it devoured and broke in pieces and stamped the residue with its feet. It was different from all the beasts that were before it; and it had ten horns" (7:7). While Daniel was considering the ten horns, a little horn came up among them and pulled up three of the first horns by the roots. In this horn "were eyes like the eyes of a man, and a mouth speaking great things" (7:8).

The Heavenly Courtroom

Then Daniel's sight was raised to a heavenly courtroom scene:

Thrones were placed and one that was ancient of days took his seat; his raiment was white as snow, and the hair of his head like pure wool; his throne was fiery flames, its wheels were burning fire. A stream of fire issued and came forth from before him; a thousand thousands served him, and ten thousand times ten thousand stood before him; the court sat in judgment, and the books were opened (7:9-10).

The angels watched as God and his heavenly council considered the cases of the human kingdoms. The fourth beast was condemned because of the blasphemous words of the little horn. It "was slain and its body destroyed and given over to be burned with fire." While the other three beasts lost their power, they were allowed to live on for a while (7:11-12). When the judgment of the human kingdoms was complete Daniel saw a new arrival at the courtroom:

Behold, with the clouds of heaven there came one like a son of man, and he came to the Ancient of Days and was presented before him. And to him was given dominion and glory and kingdom, that all peoples, nations, and languages should serve him; his dominion is an everlasting dominion, which shall not pass away and his kingdom one that shall not be destroyed (7:13-14).

Daniel was uneasy and the visions alarmed him. He asked one of the angels to interpret what he had seen. The angel answered, "These four great beasts are four kings who shall arise out of the earth. But the saints of the Most High shall receive the kingdom, and possess the kingdom for ever, for ever and ever" (7:17-18). As he was inquiring for more information about the fourth beast, the ten horns, and the little horn, he noticed that the "horn made war with the saints, and prevailed over them, until the Ancient of Days came, and judgment was given for the saints of the Most High, and the time came when the saints received the kingdom" (7:21-22).

The angel did not identify the fourth beast precisely, but he elaborated on the vision. The beast would be a kingdom which would "devour the whole earth" (7:23). The ten horns would be ten kings and the one rising after them would put down three of them (7:24). Concerning this different horn the angel declared:

> He shall speak words against the Most High, and shall wear out the saints of the Most High, and shall think to change the times and the law; and they shall be given into his hand for a time, two times, and half a time (7:25).

Daniel was informed that the horn would be judged by the heavenly court and destroyed. Then "the kingdom and the dominion and the greatness of the kingdoms under the whole heaven shall be given to the people of the saints of the Most High; their kingdom shall be an everlasting kingdom, and all dominions shall serve and obey them" (7:27). The vision still alarmed Daniel but he kept thinking about it.

A Traditional Interpretation of the Fourth Beast

Edward Young makes the interesting admission "that from the book of Daniel itself it is impossible to arrive with absolute certainty as to the identification of this fourth kingdom" (*The Prophecy of Daniel*, p. 275). But since chapter 7 is the seed plot for much of the apocalyptic material in the New Testament and is quoted once with reference to Jesus, Young has no doubt that the fourth kingdom is the Roman empire. But this is simply the old traditional method of reading the Old Testament with New Testament glasses.

"It should be noted," Young comments, "that with regard to the fourth beast, Dan. sees not only certain characteristics but also the unfolding of a history. In fact, within the history there appear to be three distinct phases or periods . 1. The beast itself is first presented to the vision. . . . 2. The period of the ten horns. . . . 3. The period of the little horn" (*The Prophecy of Daniel*, pp. 148-49). "The beast itself stands for the Roman Empire as it appeared at the birth of Christ and in the years subsequent."

Concerning the ten horns Young states:

> We are not to look for ten kingdoms which shall exist side by side when the little horn appears. If the number ten is to be pressed, all we need insist upon is that, from the time when the fourth empire lost its beast form (i.e., the destruction of the Roman Empire) to the appearance of the little horn, there have been ten kingdoms which truly partake of the character of the beast. If, however, the number ten be

regarded merely as the symbol of completeness, as I am inclined to regard it, the vs. means that from the time of the destruction of the Roman Empire to the appearance of the little horn there will be a number of kingdoms, which may truly be said to originate from the ancient Roman Empire. To seek to identify these kingdoms, when Scripture furnishes no clue as to their identity, is very precarious and probably unwarranted (*The Prophecy of Daniel*, pp. 149-50).

About the little horn, Young declares:

It is, I believe, that one of whom Paul spoke, "Let no man deceive you by any means: for that day shall not come, except there be a falling away first, and that man of sin be revealed, the son of perdition; who opposeth and exalteth himself above all that is called God, or that is worshipped; so that he as God sitteth in the temple of God, shewing himself that he is God" (2 Thes. 2:3, 4). This one is the Anti-Christ. Thus, in one remarkable picture, the entire course of history is given from the appearance of the historical Roman Empire until the end of human government" (*The Prophecy of Daniel*, p. 150).

This grandiose conjecture needs some scrutiny.

The Fourth Beast and the Little Horn

Both the Grecian and the Roman empires were terrible, dreadful, and exceedingly strong. The fact that it was different from all the beasts before it, applies first of all to the empire of Alexander. His military tactics wrote a whole new page in how to wage war. His empire, moreover, did not consist of hit-and-run raids. He set out to convert all his captured lands to Greek culture and so he left colonies of Greek scholars, teachers, and craftsmen to educate while troops maintained law and order.

Although the Romans conquered the Greek forces later on, it was the Greek culture which actually conquered the Romans. The latter certainly had some distinctive features in their culture and empire, but the contrast in style and efficiency was not nearly as distinct between them and the Greek civilization as it was between the Persian and the Greek empires.

From our armchair we can nit-pick and affirm that the Roman empire covered more square miles than Alexander's, but from the standpoint of Maccabean Daniel any army which could get clear to the Indus Valley was surely devouring "the whole earth."

The nub of the problem lies with the little horn. Young lists in parallel columns the descriptions of the little horns in chapters 7 and 8 (*The Prophecy of Daniel*, pp. 276-77). It is clear at a glance that much more is said about the horn in chapter 7, and, as Young is careful to point out, many of the statements are different. After a full page of comment and comparison Young concludes, "It would appear therefore that the 'little' horn of ch. 7 and the horn of ch. 8 are not to be identified" (*The Prophecy of Daniel*, p. 277).

The difficulty with Young's discussion is that he stresses the differences as though they were contradictory. *If it had been to his advantage to identify the two horns, you would be surprised how beautifully he could have shown that they complement each other!* The fact is that 7:25 is the most appropriate description of Antiochus Epiphanes to be found in either of the chapters. By stealing the temple vessels and desecrating the sanctuary with an altar to Zeus, he was speaking words against the Most High, the God of the Jews. In his slaughter and persecution of the Jews he most certainly wore out the saints of the Most High. He did everything he could to obliterate the religious calendar of the Jews and he forced them, if possible, to deny their faith in the law of Moses. That the Jews were in his hands for 3 1/2 years ("a time, two times, and half a time") will be more evident when we study the rest of the visions.

The saints of the Maccabean struggles expected the Most High God to bring in his own kingdom and judge Antiochus. It would last forever and the saints would reign over all the other nations. In fact, therefore, all the visions of Daniel discussed so far (chapters 2, 7, 8, 11) have terminated with the reign of Antiochus.

Jeremiah's Prophecy

In 538 B.C., the first year of Darius the Mede, Daniel "perceived in the books the number of years which, according to the word of the LORD to Jeremiah the prophet, must pass before the end of the desolations of Jerusalem, namely, seventy years" (9:2). If the 70-year period was started in 605 B.C. when Jeremiah gave the prediction then 535 was to be the year of the return. Daniel was concerned about the fulfillment of the prophecy and prayed to God. While he was praying, the angel Gabriel came to him and said, "O Daniel, I have now come out to give you wisdom and understanding" (9:22).

The Vision from Gabriel

Then Gabriel gave Daniel the vision in 9:24-27. This unit is one of the most thoroughly debated passages in the Bible. The late J. A. Montgomery declared, "The history of the exegesis of the 70 weeks is the Dismal Swamp of OT criticism" (*A Commentary on Daniel*, p. 400). So much has been written on the subject and there are so many different points of view, we will get swamped as well unless we stay with the main issues.

There are two basic groups of interpreters and each group has its specific way of translating the passage. The translation which most conservatives appeal to is represented by the *New American Standard Bible* (NASB), while liberal scholars have general agreement with the *Revised Standard Version* (RSV). In order to get an overall impression of the passage and to make possible easy comparison of the two versions we will put them in parallel columns:

RSV	*NASB*
24 Seventy weeks of years are decreed concerning your people and your holy city, to finish the transgression, to put an end to sin, and to atone for iniquity, to bring in everlasting righteousness, to seal both vision and prophet, and to anoint a most holy place.	24 Seventy weeks (units of seven) have been decreed for your people and your holy city, to finish the transgression, to make an end of sin, to make atonement for iniquity, to bring in everlasting righteousness, to seal up vision and prophecy, and to anoint the most holy *place*.
25 Know therefore and understand that from the going forth of the word to restore and build Jerusalem to the coming of an anointed one, a prince, there shall be seven weeks. Then for sixty-two weeks it shall be built again with squares and moat, but in a troubled time.	25 So you are to know and discern *that* from the issuing of a decree to restore and rebuild Jerusalem until Messiah the Prince, *there will be* seven weeks and sixty-two weeks; it will be built again, with plaza and moat, even in times of distress.
26 And after the sixty-two weeks, an anointed one shall be cut off, and shall have nothing; and the people of the prince who is to come shall destroy the city and the sanctuary. Its end shall come with a flood and	26 Then after the sixty-two weeks the Messiah will be cut off and have nothing, and the people of the prince who is to come will destroy the city and the sanctuary. And its end *will come* with a flood; even to the end

to the end there shall be war; desolations are decreed.	there will be war; desolations are determined.
27 And he shall make a strong covenant with many for one week; and for half of the week he shall cause sacrifice and offering to cease; and upon the wing of abominations shall come one who makes desolate, until the decreed end is poured out on the desolator.	27 And he will make a firm covenant with the many for one week, but in the middle of the week he will put a stop to sacrifice and grain offering; and on the wing of abominations *will come* one who makes desolate, even until a complete destruction, one that is decreed, is poured out on the one who makes desolate.

Translation Problems

The first problem is the translation "weeks of years" in the RSV. Some scholars object because the literal Hebrew word is a "heptad, unit of seven" as in NASB. They prefer to interpret the periods of weeks in a symbolic way and not get tied down to specific years. Most scholars accept the meaning "weeks of years" and so multiplying 70 x 7 we get 490 years as the period of the vision.

While both translations mention periods of 7, 62, and 1 weeks, the NASB combines 7 and 62, thus forming a 69-week period, at the end of which Messiah the Prince would come. This translation is based on a Greek translation which was pre-Christian, but not the old Septuagint translation. Apparently someone after the Maccabean period combined the two periods to give more time for a priestly Messiah to appear for the 70th week.

The RSV translation, on the other hand, is based on the punctuation of the present Hebrew text. Here "an anointed one, a prince" comes at the end of 49 years. He is a different person from the "anointed one" who is "cut off" at the end of the 62-week period. The conservatives are clearly fudging when in 9:26 they translate "the Messiah" because the Hebrew has no definite article. The RSV is correct in rendering "an anointed one." But the conservatives reject the punctuation of the Hebrew text because the marks were added by Jewish scholars after A.D. 700. They reason that since the Jews did not accept Jesus as their Messiah, their interpretation of the passage cannot be trusted.

All the arguments for the 7 + 62 combination are strained. The Hebrew had the word for "nine" and had the writer intended to indicate a 69-heptad period he would have done so directly. Moreover, since most of the conservatives who follow the combined translation interpret the building of Jerusalem to be completed within the 49-year period, then nothing happens during the 62 weeks! *If it were not for the fact that the conservatives need the 69 weeks to come down to Jesus, they would be arguing against it too.*

The Most Natural Interpretation

The simplest and most natural interpretation is to take the Hebrew text as we have it. The 62-week period of 434 years is a problem, however, because so little is said about this longest period. It is quite clear that this middle section did not figure prominently in the original vision. It is the first and third periods which are crucial, therefore our interpretation should focus on the 7 weeks and the 1 week. If these fit historical situations accurately then it is hardly possible that the period in between would be exactly 434 years.

An Anointed One, A Prince

But before we can begin measuring off the periods we must determine where to begin. The plain fact is that *in our Bible there is no explicit decree or order from God or man* "to restore and build Jerusalem." It is a general statement from Gabriel and so the next best thing is to identify the "anointed one" who was a prince.

The Hebrew word translated "prince" is *nagid* and it is used in the sense of "military leader" to describe Saul (1 Sam. 9:16; 10:1) and David (1 Sam. 25:30; 2 Sam. 5:2). Is. 45:1 refers to Cyrus as Yahweh's "anointed one." Since he was a *nagid* and had such a crucial role in making it possible for the Jews to return to Palestine, he is certainly a fitting candidate for the role. He conquered Babylon in 539 B.C., but he came to the rescue of the Jews with his decree in 538. Figuring back 49 years we come to 587.

The latest evidence indicates that Jerusalem was destroyed in the summer of 586, therefore the interval was only 48 years. But with the two systems of reckoning a king's reign differing only by one year, Daniel's data may have indicated a 49-year period. In either case, it was considered a 7-week unit. Evidently it was reasoned that the minute the city was flattened God issued orders in his heavenly council for its restoration.

A more attractive alternative to Cyrus is the legitimate Zadokite high priest Joshua (Jeshua) who came to Jerusalem with Zerubbabel. This is the view of F. F. Bruce (*Biblical Exegesis in the Qumran Texts*, p. 61). We have noted that they probably came up after the original group of exiles led by Sheshbazzar, but the way the Hebrew text reads would have led most Jewish readers in the Maccabean period to think that Joshua left Babylon in 538. Since the Hebrew word *nagid* was used also of the priest who had charge of the temple (Jer. 20:1), it applies equally well to Joshua.

An Anointed One Cut Off

The next identification to determine is the "anointed one" cut off at the end of the 62-week period. The obvious figure is the Zadokite high priest Onias III, who was slain in 171 B.C. by the order of Menelaus, the wicked priest appointed by Antiochus. This makes a 367-year period, 67 years short of the ideal 434, but as noted above, there is no reason to expect the middle period to measure out exactly. Bruce comments similarly: "That the actual count of years from 538 B.C. to 171 B.C. (the date of the murder of Onias) is considerably less than 434 (or 62 heptads) is not of great importance when we are dealing with schematic numbers" (*Biblical Exegesis in the Qumran Texts*, p. 61). With this interpretation the 62-week period is bracketed by the first and the last of the legitimate high priests after the exile. In other words, Gabriel's vision is involved with priestly Messiahs, not Davidic or kingly ones such as Jesus was claimed to be.

The Prince

The prince who started the 70th week of the vision was Antiochus. He ravaged the city of Jerusalem and the temple, and made war against the saints of the Most High. He made a covenant for a week with the Hellenistic Jews, but they were not the majority and so the reference in 9:27 to "many" is a difficulty. In any case, the week would figure 171-164 B.C. Then he caused sacrifices to stop for half a week, 168-165. This 3 1/2 years would be equal to "a time, two times, and half a time" of 7:25, and come to 1,260 or 1,274 days depending on whether the calendar used had 360 or 364 days a year. The actual length of the desecration was 3 years 10 days, as we have noted, but we could hardly expect any closer projection when dealing with multiples of seven. Furthermore, we must remember that Maccabean Daniel was writing during this last half of the 70th week. The details in 9:27 are so fuzzy, there is no clean termination for the period. The Hebrew text is very difficult to interpret and it is certain that this favorite vision suffered very much at the hands of copyists and editors over the years. Those who apply the vision to Jesus have the same problem because they cannot fit all the details into their scheme either.

What is clear is that the 70th week did not work out as expected and the Messianic kingdom did not come. Therefore, in the Maccabean or Hasmonean period there began a series of deferred hopes and reinterpretations of the last week. *This fact undoubtedly accounts for the Greek translation which is the basis for the Messianic interpretation of most conservatives.* Concerning these postponements Bruce comments:

> First this heptad appears to have been identified with the seven years interregnum in the high-priesthood between Alcimus and Jonathan (160-153 B.C.); then the chronology of the post-exilic period was recast so as to make the last heptad begin with the accession of Alexander Jannaeus in 103 B.C.; later still, when Alexander's reign proved to last much longer than seven years, the last heptad seems to have been expanded to cover the whole period of the Hasmonean (and even postHasmonean) high-priesthood" (*Biblical Exegesis in the Qumran Texts*, p. 61).

Symbolic Interpretation

Some of the conservative interpretations of Dan. 9:24-27 will be considered in later chapters, but we should describe a few here in order to get an idea of the variation.

One type thinks in terms of "heptads" and not "weeks of years." Since these units are not assigned exact numerical value, this method is usually designated the "symbolical interpretation." The first period of 7 heptads extends from 538 B.C. to the first coming (advent) of Christ, the "anointed one." The second period of 62 heptads is the time of the visible church here on earth. The last heptad is the time of tribulation, the last period of history. It begins with the advent of the Antichrist and closes with his defeat and the second advent of Christ.

The symbolical approach is too vague and general to inspire confidence and it results in some crucial differences between interpreters of the same type.

Historical-Symbolical Interpretation

A modified symbolical approach is that of Edward J. Young. He insists on "sevens" instead of "weeks of years" and no numerical values are assigned. On the other hand, he fits his interpretation into a historical framework of the past; therefore his understanding might be called "historical-symbolical interpretation."

His starting point is 538 B.C., the year of Cyrus' decree, even though the instructions were to rebuild the temple, not the city. The 49-year period would end at 489, much earlier than Nehemiah's time (445) when the walls were rebuilt. "True enough," Young admits, "but the burden of proof rests with those who insist that sevens of years are intended. Of this I am not convinced. If the sevens are regarded merely as a symbolical number, the difficulty disappears" (*The Prophecy of Daniel*, p. 206).

Young notes that *after* the 62 sevens, two events are to occur: "Whether or not these two events fall within the 70th seven is not immediately stated. One of them is the death of the Messiah and the other follows as a consequent, the destruction of Jerusalem and the Temple by the Roman armies of Titus" (*The Prophecy of Daniel*, p.220).

Jesus, as the "anointed one," makes a covenant for many and by his death "in the half (middle)" of the 70th seven he causes sacrifices to cease. The "people of the prince" are the Romans who help Titus destroy Jerusalem. This occurred in A.D. 70 and thus did not take place within the 70 sevens.

The basic objection to Young's interpretation is the one common to most conservative scholars: it follows the odd 7 + 62 combination and makes all the references to "an anointed one" apply to Jesus.

Historical-Messianic Interpretation

A recent, clear presentation of the basic traditional view is the article "The Seventy Weeks of Daniel 9:24-27" by Gerhard F. Hasel

(*The Ministry*, May 1976, pp. 5D-21D). He does not think the decree to rebuild Jerusalem should be understood as coming from God, therefore he looks for a royal decree. The decree of Cyrus in 538 B.C. had to do with the temple, not the city, and the same was true of the edict of Darius (Ezra 6:1-12). Hasel thinks the order given Ezra by Artaxerxes I in 457 B.C., the seventh year of his reign, is the proper starting point.

A copy of the official letter is found in Ezra 7:11-26. But there is *not one word* in the letter or the context about building anything. Ezra "the scribe skilled in the law of Moses" (7:6) is authorized to take a group of exiles back to Palestine. He is given money to buy animals for sacrificing in the temple and he is entrusted with the spiritual oversight of the Jews. He will teach those who are ignorant of the ways of God and those who are disobedient will be judged by him.

The Decree of Artaxerxes

Where does Hasel find a basis for his claim? He refers to Ezra 4:7-23 where it is reported to Artaxerxes that the Jews are "finishing the walls and repairing the foundations of Jerusalem" (4:12). Hasel comments:

> If this report comes from the time later than the decree of the seventh year of Artaxerxes I, namely a period of uncertain political conditions for the Persian monarch after the Egyptian revolt of 448, then one may safely conclude that the decree issued in 457 B.C. related to the restoration and rebuilding of Jerusalem (*The Ministry*, May 1976, p. 15D).

But one cannot "safely" come to Hasel's conclusion because after Artaxerxes heard the report of rebuilding he said, "Therefore make a decree that these men be made to cease, and that this city be not rebuilt, until a decree is made by me" (Ezra 4:21). Artaxerxes had authorized Ezra to start a religious reform, not rebuild the city, and so he ordered the fortification of the city stopped. If Hasel is right, then Artaxerxes was schizophrenic. There is no evidence that Artaxerxes ever followed through and authorized Ezra to rebuild Jerusalem.

The Broken Walls of Jerusalem

Hasel makes a second try by referring to the report which Nehemiah got about the broken-down walls and burned gates of

Jerusalem (Neh. 1:3). "This implies," he comments, "that the city had been rebuilt, which could hardly have started before 457, because the decrees of both Cyrus and Darius related only to the building of the Temple" (*The Ministry*, May 1976, p. 15D). It implies nothing of the kind, unless you want to believe it.

Attempts to rebuild walls were interpreted by ancient kings as fortification in preparation for revolt and they seldom authorized such activity. The Jews needed walls to protect themselves from raids and harassment by their neighbors. But these enemies were there to check what was going on and so the unofficial attempts to rebuild the walls were stopped before much could be accomplished. The battered walls and burned gates reported to Nehemiah were the rubble left from Nebuchadnezzar's destruction. The returning exiles built the temple and constructed homes in area cleared of debris, but they did little with the wall system.

A third try by Hasel is Ezra's thanks for God's love in granting "some reviving to set up the house of our God, to repair its ruins, and to give us a wall in Judea and Jerusalem" (Ezra 9:9). The whole context is spiritual and has to do with the rebuilding of the temple. There was no wall around Judea; therefore the verse cannot be interpreted in a physical sense. Ezra had brought the law of Moses and taught the people a way of life. That was a "wall of protection" for the Jews of Jerusalem and Judea even though they had no walls for physical security.

Hasel makes a fourth try by quoting from Ezra 6:14 a reference to the "decree of Cyrus, Darius, and Artaxerxes." Then he comments, "Ezra considered the third decree to be the culmination of the three decrees" (*The Ministry*, May 1976, p. 15D). The whole verse is talking about the completion of the temple in March, 515 B.C., *fifty years before Artaxerxes came to the throne.* The appearance of his name is an editorial mistake due to the passage in Ezra 4:7-23, which Hasel himself admits is misplaced. The editor did not know that the account was out of order and so he associated Artaxerxes with the earlier kings Cyrus and Darius. This notation has nothing to do with what Ezra thought.

The 49-Year Period

In other words, Hasel is building his foundation on four broken reeds and instead of supporting his theory they puncture it. Or to put it another way, if you add four zeroes you get zero. *There is not one bit of solid evidence to show that in 457 B.C. there was a royal decree, or even one from God, ordering the rebuilding of Jerusalem.* Gerhard Hasel has done as thorough a job as possible under the difficult circumstances. This critique of his views should not be taken as an attempt to "hassle" him personally. The examination is really a refutation of all the conservatives who try to start the 490 years in 458 or 457 B.C.

Starting with 457, however, Hasel comes down to 408 for the end of the 7 weeks. But he has to comment, "The paucity of information surrounding the period of about 400 B.C. inevitably precludes any verification of the accuracy of the date of 408 B.C. for the restoration of the city of Jerusalem" (*The Ministry*, May 1976, p. 15D). It is certainly strange that Gabriel picked an unknown period of Jewish history, both in the Bible and Josephus, for the shift from the first to the second period of his vision. Daniel probably did not have any information about the time either. Thus, Hasel is in trouble at the beginning and the end of the 49-year period.

Jesus and Daniel 9:24-27

Nevertheless, Hasel figures down 434 years and arrives at A.D. 27, the year of Jesus' baptism. This event, marking the beginning of his public ministry, was the start of the 70th week of 7 years. In the middle of the week, 3 1/2 years later in A.D. 31, Jesus "put a stop to the sacrifice through the termination of his ministry by his death on the cross" (*The Ministry*, May 1976, p. 16D).

Then Hasel comments: "The last half of the week comes to an end with (1) the death of Stephen (Acts 9:1), (2) the scattering of the Christians from Jerusalem, (3) the carrying of the gospel to the Gentiles, and possibly (4) the conversion of Paul" (*The Ministry*, May 1976, p. 16D). Hasel admits that his theory cannot account for the destruction of Jerusalem in A.D. 70 even though he thinks the "prince" mentioned in Dan. 9:27 was Titus.

The historical-Messianic interpretation is, in Hasel's opinion, "the only interpretation that can claim a perfect agreement between the prophecy of Daniel 9:24-27 and history, even to the year. Yet it is possible that this precise correlation between prophecy and history could be a major stumbling block to its acceptance by the modern rationalistic mind" (*The Ministry*, May 1976, p. 16D).

The "major stumbling block" is not the precision. It is the fact that his two pegs at the beginning and ending of the 49-year period are impossible, and therefore the whole computation collapses.

There is an even more compelling reason why the traditional attempt to relate Dan. 9:24-27 to Jesus is misguided: *neither Jesus nor the New Testament writers understood it that way.* If the traditionalists are correct, this vision is one of the most perfect predictions of Jesus in all of Scripture. Yet not one clause or verse of the unit is quoted by Jesus or the NT writers *as support for Christ's ministry and death.* The only reference is Jesus' prediction that there would be another "desolating sacrilege" (Matt. 24:15; Mk. 13:14). In other words, the theory developed after the early church period.

The Predictions of Maccabean Daniel

Before leaving the book of Daniel it is necessary to look at the closing part of the fourth vision. We noted in the last chapter that history broke off at Dan. 11:39. In 11:40-45 Maccabean Daniel predicted that Ptolemy VI, king of Egypt, would foolishly provoke another war with Antiochus. The Syrian king would rout him, conquer Egypt, then extend his campaign west into Libya and down south into Ethiopia. Rumors from the northeast would bring him home, but en route he would meet his death "between the sea and the glorious mountain," that is, on the coastal plain of Palestine, the country he had ravaged. The problem is that none of these things happened.

In 12:1 the scene shifts to an apocalyptic vision in which the most terrible time of persecution comes on the nations. But those whose names are found written in the book will be delivered by Michael, the patron angel of the Jews. Many will be resurrected from the dead, "some to everlasting life, and some to shame and everlasting contempt" (12:2). But "those who are wise shall shine like the brightness of the firmament; and those who turn many to righteousness, like the stars for ever and ever" (12:3). This will be the glorious kingdom of God.

With the completion of the angel's message, Maccabean Daniel is told to "shut up the words, and seal the book, until the time of the end" (12:4). When he inquires how long that would be, he is told "a time, two times, and half a time" (12:7). This is the same period of time the "little horn" would have the saints in his control (7:25). It appears that Daniel has expanded the persecution of Antiochus into a cosmic picture of tribulation among all the nations. It will last 3 1/2 years, about 1,260 days.

But the reign of Antiochus lasted longer than that. Either Daniel or someone else postponed the hope by revising the figure to 1,290 days (12:11). This addition of 30 days was the one lunar month which would have been added in 3 1/2 years to keep the lunar calendar in phase with the solar calendar. Later still, the time was revised to 1,335 days, an extra 45 days or 1 1/2 months (12:12). We have no clear idea why the writer happened to pick 45 days more.

In any case, the dream had to be postponed further yet, until finally the hope of God's kingdom was picked up by the New Testament.

Chapter 10
Apocalyptic: Old and New

Before we can discuss the prophetic systems related to end-times we must look at some of the rest of the biblical passages with an apocalyptic outlook. Two in the Old Testament merit attention: Ezek. 38-39 and Zech. 9-14. Key passages in the New Teatament are Matt. 24-25; 1 Thess. 4:15-5:2; 2 Thess. 2:1-12; 2 Pet. 3:1-13; and Rev. 1-22.

Gog of Magog

One of the strangest compilations in the OT is Ezek. 38-39. It is so apocalyptic in nature many scholars think the collection is from later times, not from Ezekiel. Be that as it may, the oracles predict, in various ways and with some repetition, the following sequence.

Gog from the land of Magog, somewhere in the north, will come against Israel as foretold by the prophets. Probably Jeremiah's prediction about a people "coming from the north country" (6:22) was one such prophecy.

When Gog reaches Israel, the jealousy and blazing wrath of Yahweh will cause a great shaking of the land. Fish, birds, beasts, and human beings will tremble and mountains, cliffs, and walls will be thrown down. In addition to Gog's soldiers killing each other, Yahweh will send torrential rains and hailstones, fire and brimstone.

With all of this cosmic destruction coming on Gog and his forces, it would seem that nothing would remain of them and their equipment. Yet so many weapons will be left in the land the people will have firewood for *seven* years. In order to cleanse the land the corpses will be buried in a valley east of the Dead Sea. It will take the people of Israel *seven* months to bury them.

The birds and beasts are commanded to gather in the mountains of Israel for the sacrificial feast prepared by Yahweh. They will eat flesh and drink blood until drunk. After this apocalyptic orgy the section closes with a statement that when the nations and the house of Israel see these events they will know that Yahweh is the sovereign God. *Not one of the exiles* will remain among the nations (39:28). Yahweh's spirit will come on the whole house of Israel. This will be the time of the kingdom.

The use of the number 7 and cosmic language indicate that we should not press the details. If the troops of Gog are in the land and Yahweh sends fire and brimstone on them, what is to protect his own people? Moreover, we know that most of the exiles never returned to Palestine.

What Ezekiel, or whoever wrote the oracles, had precisely in mind is difficult to say. In Jer. 25:9 the nation from the north was clearly Babylonia under Nebuchadnezzar and that prophecy was fulfilled. Apparently the series of oracles was a warning in apocalyptic language of what Yahweh would do if any nation dared to attack Israel after it was peacefully settled in its land again.

Zechariah Supplements

We have noted that Zech. 9-14 is not from the prophet Zechariah, but scholars are at a loss to explain who wrote it and when. The dates range all the way from preexilic times clear down to the Maccabean period. Most critical scholars relate the oracle in 9:1-7 to Alexander's campaign down the coast of Syria-Palestine in 333 B.C., and they date the rest of the book from then to 200.

The basic problem, according to Paul D. Hanson, is the failure of modern scholarship to recognize that apocalyptic seers used historical data in a much looser way than the preexilic prophets: "the conqueror acting to effect Yahweh's intentions in history in Zech. 9:1-7 is not Tiglath-pileser, Nebuchadnezzar, or Cyrus, but the Divine Warrior Yahweh himself" (*The Dawn of Apocalyptic*, p. 291). "No specific historical conquest by a specific historical conqueror is being described," Hanson claims, "nor is there anywhere in these verses as much as a hint that a foreign king is being used by Yahweh as his instrument" (*The Dawn of Apocalyptic*, p. 316). The areas and cities mentioned in 9:1-7 indicate the extent of the boundaries of ideal Israel. Even the hated Philistines will be converted and become part of Israel.

Hanson dates Zech. 9-14 between 520 and 420 B.C. He attributes the apocalyptic oracles to defrocked Levitical priests and followers of Exilic Isaiah who had been pushed out of power by the Zadokite priesthood of Joshua and his successors (*The Dawn of Apocalyptic*, p. 409). These visionaries looked for Yahweh to take up their cause and bring in his kingdom of justice. Their messages offered comfort and hope in troubled times.

Zechariah 9-11

After the opening oracle about Yahweh's victory over Israel's enemies, the seer describes Yahweh's approach to Jerusalem: "Lo, your king comes to you; triumphant and victorious is he, humble and riding on an ass, on a colt the foal of an ass" (9:9). Matt. 21:5 and Jn. 12:15 quote this verse as referring to Jesus' entry into Jerusalem on Palm Sunday.

The section 9:11-10:12 pictures God's redemption of his dispersed people, both Judah and Israel, and their return to the land where they will shine like jewels of a crown. A short oracle (11:1-3) relates the downfall of those leaders, "shepherds" who kept God's people captive.

The prose oracle of 11:4-16 has been a riddle for scholars and more than thirty theories have been proposed to explain it. Yahweh commissions the seer to become the shepherd of a flock "doomed to slaughter" because their own shepherds have no pity or concern for them. The shepherd takes two staffs: one named Grace and the other Union. In one month he destroys the three careless former shepherds of the flock, but the sheep detest him for it. Then he breaks the staff Grace, thereby annulling the covenant he made with the people.

Thirty Pieces of Silver

Oddly enough, Yahweh's shepherd had been hired by the wicked dealers of sheep. When he quits his job they pay him "thirty shekels of silver," the price of a slave (Exod. 21:32). Then on Yahweh's instructions he tosses his pay into the treasury in the house of Yahweh. The Hebrew states that he throws the money "to the potter," but since the word for "potter" and "treasury" are similar, most translations today have "treasury" because one of the ancient versions reads that way.

Matthew notes that Judas threw his thirty pieces of silver down in the temple (27:5). But the chief priests said, "It is not lawful to put them into the treasury, since they are blood money," and then after consultation they took the money and bought the potter's field in which to bury strangers (27:6-8). Matthew comments, "Then was fulfilled what had been spoken by the prophet Jeremiah, saying, 'And they took the thirty pieces of silver, the price of him on whom a price had been set by some of the sons of Israel, and they gave them for the potter's field, as the Lord directed me' " (27:9-10). How Matthew happened to attribute Zech. 11:12-13 to Jeremiah is a puzzle. Perhaps he was thinking of Jeremiah's experience at the potter's shop (Jer. 18:1-4).

In any case, the original act of throwing the money into the treasury had great significance. "By this act," comments Hanson, "the shepherd identifies the ultimate source of the corruption and exploitation which are destroying the community: the temple and its leaders are to blame!" (*The Dawn of Apocalyptic*, p. 347). Mal. 1:6-2:9 also has some very strong words against the Zadokite priests and their leadership.

Then the shepherd takes the second staff Union and breaks it "annulling the brotherhood between Judah and Israel." Some of the defrocked Levitical priests had northern roots and sympathies, therefore the shepherd is declaring that there is no possibility of Israel and Judah ever getting together again. The shepherd's mission is not complete, however, because Yahweh tells him to "take the implements of a worthless shepherd" and become a visual aid mocking the shepherd "who does not care for the perishing, or seek the wandering, or heal the maimed, or nourish the sound, but devours the flesh of the fat ones, tearing off even their hoofs" (11:15-16).

Zechariah 12:1-13:6

In far more apocalyptic language, chapters 12-14 tell of the coming great day of Yahweh when he shall purge Jerusalem of its sin and set up his universal reign.

The prose unit 12:1-13:6 makes a clear distinction between Jerusalem, which is controlled by the corrupt priesthood, and the clans of Judah, who are God's faithful people. In spite of the evil in the city of David, the seer believes that Yahweh will protect it. Jerusalem will be "a cup of reeling" so that any nations trying to capture it will stagger with drunkenness and be defeated. It is a "great stone" as well and any who try to lift it will hurt themselves.

When the nations come against Jerusalem the clans of Judah will be under siege as well. But Yahweh will make them "like a blazing pot in the midst of wood, like a flaming torch among sheaves" as they fight to protect Jerusalem. "And the LORD will give victory to the tents

of Judah first, that the glory of the house of David and the glory of
the inhabitants of Jerusalem may not be exalted over that of Judah"
(12:7). This key verse makes explicit the division between the priestly
group in Jerusalem and the apocalyptic visionaries in Judah.

Not only will Yahweh give honor to the faithful in Judah, he will
pour out on Jerusalem "a spirit of compassion and supplication" so
that the leaders will mourn when "they look on him whom they have
pierced" (12:10). Apparently one of the visionary group was killed in
the bitter disputes which occurred in Jerusalem. This great mourning,
in which the families of David and the priests participate, will be the
vindication of Yahweh's faithful ones in Judah. Jn. 19:37 quotes Zech.
12:10 as a foreshadowing that Jesus' side would be pierced.

Moreover, Yahweh will open a fountain in Jerusalem to cleanse
"the house of David and the inhabitants of Jerusalem . . . from sin and
uncleanness" (13:1). The purging will remove the idols and the false
prophets as well. The parents of any person who claims to be a
prophet will say, "You shall not live, for you speak lies in the name of
the LORD (13:3), and then they will "pierce him through when he
prophesies."

This drastic situation shows clearly the belief that true prophecy
had ceased. Anyone who felt the urge to prophesy would be
considered a false prophet; therefore he would be ashamed of his
vision and say, "I am no prophet, I am a tiller of the soil for the land
has been my possession since my youth" (13:5).

Zechariah 13:7-9

The poetic oracle in 13:7-9 relates to the shepherd theme of
chapter 11, but it was placed here because it leads into the full-blown
apocalyptic vision in 14:1-21. Yahweh orders the sword to awake and
"strike the shepherd, that the sheep may be scattered." The rebellious
sheep will have to suffer because they rejected the shepherd appointed
by Yahweh. Two-thirds of the flock will perish and the remaining
third will be refined in fire. Then Yahweh will be able to say, "They
are my people," and the people will answer, "Yahweh [the LORD] is my
God."

In Matt. 26:31 and Mk. 14:27 Jesus quotes Zech. 13:7 as a
warning to the disciples that when he is captured in Gethsemane they
will fall away and be scattered.

Zechariah 14:1-21

When the day of Yahweh comes he will gather the nations and they will capture Jerusalem, ravage it, and take half of the people into exile. But the other half will remain in the city. Then Yahweh will turn and fight the nations just as he fought "on a day of battle" at the Exodus, at Heshbon, Gibeon, and the river Kishon. As he stands on the Mount of Olives, east of the city, an earthquake will split the mountain east and west and the two halves will move apart forming "a very wide valley." Jerusalemites will flee through the valley as they fled from the great earthquake in the days of Uzziah. But later Yahweh will use the valley as the processional way for his victorious return with his "holy ones."

A secret known to Yahweh is revealed to the seer. On Yahweh's day nature will be renewed so every day will be continuous springtime with light all day. The old enemies of cold, heat, and darkness will be gone. The problem of Jerusalem's water supply will be solved by a great spring bubbling up. The excess flow will split, half going to the Dead Sea and half to the Mediterranean.

The central hill country will become a plain, except that Jerusalem will remain on its mountain. As in Is. 2:2, the mountain of Yahweh's house will be "the highest of the mountains," visible from afar. David's city will dwell in security and Yahweh will reign as "king over all the earth." "The earthly Jerusalem," Hanson notes, "has begun to be transformed into the heavenly Jerusalem located at the *axis mundi* (axis of the world) where heaven and earth are conjoined" (*The Dawn of Apocalyptic,* p. 382).

With the completed rejuvenation of Jerusalem as a Garden of Eden, the vision turns to the judgment of those nations who fought against the holy city. A plague will attack them and "their flesh shall rot while they are still on their feet, their eyes shall rot in their sockets, and their tongues shall rot in their mouths" (14:12). Even the animals of the enemies shall be plagued.

Those who survive among the nations will come up yearly to worship King Yahweh at the Feast of Booths. Those families that do not come to Jerusalem to worship will suffer drought and plague. In the glorious period of Yahweh's universal reign even the warhorses will be changed. Their bells will be inscribed "Holy to the LORD," the same motto as on the turban of the high priest (Exod. 28:36-37). All the kitchen bowls and pots will be sacred because they will be needed to take care of all the worshippers from the nations.

Never again will there be a need for a "trader" (*Hebrew* Canaanite) in the temple of Yahweh. Selling sacrificial animals was big business at the temple, and the priests got a big cut from those who were allowed to do so. Things had not changed in Jesus' day and so he felt compelled to drive out the traders.

The dreams and hopes of these early apocalyptic visionaries were dashed, but still they persisted. Maccabean Daniel revived them, as we have seen, yet they danced on ahead of his time until they were appropriated in modified form by Jesus.

Matthew 24-25

In chapters 24-25 Matthew has a collection of Jesus' sayings related to the destruction of Jerusalem and to end-times. The unit has been called "the little apocalypse," but it is not apocalyptic in the sense of secret revelations by visions with mysterious symbols.

When the disciples point out to Jesus the beautiful buildings in the temple complex, he answers, "Truly, I say to you, there will not be left here one stone upon another, that will not be thrown down" (24:2). On the Mount of Olives they ask him privately, "Tell us, when will this be, and what will be the sign of your coming (Greek *parousia*) and of the close of the age?" (24:3). Jesus' prediction was about the destruction of Jerusalem, but the question of the disciples involves his second coming and end-times. The implication is that they thought the three events would occur at the same time.

In Luke, however, after Jesus' prediction the disciples ask, "Teacher, when will this be, and what will be the sign when this is about to take place?" (21:7). This is most likely what was asked at that time. Matthew includes the other issues because his collection of sayings will deal with them.

Jesus warns the disciples not to be led astray. Many will come saying, "I am the Christ." Wars, famine, and earthquakes will come, but these will be just "the beginning of the sufferings," not the end (24:4-8). The disciples will be persecuted and put to death because of their fidelity to Jesus. The end will come when the "gospel of the kingdom will be preached throughout the whole world" (24:14).

The Destruction of Jerusalem

When the disciples see the "desolating sacrilege . . . standing in the holy place," then they are to flee to the mountains (24:15-16). We have noted already that Matthew adds the words "spoken of by the prophet Daniel," whereas they are missing in Mk. 13:14. The destruction of Jerusalem would involve another destruction of the temple.

Many conservatives project this statement about the fall of Jerusalem to end-times, but Jesus' use of "you" indicates that he is still referring to the disciples. Furthermore, Matthew's use of "so, therefore" in vs. 15 shows that the unit 15-28 is doubling back to explain what it will be like when the temple is destroyed. This is much clearer in Luke. Since he is writing for Gentiles he makes no mention of the desecration of the temple. After warning the disciples of the sufferings that await them, he answers their question, "But when you see Jerusalem surrounded by armies, then know that its desolation has come near" (Lk. 21:20). The presence of the Roman armies will be a sure sign that the temple destruction is at hand.

Time will be of the essence. Those on the housetops should not go through the house gathering things to take with them. Rather, they should go down the outside stairs and flee into the hills. It will be a very difficult time for those pregnant or nursing their young. "Pray that your flight may not be in winter or on a sabbath" (Matt. 24:20). Being driven from home will be misery enough without being cold or bearing the guilt of going beyond the sabbath limitations on travel.

The Great Tribulation

Then there will be great tribulation "such as has not been from the beginning of the world until now, no, and never will be," and unless the time of persecution is shortened no one will survive (24:21-22). Here Jesus seems to be picking up the apocalyptic theme of the awful tribulation at end-times, such as in Dan. 12:1. Evidently he thought the end of the age would be in conjunction with the destruction of Jerusalem because he continues to address the disciples: "Then if any one says to you, 'Lo, here is the Christ!' or 'There he is!' do not believe it. For false Christs and false prophets will arise and show great signs and wonders so as to lead astray, if possible, even the elect" (24:23-24).

The suffering of the people in Samaria and Jerusalem during the sieges of the Assyrians and the Babylonians was terrible, but the Roman siege will be worse. Josephus gives us some idea of the horrible conditions:

> So all hope of escaping was now cut off from the Jews, together with their liberty of going out of the city. Then did the famine widen its progress, and devoured the people by whole houses and families; the upper rooms were full of women and children that were dying by famine, and the lanes of the city were full of the dead bodies of the aged; the children also and the young men wandered about the marketplaces like shadows, all swelled with the famine, and fell down dead, wheresoever their misery seized them. . . . many died as they were burying others, and many went to their coffins before that fatal hour was come (*Wars of the Jews*, Book V, Chapter XII, paragraph 3).

Later on Josephus indicates how awful the pangs of hunger were by relating the story of a desperate woman. While nursing her infant son she was overcome with hunger and said, "O you miserable infant! for whom shall I preserve you in this war, this famine, and this sedition? . . . Come on, be my food." Then she killed her son, roasted him, and ate half of him. The other half she hid for another meal (*Wars of the Jews*, Book VI, Chapter III, paragraph 4). For those who went through the siege of Jerusalem it must have seemed like the end of the world.

The Coming of the Son of Man

After the great tribulation "the sun will be darkened, and the moon will not give its light, and the stars will fall from the heaven, and the powers of the heavens will be shaken" (24: 29). Here again Jesus is using apocalyptic language. But out of the darkness "they will see the Son of man coming on the clouds of heaven with power and great glory" (24:30). The elect will be gathered from the four winds by the angels accompanying the Son. In Dan. 7:13 the "son of man" comes on clouds to appear before the Ancient of Days in the heavenly courtroom scene. Now "the Son of man" comes to earth on clouds in order to gather his elect.

To illustrate his teaching Jesus uses his example of the fig tree: "as soon as its branch becomes tender and puts forth its leaves, you know that summer is near. So also when you see all these things, you know that he is near, at the very gates. Truly, I say to you, this generation will not pass away till all these things take place" (24:32-34).

God's Spiritual Kingdom

In another connection Jesus said, "Truly, I say to you, there are some standing here who will not taste death before they see the kingdom of God come with power" (Mk. 9:1). Jesus began his ministry with the warning, "The time is fulfilled, and the kingdom of God is at hand; repent, and believe in the gospel" (Mk. 1:15).

The Sermon on the Mount (Matt. 5-7) describes the character of God's spiritual kingdom. The qualities of kingdom members are listed in 5:1-12 and their mission as "salt" and "light" is noted in 5:13-16. Then 5:17-7:12 discusses the principles by which kingdom members are to live. Jesus gives his spiritual understanding of the law (5:17-48), religious activities (6:1-18), personal living (6:19-34), and social outreach (7:1-12). Then he closes with some warnings (7:13-27).

Jesus was convinced that his ministry to the sick and the outcasts was the beginning of God's kingdom. When some Pharisees asked him when the kingdom of God would come, he informed them that it was already in their midst (Lk. 17:21). But they did not recognize it.

Yet Jesus knew that the coming of the kingdom in power was still in the future. Thus the kingdom of God was both "now" and "not yet." Therefore he assured his disciples that all these things would take place before their generation passed away. If these are actually the words of Jesus and if his words mean anything, it is certain that he expected to return and set up God's kingdom of power and peace within the lifetime of the disciples.

Was Jesus Mistaken?

But this plain meaning of the passage is rejected by most conservatives because it means admitting that Jesus was mistaken about the time. The issue is intensified because Jesus added, "Heaven and earth will pass away, but my words will not pass away" (Matt. 24:35; Mk. 13:31; Lk. 21:33). All attempts to reinterpret "generation" are armchair approaches to solve *our* difficulty in understanding the passage. As we noted in chapter 1, the clear-cut testimony of the rest of the New Testament is that the disciples, Paul, and the early church understood Jesus literally. If Jesus really referred to events more than 1,900 years in the future, then he was playing word games with his disciples. When we look at the problem honestly there are two basic options: either Jesus was leading his disciples to think something different from what he had in mind, or he was mistaken. The latter is far more preferable because it was done in innocence and shows his true humanity.

Only the Father Knows

The humanity of Jesus is clearly acknowledged in his warning about being cocksure of the precise time of his coming. The sprouting of fig leaves will alert them to the general period, but there is *no* way to know the exact moment when the kingdom will come: "But of that day and hour no one knows, not even the angels of heaven, nor the son, but the Father only" (Matt. 24:36).

At the coming of the Son of man "two men will be in the field; one is taken and one is left. Two women will be grinding at the mill; one is taken and one is left. Watch therefore, for you do not know on what day your Lord is coming" (24:40-42). Then using the example of a thief breaking unexpectedly into a house, Jesus comments, "Therefore, you also must be ready; for the Son of man is coming at an hour you do not expect" (24:44).

This point is reinforced by two more illustrations: (1) the faithful and unfaithful servants (24:45-51); and (2) the parable of the five wise and five foolish maidens (25:1-13). In the former, the master returns *sooner* than the unfaithful servant thinks he will. In the latter, the bridegroom appears *later* than the unwise maidens expect and so they run out of oil. We will have more to say later about the idea of a "secret rapture" of God's people, but for the time being it should be noted that while the coming of the Son of man will be sudden, it will not be secret: "For as the lightning comes from the east and shines as far as the west, so will be the coming of the Son of man" (24:27). Lightning and thunder do not occur in secret.

As an example of what the disciples should do until the kingdom comes, Jesus tells the parable of the talents (25:14-30). They must make the greatest use possible of their abilities in order to have some results from their lives. To the servant who hid his talent the master of the house says, "Then you ought to have invested my money with the bankers, and at my coming I should have received what was my own with interest" (25:27). The talent is taken from the worthless servant and then he is sent away into outer darkness, where people "will weep and gnash their teeth."

The Great Judgment

When the Son of man comes with his angels in glory "he will sit on his glorious throne" (25:31), and all the nations will be gathered before him. In Dan. 7:9 the Ancient of Days was on the throne during the courtroom scene, but now the Son of man takes his place. Like a shepherd, the Son separates the sheep from the goats. To the sheep, on the right, he says, "Come, O blessed of my Father, inherit the kingdom prepared for you from the foundation of the world" (25:32-34).

The criterion for judgment is astonishing, especially in the light of what is said elsewhere in the gospels. Their fate rests solely on whether they have fed the hungry, given the thirsty a drink, clothed the naked, and visited the sick and prisoners. The sheep are amazed when the Son tells them that they have done all these things for him. "Truly, I say to you," He assures them, "as you did it to one of the least of these brethren, you did it to me" (25:40). These righteous ones will have eternal life, but to the goats the Son orders, "Depart from me, you cursed, into the eternal fire prepared for the devil and his angels (25:41).

Jesus the Apocalyptist

Thus end Jesus' statements about the future. There are many difficulties in the two chapters and perhaps some of the views of the early church have colored the quotations from Jesus. The older liberals tried to make Jesus into one of their own kind with primary concern for bringing the kingdom of social justice here on earth. It was the early church, so they said, which attributed all these apocalyptic ideas to Jesus.

But there is too much evidence to show that Jesus had a definite apocalyptic point of view. Furthermore, the influence of Jesus on the early church is so clear in other areas it is very difficult to account for their views on eschatology without admitting that Jesus was the source of their outlook.

The conservatives, on the other hand, have accepted the apocalyptic outlook of Jesus but pushed it into the distant future because the kingdom did not come in the 1st century A.D. The most objective estimate of the biblical evidence is that Jesus was an apocalyptist, but that he was mistaken in his timing of the end of the age.

Before closing the discussion about Jesus and his views it should be noted that just before his ascension the disciples ask him, "Lord, will you at this time restore the kingdom to Israel?" (Acts 1:6). He informs them that it is not for them to know the times and seasons fixed by God's authority. They will receive the power of the Holy Spirit and be witnesses "in Jerusalem and in all Judea and Samaria and to the end of the earth" (1:8). When Jesus is taken out of their sight in a cloud, two men "in white robes" say, "Men of Galilee, why do you stand looking into heaven? This Jesus, who was taken up from you into heaven, will come in the same way as you saw him go into heaven" (1:11).

Paul's Eschatology

To those Thessalonians concerned about their loved ones who have died, Paul gives words of comfort:

> For the Lord himself will descend from heaven with a cry of command, with the archangel's call, and with the sound of the trumpet of God. And the dead in Christ will rise first; then we who are alive, who are left, shall be caught up together with them in the clouds to meet the Lord in the air; and so we shall always be with the Lord (1 Thess. 4:16-17).

He reminds them that they have no need for instructions about "the times and the seasons" because they know "the day of the Lord will come like a thief in the night" (5:1-2). Paul is echoing the sentiments of Jesus: the Lord will come suddenly and in his own lifetime.

Later on, the word spread among the Christians at Thessalonica that Paul was claiming that the Lord had already come. Apparently the rumor got started by some ecstatic person or a forged letter (2 Thess. 2:1-2). In either case, Paul warns them not to be deceived and then he reminds them of what he told them when he was there:

> That day will not come, unless the rebellion comes first, and the man of lawlessness is revealed, the son of perdition, who opposes and exalts

himself against every so-called god or object of worship, so that he takes his seat in the temple of God, proclaiming himself to be God (2:3-4).

The "mystery of lawlessness is already at work," but "the man of lawlessness" has not appeared because he is being restrained by someone or something. Evidently Paul had explained this point when he was with them and so he does not elaborate further. The three main identifications which tantalized commentators have suggested are: (1) a supernatural power; (2) Satan himself; or (3) the Roman empire and emperor.

In any case, when the restraint is removed "the lawless one" will come and be helped by Satan. His "pretended signs and wonders" will deceive those who refuse to love the truth and be saved, because God will send "upon them a strong delusion, to make them believe what is false" (2:9-11).

In connection with comments on the resurrection, Paul informs the Corinthians, "Lo! I tell you a mystery. We shall not all sleep, but we shall be changed, in a moment, in the twinkling of an eye, at the last trumpet. For the trumpet will sound, and the dead will be raised imperishable, and we shall be changed" (1 Cor. 15:51-52).

Our knowledge of Paul's eschatology is derived from remarks made in connection with other issues. We do not know how extensively he had thought out the details because he never spells them out in a systematic way.

2 Peter 3:1-13

With the delay of Christ's coming (*parousia*) scoffers begin to taunt the Christians with the question, "Where is the promise of his coming? For ever since the fathers fell asleep, all things have continued as they were from the beginning of creation." The author of 2 Peter reminds his readers that God has a "day of judgment and destruction" for these ungodly men.

God is not really slow about his promise because he is patiently waiting for others to come to repentance. After all, in God's sight a 1,000 years are like a day. We noted in Chapter 1 that this rationale is not very helpful for mortals who live 70-80 years, but apparently it was considered a good answer for the scoffers.

Be that as it may, "the day of the Lord will come like a thief, and then the heavens will pass away with a loud noise, and the elements will be dissolved with fire, and the earth and the works that are upon it will be burned up" (2 Pet. 3:10). Apocalyptic literature outside the Bible has numerous references to the destruction of the world by fire, and there is no doubt that the writer shares this outlook.

He encourages his readers to live "lives of holiness and godliness" while they eagerly wait for "the coming of the day of God, because of which the heavens will be kindled and dissolved, and the elements will melt with fire!" (3:11-12). After this will come the "new heavens and a new earth in which righteousness dwells."

Second Peter, like most of his contemporaries in the early church, was thoroughly apocalyptic in his expectations. But the grandest apocalypse of them all is The Revelation of Jesus Christ to John.

Chapter 11
The Revelation to John

The grandest of the apocalypses has a sweeping introductory verse: "The revelation of Jesus Christ, which God gave him to show to his servants what must soon take place; and he made it known by sending his angel to his servant John." This *apocalypsis* originated with God and was passed via Jesus and an angel to John.

The writer could have saved the church an enormous amount of time, energy, and argument by identifying himself more explicitly, but he did not. Was he John the Apostle or John the Elder? In either case, he was using his own name and not a pseudonym.

The Time is Near

Those who read, hear, and live by the revelation will be blessed for "the time is near" (1:3). It is certain, therefore, that John expected the events of the revelation to occur in the not too distant future. He informs the seven churches in Asia Minor that Jesus Christ "is coming with the clouds, and every eye will see him, every one who pierced him; and all tribes of the earth will wail on account of him. Even so. Amen" (1:7). John indicates the urgency of his warning with a double assurance in Greek "Even so" and Hebrew "Amen."

The statement "every one who pierced him" is John's reinterpretation of Zech. 12:10. He seldom quotes more than a few words from the Old Testament, but he shows a remarkable knowledge of Scripture by his many allusions and combinations of references. John is a creative interpreter.

What does he mean, however, that "every eye will see him"? This detail is hard to square with the claim that Jesus will return the same way he ascended from the Mount of Olives (Acts 1:11). We need to keep alert to the danger of pressing the details of apocalyptic material too far.

John explains that while on the island of Patmos, where he was patiently suffering tribulation, he "was in the Spirit on the Lord's day" (1:10). The expression "in the spirit" indicates an ecstatic experience. Since it occurs also in 4:2; 17:3; and 21:10, John is telling us that he had four visions: 1:9-3:22; 4:1-16:21; 17:1-21:8; and 21:9-22:5. These he

places between the introduction (1:1-8) and an epilogue of
exhortations and warnings (22:6-21).

Events Leading to the End-Time

Proper interpretation of the book demands an understanding of
its overall pattern and structure. The most difficult vision is the
second. The effect is staggering because the long series of apocalyptic
scenes seem to follow each other endlessly. Are these chronologically
consecutive or are they varying ways of describing the same cluster of
events?

One of the most readable and instructive commentaries on
Revelation is *The Most Revealing Book of the Bible* (1974) by
Vernard Eller. He suggests, for example, that the visions of the seven
seals, trumpets, and bowls are to be understood as a spiral with each
group covering in different ways the same events leading up to the
end time. His outline (on the inside of the back cover) is very helpful
in establishing an overview of the book:

I. The Introduction to the Book (1:1-20)
   A. The Commission (1:1-3)
   B. The Greeting (1:4-8)
   C. John and the Revealer (1:9-20)

II. The Revealer's Letters to Seven Actual Churches of the
    End-Time (2:1-3:22)
    A. To Ephesus (2:1-7)
    B. To Smyrna (2:8-11)
    C. To Pergamum (2:12-17)
    D. To Thyatira (2:18-29)
    E. To Sardis (3:1-6)
    F. To Philadelphia (3:7-13)
    G. To Laodicea (3:14-22)

III. The Control of History in the End-Time (4:1-5:14)
    A. The Throne of God (4:1-11)
    B. The Scroll of the Future (5:1-5)
    C. The Lamb (5:6-14)

IV. The End-Time as Seven Seals (6:1-8:1)
    A. Seal 1 (6:1-2)
    B. Seal 2 (6:3-4)
    C. Seal 3 (6:5-6)   } The Four Horsemen
    D. Seal 4 (6:7-8)
    E. Seal 5 (6:9-11)
    F. Seal 6 (6:12-17)   } The Saints and the Kings
    G. The Seal Interlude: The Church—Below and Above
       (7:1-17)
       Part A: The Church of the Living (7:1-8)
       Part B: The Church of Those Who Have Died (7:9-17)
    H. Seal 7: The Coming of the End (8:1)

V. The End-Time as Seven Trumpets (8:2-11:19)
    A. Introduction to the Trumpets (8:2-6)
    B. Trumpet 1 (8:7)
    C. Trumpet 2 (8:8-9)
    D. Trumpet 3 (8:10-11)   } The Four Plagues
    E. Trumpet 4 (8:12)
    F. Trumpet 5: The Warrior Locusts (8:13-9:12)
    G. Trumpet 6: The Demonic Cavalry (9:13-21)
    H. The Trumpet Interlude: The Scroll and Its Contents
       (10:1-11:13)
       Part A: The Eating of the Scroll (10:1-11)
       Part B: The Fate of the Church (11:1-13)
    I. Trumpet 7: Victory to Our God (11:14-19)

VI. The End-Time in Freehand Sketch (12:1-14:20)
    A. The Woman and Her Child (12:1-6)
    B. The Dragon Thrown Down (12:7-17)
    C. Enter, the Beast (13:1-10)
    D. And Another, the Unholy Spirit (13:11-18)
    E. The Lamb and His Hundred Forty-Four Thousand
       (14:1-5)
    F. The Collapse of Evil's Kingdom (14:6-13)
    G. The Parousia as Harvest (14:14-20)

VII. The End-Time Intensification as Seven Bowls (15:1-16:21)
  A. Introduction to the Bowls (15:1-16:1)
  B. Bowl 1 (16:2) ⎫
  C. Bowl 2 (16:3) ⎪
  D. Bowl 3 (16:4-7) ⎬ The Worst Plagues of All
  E. Bowl 4 (16:8-9) ⎪
  F. Bowl 5 (16:10-11) ⎭
  G. Bowl 6: The Mobilization at Armageddon (16:12-14, 16)
  H. The Bowl Interlude: An Exhortation (16:15)
    Part A: The Day I Come (16:15a)
    Part B: Stay Awake (16:15b)
  I. The Collapse of the War Effort (16:17-21)

VIII. The Events of the End (17:1-20:3)
  A. The Great Whore, Babylon (17:1-6)
  B. The Whore and Beast Explained (17:7-8 & 18)
  C. The Nero Ciphers (13:18 and 17:9-17)
  D. The Fall of Babylon (18:1-8)
  E. Lament Over Babylon (18:9-24)
  F. Exultation and the Promise of the Wedding Supper (19:1-10)
  G. The Parousia of the Rider (19:11-20:3)

IX. The Apportioning of Mankind (20:4-15)
  A. LIFE: The Millennial Resurrection (20:4-10)
  B. DEATH: The Final Sentencing to the Lake of Fire (20:11-15)

X. The New Heaven and the New Earth (21:1-22:21)
  A. Introductory Overview (21:1-8)
    1. The New Jerusalem (21:1-4)
    2. The New World (21:5)
    3. Exhortations (21:6-8)
  B. The New Jerusalem in Detail (21:9-27)
  C. The New World Attempted (22:1-5)
  D. Closing Exhortations (22:6-21)

Types of Interpretation

As would be expected, the difficult Book of Revelation has been a battleground in the history of the church. The various attempts to understand it can be grouped into five types. One view believes that the visions are symbolical and offer a message of comfort to the suffering saints of every generation that good will triumph over evil. Another view is that the visions applied only to the 1st century A.D. and have no long-range predictions at all.

A third view takes the visions as a prophecy of the history of the church. A fourth interpretation understands the letters to be historical, chapters 4-6 as leading up to end-time, and 7-22 as the description of what will happen at the end of human history. A fifth view takes a more futuristic stance and sees chapters 4-22 as describing the great tribulation and events at end-times.

The First Vision

Some of these views and their implications and identifications will be discussed in later chapters, but in preparation it will be helpful to become acquainted with the main characters and the plot of the drama.

While John was "in the spirit" on Patmos he heard a trumpetlike voice ordering him to write what he saw and send it to the seven churches. When he turned to see who was speaking to him he saw "one like a son of man" standing among seven golden lampstands. "In his right hand he held seven stars, from his mouth issued a sharp two-edged sword" (1:12-16).

Just as Daniel was stunned by the visions he saw, John fell at the Son's feet as though dead. As the angels had comforted Daniel and set him on his feet, so the Son of man touched John, saying, "Fear not, I am the first and the last, and the living one; I died, and behold I am alive for evermore, and I have the keys of Death and Hades" (1:17-18). Then he explained the vision: the seven lampstands are the seven churches and the seven stars their angels.

The Seven Churches

The unit 2:1-3:22 contains the messages to seven actual churches in Asia Minor. Where at fault they are warned and where faithful they are praised. The section closes with an exhortation and a promise:

Behold, I stand at the door and knock; if any one hears my voice and opens the door I will come in to him and eat with him and he with me. He who conquers, I will grant him to sit with me on my throne, as I

myself conquered and sat down with my Father on his throne. He who
has an ear, let him hear what the Spirit says to the churches (3:20-22).

The Throne of God

After the vision about the seven churches John sees an open door
in heaven and the trumpetlike voice says, "Come up hither, and I will
show you what must take place after this" (4:1). At once John is "in
the spirit" and, like Ezekiel's quick trip to Jerusalem, he is transported
to heaven. There he sees God seated on his throne and around are 24
elders seated on their thrones. No doubt they represent the people of
God, the double 12 meaning both the 12 tribes of Israel and the 12
apostles of the church.

Also around the throne of God are four living creatures like a
lion, an ox, a man, and a flying eagle. Each of them has 6 wings and
is full of eyes to observe what is transpiring. Day and night they
never cease to sing, "Holy, holy, holy, is the Lord God Almighty, who
was and is and is to come!" These creatures seem very strange, yet they
are simply John's combination of those described in Ezekiel 1 and
Isaiah 6.

In the right hand of God is a scroll written on both sides and
sealed with seven seals. John weeps because no one is worthy to open
the scroll and break its seals. One of the elders tells him not to weep
because "the Lion of the tribe of Judah, the Root of David, has
conquered, so that he can open the scroll and its seven seals" (5:5).

Then in the crowd around the throne John spots "a Lamb
standing as though it had been slain." He takes the scroll and the
heavenly citizens shout, "Worthy is the Lamb who was slain to receive
power and wealth and wisdom and might and honor and glory and
blessing!" (5:12).

The Seven Seals

The first four seals are horsemen riding different colored horses.
Some understand the rider of the white horse to be Jesus Christ, but
the thrust of the whole passage indicates that the rider is the
Antichrist. War rides the red horse, Famine the black, and Death and
Hades ride double on the pale horse. These woes come on humanity
because of their sinful ways. Judgment comes in the form of a great
earthquake (the 6th seal):

The sun became black as sackcloth, the full moon became like blood, and the stars of the sky fell to the earth as the fig tree sheds its winter fruit when shaken by a gale; the sky vanished like a scroll that is rolled up, and every mountain and island was removed from its place (6:12-14).

Chapter 7 is an interlude which describes God's people: 144,000 on earth sealed with the mark of God on their foreheads and a great multitude in heaven who have come through the great tribulation. The 7th seal results in "silence in heaven for about half an hour" (8:1).

The Seven Trumpets

The first four trumpets convulse nature so that a third of the earth is destroyed, a third of the seas turn to blood, a third of the water supply turns to wormwood bitterness, and a third of the light is extinguished (8:7-12). The next three trumpets are to bring greater woe.

Vernard Eller likens these fantastic "visions of trauma" to Picasso's painting *Guernica*. The artist pictures in his inimitable style the horrors of Franco's bombing of the Basque town Guernica on April 28, 1937. Yet the tragedy of that day is preserved in a way that can speak to the horrors of war any place and any time. Eller comments:

> But if a person insists on trying to read *Guernica* as though it were a photograph, he's headed for nothing but trouble. His fascination in trying to sort out and make sense of the details will forever prevent him from feeling the impact or getting the message of the whole. He'll hang on that bull with the eye underneath its ear until he either invents some wild-eyed theory to "explain" it or else concludes that the whole freaky painting is a bunch of bull.

Then he adds:

> It is obvious to us that, if even the tiniest of stars moves anywhere close to the earth, the earth will give way rather violently. Yet, in John's picture, the earth goes right on (and with people living on it); and in subsequent scenes he again has stars falling to earth. How irrational will Revelation (and *Guernica*) become if one refuses to let the author speak in his own way and instead determines that he has to be a photographer! (*The Most Revealing Book of the Bible*, p. 89).

After the 5th trumpet, a horde of locusts with the sting of a scorpion and "like horses arrayed for battle" torture humanity for 5 months (9:1-11). With the 6th trumpet 200 million cavalry troops are released to kill a third of mankind (9:13-19). In spite of the awful judgment, the human survivors do not repent (9:20-21). What more graphic description could be given of our world! Wars devastate us and yet we continue to do those things which bring more judgment as a consequence.

The Second Interlude

In the interlude before the last trumpet an angel brings a small scroll to John and, like Ezekiel (3:1-3), he is ordered to eat it. It is sweet in his mouth because it is God's word, but it is bitter in his stomach because of the awful judgments to come (10:1-11).

The contents of the scroll are given in 11:1-13. The outer court of the temple will be trampled by the nations for 42 months = 3 1/2 years. Two witnesses, resembling Zerubbabel and Joshua, and Elijah and Moses, prophesy repentance for 1,260 days; then the beast from the bottomless pit, the Antichrist kills them and their bodies lie 3 1/2 days in the street of the city "where their Lord was crucified." While people rejoice over the dead prophets, they come to life and ascend to heaven. An earthquake of judgment destroys a 10th of the city and 7,000 people perish. Those that survive are terrified, but they give glory to God.

At the 7th seal there was silence in heaven. With the 7th trumpet heaven rings with the song of victory because those who have persecuted God's saints have been punished. "Then God's temple in heaven was opened, and the ark of his covenant was seen within his temple; and there were flashes of lightning, loud noises, peals of thunder, and earthquake, and heavy hail" (11:19). While John is a Christian, yet he sees the model of the ark in heaven. Evidently he is affirming that the commandments of God, which were housed in the ark, are still valid.

The Great Red Dragon

A woman "clothed with the sun" and with "a crown of 12 stars" brings forth a male child "who is to rule all the nations." A great red dragon "with seven heads and ten horns" attempts to devour the son, but he is "caught up to God and his throne" (12:6). Jesus, who came from Israel, was resurrected and ascended to heaven before the Devil, Satan, could kill him.

When Satan and his angels start war in heaven, Michael and his angels defeat them and throw them down to earth. The Devil is very angry because he knows his time is short (12:7-12). He pursues the woman (now the church with Jews and Gentiles) but she escapes into the wilderness where she is "nourished for a time, and times, and half a time" (12:14).

The Two Beasts

While Satan stands on the seashore, a beast rises from the sea. It has "ten horns and seven heads, with ten diadems upon its horns and a blasphemous name upon its heads" (13:1). It is a composite of the four beasts in Daniel 7. Satan gives it his power, throne, and authority. One of the beast's heads is wounded severely, but the wound heals. He rules for 42 months in which he blasphemes God and persecutes the saints (13:5-10).

Another beast, the third of the evil triumvirate, rises from the earth. It has two horns like a lamb, but it speaks like a dragon (13:11). Later on it is identified as the False Prophet. He forces the world to worship the first beast and his image or be slain (13:12-15). Emperor worship began in Pergamum, the city of one of the seven churches. Later on, Christians in various parts of the Roman empire lost their lives by refusing to worship the emperor. In John's vision the False Prophet extends his control by ordering that no one can buy or sell without the mark of the beast on his forehead or right hand. Then appears a curious note which is different in style and tone from John's: "This calls for wisdom: let him who has understanding reckon the number of the beast, for it is a human number, its number is 666" (13:18). Further clues to this puzzle are given later on, therefore we will deal with it then.

Another Interlude

Chapter 14 has three visions to encourage the suffering church. In contrast to those with the mark of the beast, the Lamb gathers on Mt. Zion the faithful 144,000 who bear the marks of God and the Lamb. They sing a new song which only the redeemed of earth could learn (1-5).

Then in 14:6-13 the downfall of evil is pictured. An angel "with an eternal gospel to proclaim" warns all the nations "Fear God and give him glory, for the hour of his judgment has come; and worship him." Another angel announces, "Fallen, fallen is Babylon the great, she who made all nations drink the wine of her impure passion." A third angel declares that anyone who received the mark of the beast will suffer eternal punishment.

The double harvest of Christ's coming is described in 14:14-20. One "like a son of man" comes on a cloud and reaps the harvest of the saints, while an angel harvests the grapes and puts them "into the great wine press of God." Blood flows from the press "as high as a horse's bridle, for 1,600 stadia (about 200 miles)" (14:20). "For calendarizers who might be interested," Eller notes, "I can report that some clever head has figured out the amount of blood that could be squeezed from an average human being and divided that into the volume of a puddle two hundred miles in radius and as deep as a horse's bridle. His conclusion is that, even if everyone went through the press of wrath, the cumulative population of the world still has not been nearly enough to provide the juice. It's a bloody shame!" (*The Most Revealing Book in the Bible*, p. 144).

The Seven Bowls

The seven bowls, like the seals and trumpets, originate from heaven, but the scene is like the victory song of Moses after being freed from Egypt. From the heavenly model of the old "tent of witness," the tabernacle of the wilderness, come seven angels with seven plagues like those which came on Egypt. They are given seven bowls from which to pour the plagues on the earth (15:1-8).

The first bowl results in terrible sores on all who have the mark of the beast. After the second bowl the sea becomes like the blood of a dead person and all sea life dies. The rivers and springs become blood when the third bowl is poured out because people "have shed the blood of saints and prophets." The fourth bowl brings scorching heat from the sun. People curse God, but they do not repent. The throne of the beast is plagued by the fifth bowl and darkness comes over his kingdom. The citizens are in anguish and curse God, but they do not repent even though the opportunity exists (16:1-10).

The sixth bowl dries up the Euphrates river, thus preparing the way for the kings of the east. Demonic spirits come from the mouths of the unholy trinity (the dragon, the beast, and the False Prophet). These spirits perform wonders and assemble the kings of the whole world for battle at Armageddon, "Mt. Megiddo," on the great day of God Almighty (16:12-16). Verse 15 implies that Christ's coming will occur about the time of this military buildup: "Lo, I am coming like a thief! Blessed is he who is awake, keeping his garments that he may not go naked and be seen exposed!"

As the seventh bowl is poured into the air a great voice from the throne temple says, "It is done!" Then occurs the most awful storm and earthquake ever experienced by human beings. Islands and mountains vanish as 100-pound hailstones rain down. Apparently Mt. Megiddo is bombed out and the battle never occurs. The "great city" (Rome, Jerusalem, or Babylon?) is split into 3 parts, cities of the nations fall, and great Babylon drinks the cup of God's fury (16:17-20). Thus ends the long second vision with its threefold description of end-time trauma.

The Great Harlot

The third vision (17:1-21:8) relates the events that will occur at the end. The first theme is the fall of Babylon, the great harlot. She is arrayed in beautiful clothing and jewels, and she rides on "a scarlet beast" which has seven heads and ten horns. Moreover, she is drunk with the blood of the saints and the martyrs of Jesus. John marvels at the sight, but an angel explains the mystery. The beast is described in 17:8 and the woman in 17:18.

The section 17:9-17 begins, "This calls for a mind with wisdom," and it seems very similar to the riddle verse in 13:18. Then the explanation follows:

> The seven heads are seven hills on which the woman is seated; they are also seven kings, five of whom have fallen, one is, the other has not yet come, and when he comes he must remain only a little while. As for the beast that was and is not, it is an eighth but it belongs to the seven, and it goes to perdition (9-11).

Here the harlot and the beast are clearly identified with Rome.

The Number of the Beast

Eller considers the two riddle passages as later additions by an editor. The last of the five kings was Nero, the one ruling is Vespasian, and the one to come is Titus. The eighth king, who is also one of the seven, will be Nero. The editor is making explicit the old Roman myth that the evil emperor Nero would revive and rule (*The Most Revealing Book of the Bible*, pp. 159-64). The numerical value of the letters in *Neron Caesar*, spelled in Hebrew, comes to 666. If *Nero* is used instead of *Neron*, the loss of the "n" drops the total to 616, a variant reading found in some Greek texts.

Eller thinks it is strange that the magic number results from the name in Hebrew, not Greek or Latin, and so he uses the ancient game of *triangular numbers* (counting dots in various sized triangles) to show that 666 = 8. The secret numbers of the two inserted passages are equal and prove that Nero was intended. Eller's whole point is that in John's mind Babylon meant Babylon. He picked the city because it was in ruins in his time and its past history as the center of worldly power and wealth made it an ideal type for anti-God ways of thinking and acting. It is the editorial additions, not John, that give support to those who relate the characters in Revelation to specific historical entities. Eller is adamant against this timetable approach to eschatology.

The Fall of Babylon

An authoritative angel from heaven shouts:

Fallen, fallen is Babylon the great!
It has become a dwelling place of demons,
a haunt of every foul spirit,
a haunt of every foul and hateful bird;
for all nations have drunk the wine of her impure passion,
and the kings of the earth have committed
    fornication with her,
and the merchants of the earth have grown rich
    with the wealth of her wantonness (18:2-3).

Another voice from heaven urges, "Come out of her, my people, lest you take part in her sins, lest you share in her plagues; for her sins are heaped high as heaven." God remembers how she dealt out double punishment to her captives and so he will "repay her double for her deeds" (18:4-6).

The kings of the earth, who patronized the harlot, weep and wail when they see her burning. The merchants of the earth weep and mourn because their best customer is gone. There is no one to buy their wide assortment of goods. Shipmasters, seamen, and traders throw dust on their heads and mourn. All these groups cry out, "Alas, alas for the great city. . . . In one hour she has been laid waste" (18:9-20).

A mighty angel takes up a large stone and throws it into the sea, saying, "So shall Babylon the great city be thrown down with violence, and shall be found no more. The happy round of human activity will cease forever" (18:21-24).

The Victory Song and the Wedding Supper

In contrast to the mourning of the harlot's customers is the victory song of the multitude in heaven. They praise God that judgment has come on the one who corrupted the earth (19:1-5).

Then rejoicing is heard because of the approaching wedding of Christ, the Lamb, and his bride, the church:

Hallelujah! For the Lord our God the Almighty reigns.
Let us rejoice and exult and give him the glory,
for the marriage of the Lamb has come,
and his Bride has made herself ready (19:6-7).

Then John is instructed to write, "Blessed are those who are invited to the marriage supper of the Lamb." Then the angel adds, "These are the true words of God." The invitation is still open for John's readers and he is encouraging them to prepare for the wedding feast.

Because of the emotional setting John falls down at the angel's feet and worships him. "You must not do that!" he says, "I am a fellow servant with you and your brethren, who hold the testimony of Jesus. Worship God" (19:10). The book of Hebrews shows that the worship of angels became a serious threat in the early church. Evidently John is taking aim at the heresy also because he adds as his comment to the incident, "For the testimony of Jesus is the spirit of prophecy."

The Coming of "The Word of God"

When heaven opens again, John sees a white horse with a rider named "The Word of God." The rider is also named "Faithful and True" and he has still another name which only he knows. His eyes are like a flame of fire. He wears many diadems and a blood-dipped robe. Following him are the armies of heaven on white horses. A sharp sword, the instrument of judgment and authority, issues from his mouth. On his robe and his thigh is inscribed the title "King of kings and Lord of lords" (19:11-16).

"The Word of God" and his armies come down to fight the combined army of the beast (the Antichrist) and the kings of the earth. "Come," shouts an angel to the birds, "gather for the great supper of God." This recalls the similar invitation to the birds and beasts when Gog was defeated (Ezek. 39:17). The beast and the False Prophet, his associate, are captured and "thrown alive into the lake of fire that burns with brimstone." But the rest are slain by the sword of "The Word of God" and the birds gorge themselves on the flesh (19:17-21). Thus, two of the unholy trinity are gone.

The rider of this white horse is clearly different from the one in Rev. 6:1-2. There the rider was armed with "a bow" and he was in the company of war, famine, and death. He was the Antichrist. The numerous names and title make it obvious that the rider of this white horse is Christ, the Lamb.

The battle scene has some similarities to the one at Armageddon (16:12-16), but there are some differences. There the demonic spirits of the evil trinity gathered the kings of the whole world for battle. The opponent appeared to be the kings of the east, and yet if the army actually included the "kings of the whole world," then they were opposing God.

The comment in 16:15 "Lo, I am coming like a thief!" was apparently John's clue for associating the great, final battle of history with the coming of Christ. The difficulties in trying to harmonize the differences in detail alert us again to the fact that we are dealing with apocalyptic literature. The pieces of these fantastic visions cannot be fitted together neatly into one jigsaw puzzle. One part of the puzzle is plain, however. John is telling his readers that they have a choice between two, and only two, suppers or feasts: they can share the joy of the Lamb's wedding or be the food for the birds.

The Chaining of the Dragon

The condition of the unholy trinity is *two down and one to go*. An angel comes from heaven with "the key of the bottomless pit and a great chain." He chains the dragon "that ancient serpent, who is the Devil and Satan," and imprisons him in the pit for 1,000 years. The nations will have some peace without his deceptive activities (20:1-3).

The Millennium

After taking many chapters to describe the events leading up to and during end-time, John covers the 1,000 year reign of Christ in just three verses (20:4-6). That is really speeding up the pace of the drama! But unfortunately the message gets garbled like a fast tape. He sees thrones and judges sitting on them. It reminds us of the heavenly courtroom scene in Daniel 7, yet John never tells us explicitly whether the scene is in heaven or on earth. He sees the souls of the martyrs who died witnessing for Jesus and the souls of those who, while refusing to worship the beast and accept his mark, were not martyred. These come to life and reign with Christ during the millennium. The problems come with 20:5-6:

> The rest of the dead did not come to life until the thousand years were ended. This is the first resurrection. Blessed and holy is he who shares in the first resurrection! Over such the second death has no power, but they shall be priests of God and of Christ, and they shall reign with him a thousand years.

Just how does one make sense out of this series of contradictions? If God's dead are raised and reign with Christ, then "the rest of the dead" would seem to be those who backed the evil forces. Yet those who share in "the first resurrection" at the end of the millennium are called "blessed and holy" because they will not be subject to "the second death." These must be God's people as well! It would appear, then, that in spite of the literal sense of the passage the first resurrection has two phases: one at the beginning of the millennium and one at the end.

The Meaning of the Millennium

Eller follows the general intent of the passage by having the martyrs resurrected at the beginning of the millennium and the rest of the deceased saints at the end. The martyr-saints "deserve some special recognition and honor." The other reason John brings in the millennium, according to Eller, is to give the saints a chance to reign.

The Antichrist and his allies have had their reign, now it is time for Christ and the saints to have theirs. Since the former is on the earth, Eller believes that the millennium is on earth as well (*The Most Revealing Book of the Bible*, pp. 183-87).

The meaning and the length of the millennium have been vigorously debated and, as we shall see in the following chapters, the debate is not over. Eller's understanding makes the most sense out of the confusing three verses. He is convinced, moreover, that John never intended the 1,000 to be literal years. Since John covers the period so quickly and says so little about it, the 1,000 is to be taken as "a large, full number" in contrast to the 3 1/2 years the evil forces reigned.

The End of the Evil Trinity

After the millennium, Satan is released from the pit and goes out to deceive the nations (20:7). Where do these people come from? Supposedly all human beings following Satan and the Antichrist died at the *parousia* of Christ. Apocalyptic visions have caused us a number of "hang-ups" so far, and it looks like they intensify near the end of the Bible. To compound the problem, the nations at the four corners of the earth are none other then "Gog and Magog," as numberless as the sand of the sea (20:8).

In Ezekiel 38-39 Gog's forces from Magog in the north and his allies from the earth come down against God's people in the land of Israel. For his name's sake and as evidence for the nations and his own people, Yahweh defeats Gog. Then his kingdom comes when his spirit is poured on his people. John has Gog and Magog "surround the camp of the saints and the beloved city" (20:9). By having the confrontation after the millennium and before the final judgment, John is reinterpreting Ezekiel 38-39.

Fire comes down from heaven and consumes all the enemy except the Devil. He is thrown into the lake of fire where he joins his two henchmen, the Antichrist and the False Prophet, to suffer torment "day and night for ever and ever" (20:10).

The Final Judgment

The heavenly courtroom scene expands, pushing earth and sky aside. John sees all the dead, from the land and the sea, standing before "a great white throne." The unnamed judge is probably God because John does not like to associate Christ with the punishment of evil. It was an angel, not the "son of man," who executed God's wine press of wrath (14:17-20).

Tradition has usually interpreted this scene to involve the judgment of all persons, good and bad. But God's saints have been resurrected and are beyond the power of "the second death" (20:6). The dead are clearly the evil dead. Note that there is no mention of them being resurrected even if they are all gathered before the throne!

God has the records of all the deeds of all his creatures (like Dan. 7:10). If some of the dead plead to be acquitted, the books testify against them. The book of life is double proof—their names are not recorded there. Then they are thrown into the lake of fire. Also Death and Hades are thrown into the lake of fire, the second death (20:12-15).

The Holy City, New Jerusalem

Then John sees a new heaven and a new earth as depicted in Is. 65:17; 66:22. The sea, that chaotic, restless force and source of evil is gone. The holy city, new Jerusalem, comes down from God "prepared as a bride adorned for her husband" (21:1-2). A great voice from the throne declares:

> Behold, the dwelling of God is with men. He will dwell with them, and they shall be his people, and God himself will be with them; he will wipe away every tear from their eyes, and death shall be no more, neither shall there be mourning nor crying nor pain any more, for the former things have passed away (21:3-4).

God adds, "Behold I make all things new," implying that the earth and everything outside the holy city are renewed. He then tells John, "It is done! I am the Alpha and the Omega, the beginning and the end. To the thirsty I will give water without price from the fountain of the water of life" (21:6).

The Fourth Vision

One of the angels says to John, "Come, I will show you the Bride the wife of the Lamb." Then "in the spirit" of his fourth vision he is taken to a great, high mountain. There he has a marvelous view of the holy city Jerusalem coming down from heaven.

It has the radiance of a jasper, just like God's glory (4:3). As Ezekiel was told to measure the temple complex, so John is told to measure the city. It is the shape of a cube or a pyramid with each dimension measuring 12,000 stadia (about 1,500 miles). It has 12 gates of pearl, 3 on each side, with an angel at each gate. A name of one of the 12 tribes of Israel is inscribed on each of the gates.

There are 12 foundations of the city, each adorned with a precious stone similar to the 12 stones in the high priest's breastplate (Exod. 28:17-20). A name of one of the 12 apostles of the Lamb is written on each of the 12 foundations. Moreover, the streets are paved with gold. This is all very lovely, but the essence of the description is that the Bride consists of the people of God, both Jewish and Gentile.

Ezekiel's vision of the restored temple plays a great role in John's vision, but he has to make a number of revisions to make things fit. The temple was the focal point of Ezekiel's description. There is no temple in John's, however, because there is no more need for mediation between God and his people (21:22). They see his face and have immediate, perfect communion together (22:4). Neither are the sun and moon needed inasmuch as the glory of God and the Lamb furnish the light.

Ezekiel's river of life flowed from the temple (47:1), but since John has no temple he has the river of the water of life flowing from the combined throne of God and the Lamb. Another complication is that in Ezekiel's vision there were many trees on either side of the stream (47:7), yet John wants to make these "the tree of life" which humanity forfeited when driven from the Garden of Eden. It produces a different kind of fruit each month.

The Healing of the Nations

A most interesting observation about the tree of life is that its leaves are "for the healing of the nations" (22:2). But the nations have been cast into the lake of fire. Furthermore, there is the startling statement that "the kings of the earth," those who were the customers of the harlot Babylon, bring their glory into the New Jerusalem (21:24). It is not likely that anyone in the city wants to go out because the road leads to the lake of fire. Yet the gates are open all the time. Evidently they are intended for incoming traffic. Nothing unclean can enter the city, therefore something must have happened to the kings of the earth.

The Universalistic Possibility

When John refers to "the first resurrection" he seems to imply a second resurrection—yet he never mentions it explicitly. Eller feels that 21:24-27 fits the description. He shows "the possibility of a continuing traffic from the lake of fire into the New Jerusalem. It can only be labeled as a 'resurrection'; for the lake of fire is second-order DEATH and the New Jerusalem second-order LIFE, and by what conceivable means could a person get from one to the other except by 'resurrection'?" (*The Most Revealing Book of the Bible*, p. 201).

Thus Eller is suggesting that John holds to a "universlistic possibility." But this modified universalism does not claim that all persons will eventually be saved. Eller notes five conditions:

1. John is not proposing the possibility of salvation apart from faith in Jesus Christ;

2. He does not underestimate the power of evil and the pervasiveness of its influence among men. He does not show us a world that every day in every way is getting better and better;

3. John is fully aware of the *seriousness* of sin. It is not something that can simply be ignored or brushed aside;

4. John knows, too, that God's love cannot be true unless it includes *justice*; he understands the propriety and rightness of *punishment*;

5. John never could be accused of the sort of universalism that undercuts the evangelistic *urgency of decision*. When the picture is drawn John's way, no one in his right mind is going to put off accepting Christ on the grounds that it will be just as easy to do it later—after being eaten by vultures and spending time in the lake of fire, maybe? (*The Most Revealing Book of the Bible*, p. 203).

Eller comments further, "But as it would be wrong to assert that he (John) teaches that *all men will be saved*, just as wrong would it be to assert that *some men can never be saved*; he doesn't say that either!" "What we can and must say," Eller concludes, "is that John attributes to and leaves with God 'the universalistic possibility.' " (*The Most Revealing Book of the Bible*, p. 204).

The End Is Near

Eager expectancy is expressed a number of times in the final exhortations. The words of the book "are trustworthy and true" and they "must soon take place" (22:6). The assurance of Jesus is added in 22:7, "And behold, I am coming soon. Blessed is he who keeps the words of the prophecy of this book."

John is instructed, "Do not seal up the words of the prophecy of this book, for the time is near" (22:10). The message is to be shared, but those who hear and read have the right to make their own decisions: "Let the evildoer still do evil, and the filthy still be filthy, and the righteous still do right, and the holy still be holy" (22:11). "Behold, I am coming soon," Jesus reiterates, "bringing my recompense, to repay every one for what he has done" (22:12). Justice will match the deed.

John's "now" tingles with the hope that soon the "not yet" will appear. Jesus pronounces a "blessing" on those who keep "the words of the prophecy." Woven throughout the book is the invitation to repent and live according to God's will. Sinful ways always bring plagues and suffering. Those who "wash their robes" (22:14) will have the right to "the tree of life." That is the only way to be true to the book. *There is no blessing promised for those who try to figure out the times.* The all-important matter is to be prepared for Christ's coming.

"I am the Alpha and the Omega," Jesus reaffirms; "I am the root and offspring of David, the bright morning star" (22:13, 16). He is the answer to the hopes of the Old Covenant and he is the bright future of the New Covenant.

The eager Bride, the church, says to Jesus, "Come." Those who hear are encouraged to say, "Come," and those who are thirsty are invited to come drink of the water of life (22:17).

In line with an old warning not to add to or take from God's commands (Deut. 4:2) a severe warning is given to those tempted to tamper with the record. Those who add any words will suffer the plagues described in it and if anyone deletes any portion he will cut himself out of "his share in the tree of life and in the holy city" (22:18, 19).

For the third time Jesus promises, "Surely, I am coming soon." "Amen," John exclaims, "Come, Lord Jesus!" Then John adds his benediction: "The grace of the Lord Jesus be with all the saints. Amen."

And still the Bride waits!

Chapter 12
The Story of Dispensationalism

One of the most pervasive prophetic systems today, especially in the United States, is that of "dispensationalism." Its roots go back to John Nelson Darby (A.D. 1800-1882). This Irishman, educated at Trinity College, Dublin, began a law career, but about 1820 he entered a period of spiritual distress. He gave up his legal profession in 1823 and two years later was ordained as a priest in the Church of England.

Darby's Conversion

His first assignment was among Irish Catholics in "a wild and uncultivated district" where he ministered for 27 months. In 1827 he had a serious leg injury which required surgery in Dublin and a long period of recovery. During this period of inactivity he had a religious experience which delivered him from his anxiety. He felt that he was "united to Christ in heaven" (Eph. 2:6) and that his wretched attempts to live by the law were past.

Darby's "revelation" gave him, as it were, a new pair of glasses through which to view Scripture and the world around him. The only true "church of God" consisted of those who had been united with Christ as he had. Christendom, the visible church, was really the world, therefore he renounced his ordination. He even refused to join the dissenting groups.

The dominant eschatological view in the church since Augustine had been some form of "postmillennialism," that is, the church was in the millennium and Christ would return *after the millennium* (whether 1,000 years or not) was completed. The unrest after the Napoleonic wars resulted in an apocalyptic period of great dissatisfaction with the established church. The expectancy of the Lord's return was the hope which appealed to these disillusioned people. Cell groups formed in a number of towns and cities in Ireland and England, and so Darby joined one of them. Later on, these groups acquired the name "Plymouth Brethren" because of Darby's leadership of the cell at Plymouth, England.

While Darby could not doubt his experience of heavenly union with Christ, he had to admit that Isaiah 32 spoke of a kingdom of God on earth. He did not understand the implications of his insight, but the key idea was there in 1827: God had two plans and two groups of people with whom to work. Israel was God's kingdom here on earth and the church was God's heavenly kingdom. From the start, therefore, Darby's thinking was governed by the revelation of his conversion experience during the convalescence. Accordingly, his whole system stands or falls on his ecclesiology (doctrine of the church) and his eschatology (doctrine of last things).

Darby's Influence Expands

Darby began writing articles in 1829 and he continued writing and teaching for more than 50 years. About 1830 the logic of his presuppositions led to a new understanding of 2 Thess. 2:1-2: the saints of the church would be "raptured" (taken out) from the world to meet Jesus Christ. This "rapture of the saints" would take place *a period of time before* the judgment day of the Lord. Controversy resulted from Darby's teachings, especially his separation of Israel and the church. However, he was victorious over his chief adversary, B. W. Newton, and went on to be the commanding leader of the Plymouth Brethren.

Darby's most faithful propagandist in England was William Kelly (1821-1906). He was convinced of the superiority of Darby's system of interpretation and he urged everyone to read his writings. In order to make them more accessible, he published (1857-1867) 32 volumes of his writings. Furthermore, *The Bible Treasury*, a monthly paper Kelly edited in 1856-1906, helped spread the new system of prophecy.

Darby in America

Some of the Brethren emigrated to America around 1850 and brought Darby's views with them. More influential in spreading Darbyism in America was James Inglis, editor of *Waymarks in the Wilderness*. He carried a succession of prophetic articles, many of which bore the Darby stamp.

Most influential of all, however, were Darby's seven extended visits to Canada and the United States (1862-1877). During this 15-year period he spent a total of six years west of the Atlantic. His novel ideas and his method of quoting numerous verses from Scripture convinced many listeners of the truth of his teaching.

News spread and prominent clergymen opened their churches to Darby. He held a number of meetings and Bible studies in New York, Boston, and St. Louis, and he was thrilled with the success of his teachings. But he was very disappointed when the ministers and their congregations did not leave the mainline churches and form Plymouth Brethren groups. He believed that the Lord was "about to come" and he wanted his hearers to leave the apostate church and get ready for Christ's return.

It is ironic that the failure of Darby's dream contributed to the widespread influence of his prophetic system. While most of his hearers were not leaving the churches, they were spreading his views among the mainline denominations. Darby's desire for a publication outlet in America became reality when Paul and Timothy Loizeaux, converts to Brethrenism, founded the Loizeaux Brothers publishing house. It became the main source for Plymouth Brethren writings in the United States and its publications were distributed widely.

James H. Brookes

The most effective propagandist for Darbyism in the 19th century was James H. Brookes, pastor for 33 years of two large Presbyterian churches in St. Louis. He invited Darby a number of times to preach to his congregation. His book *Maranatha, or The Lord Cometh* appeared in 1870 and sold rapidly. One of his key ideas was the two-phase coming (*parousia*) of Christ. He could come at any moment *for* his saints, but he would not return *with* his saints until the signs of his coming had occurred. In other words, the "rapture" of the saints was not dependent on any events or signs.

One would get the idea that the "any-moment coming of Christ" was Brookes' idea, yet Darby had been teaching it all along. A great deal has been written trying to explain why Brookes failed to indicate the source of his ideas. The most plausible is that he was trying to protect Darby's views from the backlash of criticism resulting from the inner fighting of the Brethren. Brookes noted their "hairsplitting and nonsensical divisions" and claimed that they were just as "wrecked" as the denominations they were opposing. Robert Cameron, a personal friend of Brookes, stated explicitly that Brookes got the idea of the "any-moment coming" from Darby and the Brethren writers.

The Niagara Bible Conferences

From 1875 until his death in 1897, Brookes was prominent in the summer series of conferences which came to be known as "The Niagara Bible Conferences." Year after year the speakers rang the changes on dispensational distinctives, especially the "any-moment return of Christ." They got great results for a while by claiming that Jesus might return before the next morning or even before the service was over.

The psychological pressure wore thin with the passing of the years, however, and even the speakers had to "psych" themselves up to keep parroting the old line. In fact, it was a series of defections from the old party line which was instrumental in the demise of the conference. Robert Cameron, Nathaniel West, and W. J. Erman could no longer accept the idea of Christ's coming at "any moment," and they said so publicly.

When Cameron, the editor of the popular prophetic monthly *Watchword and Truth*, first came under the influence of the Brethren he was entranced by their devotion and he accepted everything they said or wrote without the slightest doubt. His intellectual conversion came when he began reading some writers critical of Darby. This type of gullibility and reaction point up the need for checking out any system before buying into it.

Darby's method contributed to the problem. In his writing and teaching he preferred to quote a number of verses from different parts of the Bible. When the issue was raised why he did not take fewer passages and expound them more thoroughly, Darby explained that in his method the faith of the hearers was grounded in "the power of God" and not "the wisdom of man." This sounds very pious, but the plain fact is that a well-meaning person can string together a number of prooftexts in such a way as to do violence to the context of the verses. His prooftext method was still "the wisdom of man," namely Darby. Had he used a thorough inductive method of examining various passages, his followers would have been able to pick up the defects of his system more quickly.

Cyrus Ingerson Scofield and Arno C. Gaebelein

Brookes multiplied himself greatly through Cyrus Ingerson Scofield (1843-1921), a young lawyer who studied with him. For three years after his conversion in 1879, Scofield came to Brookes' home for tutoring about the dispensational system. At the 1888 Niagara Conference he delivered a prophetic message "Rightly Dividing the Word of Truth," and steadily his influence increased. He got the idea of a reference Bible with dispensational notes and tried to rally the Conference leaders in support of his project. When he failed, he published his own correspondence course and circulated it widely.

A new recruit for Darbyism was the German immigrant Arno C. Gaebelein. While ministering to New York Jews he came in contact with three Plymouth Brethren business men. Gaebelein was just as entranced as Cameron had been, and he considered his new teachers "next to the Apostles" in soundness and spirituality. He found his ministry was more effective when he began to teach the literal fulfillment of the prophecies about Israel, and he began to share his new faith in his monthly magazine *Our Hope.*

The Scofield Reference Bible

After the Niagara Conference collapsed, Gaebelein and Scofield started a new series in 1901 at Sea Cliff, Long Island, N. Y. There Scofield mentioned to Gaebelein his idea of a reference Bible. It was suggested to Mr. Ball and Mr. Pirie, two of the business men who had influenced Gaebelein, and they agreed to support the project. Scofield was able to spend all his time editing the notes and references. He requested Gaebelein's help in dealing with some difficult passages and so when the *Scofield Reference Bible* (SRB) appeared in 1909, Arno C. Gaebelein was listed among the Consulting Editors.

Scofield had made contact with some scholars on both sides of the Atlantic and he expressed his indebtedness to "a very wide circle of learned and spiritual brethren in Europe and America." Then he did a little name-dropping: "It may not be invidious to mention among these Professor James Barrellet of the Theological Faculty of Lausanne, Professors Sayce and Margoliouth of Oxford, Mr. Walter Scott, the eminent Bible teacher, and Professor C. R. Erdman, of Princeton" (Introduction).

This window dressing was designed to give the impression of wide scholarly support for the Bible, but such was not the case. Scofield even went so far as to include William J. Erdman and W. G. Moorehead as Consulting Editors when both of them were opposed to the pretribulation rapture taught in the SRB. Far more influential in shaping the notes was Walter Scott, a member of the Plymouth Brethren. Scofield does give credit to William Erdman for his outline of Revelation, but he does not explain that by his various section headings he has reinterpreted Erdman.

"Thus it is obvious," Daniel P. Fuller comments, "that Scofield took the liberty of using Erdman's outline of Revelation and shaping its wording and interpretation to suit his own Darbyistic views. All this was done without Erdman's knowledge, for his son, C. R. Erdman of Princeton, asserts that without any prior knowledge on his father's part, Scofield included his name among the list of consulting editors" (*The Hermeneutics of Dispensationalism*, p. 118).

Nevertheless, the SRB was an immediate success. The section headings and parallel passages opened up the format of the text and made reading much easier. The notes and references laid out in clear fashion the dispensational system of prophecy. A revised edition appeared in 1917.

Lewis Sperry Chafer

The next in the apostolic succession of Darby was Lewis Sperry Chafer (1871-1952). In his twenties he was a song leader and an evangelist. In 1903 he joined the faculty of Northfield School, Dwight L. Moody's school for boys in E. Northfield, Mass. While leading the music for the summer Bible Conferences at Northfield, he met Scofield and they became close friends. Scofield realized that he had "the makings of a good Bible teacher," and in 1914 he laid his hands on him and dedicated him to the Lord for that purpose.

When Scofield founded the Philadelphia School of the Bible in 1919, Chafer joined the faculty. Scofield had planned on writing a book on the religious theme "Grace," but with his failing health he asked Chafer to do it for him.

Since dispensationalists considered most theological seminaries apostate, they formed many Bible Schools and Institutes after World War I in order to train their own people. Chafer was convinced that there was a need for a more advanced dispensational school, and so in 1924 he helped found the Evangelical Theological College and became its first President. In 1936 it was renamed Dallas Theological Seminary. The next year he began writing his *Systematic Theology*, a project that took a decade and ran to 8 volumes.

The Success of Dispensationalism

By 1950, not long before his death, Chafer had brought dispensationalism to its greatest prominence. The popularity of the system was due in large measure to the zeal of its promoters and the inbreeding of the schools. They were essentially "training schools," not "educational institutions." The curriculum was basically a "one-way program" where the major goal was to learn the details of the system. Alternative possibilities of interpreting the Bible were mentioned only in the interest of how to refute them, not to learn from them. Daniel Fuller comments very cogently:

> Ignorance is bliss, and it may well be that this popularity would not be so great if the adherents of this system knew the historical background of what they teach. Few indeed realize that the teaching of Chafer came from Scofield, who in turn got it from Brookes, who got it through the writings of Darby and the Plymouth Brethren (*The Hermeneutics of Dispensationalism*, p. 136).

Chapter 13
The Dispensational System

In 1917, eight years after the appearance of the *Scofield Reference Bible* (SRB), the Oxford University Press decided to reset the entire Bible in new type. Scofield took advantage of this opportunity to make some changes in format and to add new material.

The New Scofield Reference Bible

The *New Scofield Reference Bible* (NSRB) appeared in 1967, the 50th anniversary since the last edition. The nine-man Editorial Committee was chaired by E. Schuyler English. While the essence of the Scofield system is retained, some excesses are eliminated or toned down. One obvious change is the elimination of Bishop Ussher's dates. In place of 4004 B.C. at Gen. 1:1, appears the note: "Scripture gives no data for determining how long ago the universe was created." In our discussion of dispensational distinctives, we will generally note where the NSRB revises the SRB.

Seven Dispensations and Eight Covenants

A "dispensation" is defined as "a period of time during which man is tested in respect to his obedience to some specific revelation of the will of God" (note at Gen. 1:28). NSRB has extensive new notes to clarify the definition and remove the ambiguity. "These different dispensations," for example, "are not separate ways of salvation. During each of them man is reconciled to God in only one way, i.e. by God's grace through the work of Christ that was accomplished on the cross and vindicated in His resurrection." "The purpose of each dispensation, then, is to place man under a specific rule of conduct, but such stewardship is not a condition of salvation."

Closely linked with the dispensations are eight covenants which God made with various individuals or groups. A covenant is defined as "a sovereign pronouncement of God by which he establishes a relationship of responsibility" (note at Gen. 2:16). "Covenants are normally unconditional in the sense that God obligates Himself in grace, by the unrestricted declaration, 'I will,' to accomplish certain announced purposes, despite any failure on the part of the person or people with whom he covenants." Thus, "human failure is never permitted to abrogate the covenant or block its ultimate fulfillment."

NSRB retains seven basic dispensations, but it revises one name and five starting points of those in SRB. For ease of comparison the two categories are listed in parallel columns:

Dispensations	*Covenants*
1. Innocence (Gen. 1:28);	1. Edenic (Gen. 2:16);
2. Conscience or Moral Responsibility (Gen. 3:7), instead of 3:23;	2. Adamic (Gen. 3:15);
3. Human Government (Gen. 8:15), instead of 8:20;	3. Noahic (Gen. 9:16);
4. Promise (Gen. 12:1);	4. Abrahamic (Gen. 12:2);
5. Law (Exod. 19:1), instead of 19:8;	5. Mosaic (Exod. 19:5);
6. Church (Acts 2:1), instead of Grace (John 1:17); and	6. Palestinian (Deut. 30:3);
7. Kingdom (Rev. 20:4), instead of Eph. 1:10.	7. Davidic (2 Sam. 7:16); and
	8. New Covenant (Heb. 8:8).

The general idea of various dispensations and covenants is not unique with the dispensationalists. Because the term "Testament" has been understood as "Covenant" or "Dispensation," all Christians have recognized at least the Old and New periods of God's activity with his people. What distinguishes dispensationalism is the large number of categories and the sharp distinctions which are often made between them.

Authority for Dispensational Division

For Scofield and Gaebelein, the key "prooftext" authorizing this division of Scripture was "rightly dividing the word of truth" (2 Tim. 2:15). But this *King James Version* rendering was an attempt to translate the Greek verb meaning "to cut straight." The idea is to be right and straightforward in handling of Scripture, *not in compartmentalizing it.*

Dispensationalists recognized that their views were different from those which the church had held for centuries. They assumed, however, that the ideas had been lost, and so they searched the writings of the early church fathers to find ancient authority for their position. They turned up a number of references to "dispensation" and tried to make a case for their claim, but on examination each of them is a general use of the term and has nothing to do with the refinements of the dispensational system.

In Part X of his "Introduction," Scofield makes a valiant effort to justify the distinctions by quoting Augustine: "Distinguish the ages and the Scriptures harmonize." This is a misleading translation, however, because "the ages" should be "times." Augustine made this statement when trying to harmonize two apparently contradictory passages of Scripture. A proper recognition of the "time" or "circumstance" of the statements resolved the difficulty. In no way was he referring to distinctive "ages" or "periods of time" in the history of God's dealing with his people. Even if this quotation was made in innocence, it was cheating on the truth, and fortunately the NSRB has removed it. The plain fact is that *there is no historical authority for the distinctives of the dispensational system—they begin with Darby in 1827, not before.*

Dispensational Distinctives

The SRB and NSRB have many helpful, accurate notes concerning God's redemptive activity throughout the Old and New Testaments, and it is obvious that dispensationalists share many ideas with traditional Christianity. The purpose here, however, is to examine their distinctive ideas, especially with reference to prophecy and prediction.

The basic difference is Darby's "revelation" that God has different purposes and plans for Israel and the church. This assumption results in the following distinctive interpretations of Scripture: (1) the literal fulfillment of all the covenants and promises concerning Israel; (2) prophecy applies only to Israel; (3) the church is a "mystery" revealed first to Paul; (4) the church is a "parenthesis" (interruption) of God's earthly plans for Israel; (5) since the Church will *not* go through the tribulation, Christ's coming or advent must be in two phases; and (6) the coming of Christ for his saints could happen at "any moment."

Literal Understanding of Scripture

Dispensationalists have claimed to take the Bible literally. It is obvious to everyone, however, that this is impossible. For example,

Jesus commanded, "If your right hand causes you to sin, cut it off and throw it away" (Matt. 5:30). Most people interpret this command figuratively or spiritually.

The crucial factor in interpretation is to know when to take a passage literally and when spiritually. The clues should come from the passages being studied. But because of the dispensationalists' absolute view of prophecy, they determine ahead of time that all prophecies will be interpreted literally. In other words, their assumption has already determined the outcome, no matter what the passage says.

Where a verse or passage contradicts the system the tendency is to reinterpret the section or to spiritualize it by resorting to "types" and "antitypes." "A type," according to Scofield, "is a divinely purposed illustration of some truth" (note on Gen. 1:16). It may be a person, event, thing, institution, or ceremonial. "Types occur most frequently in the Pentateuch," Scofield notes, "but are found, more sparingly, elsewhere. The antitype, or fulfillment of the type, is found, usually, in the New Testament."

In Gen. 1:16, for example, the "greater light" is a type of Christ, while the "lesser light" represents the church. Types of the church are found all over the Old Testament and yet the Old Testament is supposed to know nothing about God's plans for the church. Did God place these "divinely purposed" illustrations of truth there solely for the benefit of the dispensationalists?

Does Prophecy Apply Only to Israel?

A correlative of this rigid view of prophecy is that the promises of the prophets apply only to Israel. Thus, in Dan. 9:24-27 the first 69 weeks go down to the crucifixion of Christ, but the 70th week must be postponed until the close of the church age. This drastic separation of a unified prophecy is the supreme example of how arbitrary the dispensational method is. It is true that the book of Revelation picks up some details from Daniel, but these are reinterpretations of John for his time, not some distant future.

In answer to such a suggestion, the conservative patriarch Ernst W. Hengstenberg comments, "*Exactly* seventy weeks in all are to elapse; and how can any one imagine that there is an interval between the sixty-nine and the one, when these together make up the seventy?" (*Christology in the Old Testament*, Vol. III, p. 143).

Dispensational Interpretation of the 70 Weeks

Because the 70th week is projected into the future, dispensationalists have 483 years until the crucifixion of Christ. Thus, instead of
beginning in 458/457 B.C. with the traditional conservatives, they start
at 445, the year Nehemiah requested Artaxerxes I for permission to
rebuild Jerusalem (Neh. 2:5). A note on this verse in NSRB states
accurately, "This is the only decree actually recorded in Scripture
which relates to the restoring and rebuilding of the city of Jerusalem."

But aside from this more accurate starting point, the dispensationalists have some of the same troubles the traditionalists have
because they accept the 7 + 62 combination of weeks. There is nothing
to authenticate the end of the 49-year period. The full 69 weeks = 483
years come down to about A.D. 38, a number of years after the
crucifixion of Christ. NSRB accounts for the extra years by figuring
each year as 360 days, not 365 1/4. In this same note it adds (note 4
for Dan. 9:24), "In this connection it should be remembered that, in
the grand sweep of prophecy, prophetic time is invariably so near as to
give full warning, so indeterminate as to give no satisfaction to mere
curiosity." In other words, some discrepancy in details is not
important "in the grand sweep of prophecy."

Concerning the 70th week NSRB comments (p. 913), "The proof
that this final week has not yet been fulfilled is seen in the fact that
Christ definitely relates its main events to His second coming (Mt.
24:6, 15)." As we noted in chapter 10, Jesus was predicting another
"desolating sacrilege" in the near future. That was fulfilled in A.D. 70
and has no future reference. Jesus thought the rest of the apocalyptic
events would happen within the lifetime of his disciples, but they
didn't. The "proof" happens to be in the dispensational presupposition, not in an accurate understanding of Matt. 24-25.

The "Mystery" of the Church

Dispensationalists claim that the church is a unique "mystery,"
unknown to the Old Testament prophets, predicted by Jesus (Matt.
16:18), but not fully explained until it was revealed to Paul. Their
basis is Eph. 3:4-6:

When you read this you can perceive my insight into the mystery of
Christ, which was not made known to the sons of men in other

generations as it has now been revealed to his holy apostles and prophets by the Spirit; that is, how the Gentiles are fellow heirs, members of the same body, and partakers of the promise in Christ Jesus through the gospel.

Paul is claiming that his ministry to the Gentiles roots in the revelation that the Gentiles become peers on equal footing with the Jews and members of the same body of God's people by faith in the gospel of Jesus Christ. There is a continuity, therefore, between the Jewish people of God and the more inclusive people of God, the church.

But notice how the NSRB note on Eph. 3:6 twists the whole passage to fit the system:

The mystery "hidden in God" was the divine purpose to make of Jew and Gentile a wholly new thing—"the Church, which is his (Christ's) body," formed by the baptism with the Holy Spirit (1 Cor. 12:12-13) and in which the earthly distinction of Jew and Gentile disappears (Eph. 2:14-15; Col. 3:10-11).

It is true that Christ broke down the wall between Jew and Greek, but the passage says nothing about making "a wholly new thing." The new thing is that Gentiles are on a par with the Jews and able to share in the blessings of God's people.

God's Olive Tree

The best answer to this dispensational interpretation is Paul himself. In Rom. 11:17-24 he notes that because of unbelief, Jewish branches were broken off from God's "olive tree" and Gentile branches from a "wild olive tree" were grafted in their place. Later on he declares that Jews who believe will be grafted back into the cultivated tree.

Paul makes it clear that *God has only one olive tree.* It started growing in OT times. When Gentiles accepted Jesus as Christ they were grafted into the same tree, not another "wholly new" tree, and they continue there by faith. This analogy of Paul explains what he meant in Eph. 3:4-6: there is only one people of God and it is composed of Jews and Gentiles alike. *The church, therefore, is an extension of the OT people of God, not a unique creation completely separate from Israel.*

Darby attempted to get around this clear-cut illustration by identifying the grafted wild branches as "the professing Church," which would be destroyed just prior to the second coming. This is a slanderous misinterpretation of Paul because most of his Gentile converts were true Christians, not just professing hypocrites. NSRB claims (p. 1225), "Israel is judicially broken off from the good olive tree, Christ (vs. 17-22)." But nowhere do these verses identify the olive tree with Christ. Paul says explicitly that believing Jews will "be grafted back into their own olive tree" (11:24). *The olive tree is true Israel!*

NSRB goes on to stress the fact that Christians are "the heavenly seed of Abraham" who share in "the spiritual blessings of the Abrahamic covenant." The punch line is the backhanded comment, "That the Christian now inherits the distinctive Jewish promises is not taught in Scripture." Nor is it taught in the New Testament that all "the distinctive Jewish promises" have eternal validity for Jews. This quotation is more dispensational schizophrenia in which the church is heavenly and completely distinct from earthly Israel. People of faith, true children of Abraham, whether Jew or Gentile, have been part of God's good olive tree since the call of Abraham.

The Jerusalem Council

One more key passage for dispensationalists is Acts 15:13-18. "Dispensationally," Scofield claims, "this is the most important passage in the N. T." (SRB, p. 1169). At the Jerusalem Council Peter (Symeon), Barnabas, and Paul relate what wonderful things God has performed through them among the Gentiles. James, the leader of the Jerusalem church, replies, "Brethren, listen to me. Symeon has related how God first visited the Gentiles, to take out of them a people for his own name. And with this the words of the prophets agree, as it is written,

> After this I will return,
> and I will rebuild the dwelling of David, which has fallen;
> I will rebuild its ruins,
> and I will set it up,
> that the rest of men may seek the Lord,
> and all the Gentiles who are called by my name,
> says the Lord, who has made these things known
>   from of old" (Amos 9:11-12).

The pressing question at the council is whether Gentile Christians should be circumcised. "Therefore my judgment is," James declares, "that we should not trouble those of the Gentiles who turn to God" (Acts 15:19). The basis for his decision is that "with this," God's visits to the Gentiles, "the words of the prophets agree." The words happen to be the Septuagint version of Amos 9:11-12. They differ considerably from the Hebrew, but they say what James is trying to get across. Long ago the Lord prophesied that the Gentiles would be called by his name, therefore who are we to stand in God's way?

Observe how the NSRB twists the passage: "Amos 9:11 begins with the words 'in that day.' James introduced his quotation in such a way as to show what day Amos was talking about, namely, the time after the present worldwide witness (Acts 1:8), when Christ will return. James showed that there will be Gentile believers at that time as well as Jewish believers; hence he concluded that Gentiles are not required to become Jewish proselytes by circumcision" (p. 1186).

In other words, dispensationalists are claiming that "this" refers to the "out-calling" of the church and "I will return" to the return of Christ. Pray tell, what would this double-talk have meant to the people of the council? Fuller comments, "Thus, if the Jerusalem council understood James' quotation as Dispensationalists do, circumcision would have remained in effect for Gentiles, and the Gospel of grace would have been nullified. The only logical position to take is that James quoted Amos 9:11-12 because this was actually being fulfilled right then and there" (*The Hermeneutics of Dispensationalism*, p. 347, note 18).

Another reason why dispensationalists project James' quotation into the distant future is the reference to rebuilding "the dwelling of David." This must refer, so they say, to the restoration of the Messianic kingdom here on earth. The author of 9:11-12, who most likely was not Amos, was definitely looking forward to the establishment of the Davidic kingdom. But James had no such idea in mind. Either he ignored this part of the quotation or he was understanding the rebuilding of David's dwelling as the work of God in raising up the Gentile Christians.

The only meaningful antecedent of "this," both in James' statement and in the quotation, is the fact of God's calling the Gentiles in the days of Peter, Barnabas, Paul, and James. But the system of the dispensationalists incapacitates them for *really* standing in the historical context of the early church. Their eyes and sentiments are focused on the future.

The Church, An Interruption of God's Plans

In the NSRB the "church" is listed as the 6th dispensation. Darby was more accurate when he called the church "a parenthesis." God's main timeline, according to him, concerns Israel; therefore there are only six dispensations about God's earthly people. Thus, the church, that unique act of God, is really an interruption, not another dispensation.

It is quite evident that the Gospel of Matthew was written for Jews. Dispensationalists consider it as thoroughly dispensational; therefore they interpret its structure as an accurate description of God's activities in the 1st century A.D. and also his plans for the future.

John the Baptist announces, "Repent, for the kingdom of heaven is at hand" (Matt. 3:2) and later Jesus preaches the same message (4:17). He states the principles of the kingdom (chapters 5-7) and shows by word and deed what kind of kingdom he is offering. But the Jews reject the kingdom and Jesus their king; therefore God postpones the kingdom and begins to call out the church. In this new phase Jesus changes his approach by offering comfort to the weary and oppressed: "Come to me, all who labor and are heavy laden, and I will give you rest" (11:28).

The Kingdom of Heaven

Old dispensationalists like Scofield made a sharp distinction between the kingdoms of "heaven" and of "God." "The kingdom of God is universal," says Scofield, "including all moral intelligences willingly subject to the will of God, whether angels, the Church, or saints of past or future dispensations . . . while the kingdom of heaven is Messianic, mediatorial, and Davidic, and has for its object the establishment of the kingdom of God in the earth" (SRB, p. 1003).

"The phrase, kingdom of heaven (lit. of the heavens)," Scofield comments, "is peculiar to Matthew and signifies the Messianic earth rule of Jesus Christ, the Son of David. It is called the kingdom of heaven because it is the rule of the heavens over the earth" (SRB, p. 996). Scofield ignores the most probable reason for Matthew's usage and then reads in his own interpretation.

Before the exile, the Jews thought they had God boxed in the temple, but during the exile they made a complete shift from an extreme immanence to an extreme transcendence. God now was so other-worldly they dared not even mention his name "Yahweh" or use his title "God." Accordingly, the place where God abides was substituted for his name: "the kingdom of Yahweh (God)" became "the kingdom of heaven."

Where the same "kingdom" passage occurs in each of the first three gospels, Matthew has "the kingdom of heaven," while Mark and Luke have "the kingdom of God." There is no distinction in meaning at all. Matthew's unique expression is simply his attempt to abide by the taboo which conservative Jews practiced.

But strangely enough, "the kingdom of God" appears in five passages in Matthew (6:33; 12:28; 19:24; 21:31, 43). Matt. 6:33 is doubtful, however, because some Greek manuscripts have either "kingdom" or "kingdom of heaven." The remaining instances are in direct quotations from Jesus, and perhaps Matthew took them directly from his sources without any editing. In any case, there is nothing decisive in the contents to indicate an explicit difference in meaning. It should be noted that while the NSRB tones down the sharp contrast in SRB, it still retains the emphasis on the Jewish aspects of the kingdom of heaven.

The Sermon on the Mount

Since Christians, who belong to the kingdom of God, have nothing to do with the Jewish kingdom of heaven, according to Scofield, "the Sermon on the Mount in its primary application gives neither the privilege nor the duty of the church. These are found in the Epistles" (SRB, p. 1000). At the Lord's Prayer petition "And forgive us our debts, as we forgive our debtors" (6:12), Scofield comments, "This is legal ground. Cf. Eph. 4:32, which is grace. Under law forgiveness is conditioned upon a like spirit in us; under grace we are forgiven for Christ's sake and exhorted to forgive because we have been forgiven" (SRB, p.1002).

This sharp line between law and grace is the logical outgrowth of the separation between Israel and the church, but it certainly perpetrates a lot of nonsense. The NSRB still holds that the Sermon on the Mount is law, that it cannot save sinners, and that Christians are not under it, but NSRB tones down Scofield's extremes by noting, "Both the Mosaic law and the Sermon on the Mount are part of Holy Scripture which is inspired by God and therefore 'profitable for doctrine, for reproof, for correction, for instruction in righteousness' (2 Tim. 3:16) for the redeemed of all ages" (p. 997).

In the early stages of his ministry, the only place Jesus could begin was with the proper understanding of the Mosaic law. On that foundation his followers would rest until the redemptive aspects of his death and resurrection were made known. The ministry of Jesus was the bridge between Israel and the church. Instead of it being split into two distinct phases, it was a transition linking two periods of God's activity with his people. *The kingdom was not postponed—it was raised to a new level in the church!*

The Kingdom Is at Hand

In attempting to get around the plain statement that the kingdom was "at hand," both the SRB and NSRB comment:

> The Bible expression "at hand" is never a positive affirmation that the person or thing said to be at hand will immediately appear, but only that no known or predicted event must intervene. When Christ appeared to the Jewish people, the next thing, in the order of revelation as it then stood, should have been the setting up of the Davidic kingdom. In the knowledge of God, not yet disclosed, lay the rejection of the kingdom and King, the long period of the mystery-form of the kingdom, the world-wide preaching of the cross, and the out-calling of the Church. But this was as yet locked up in the secret counsels of God (SRB, p. 998; NSRB, p. 996).

This is simply another weasel explanation to fit their unbiblical definition of the kingdom. As we noted earlier, Jesus told the Pharisees that the kingdom was in their midst. He was convinced that his teachings and deeds were the beginning of God's kingdom.

The Mystery-Form of the Kingdom

Since the kingdom has supposedly been postponed and the church age is beginning, dispensationalists have had to invent a hybrid kind of kingdom in order to explain Matthew 13. Both the SRB and NSRB comment:

> The seven parables of ch. 13, called by our Lord "mysteries of the kingdom of heaven" (v, 11), taken together describe the result of the presence of the Gospel in the world during the present age, that is, the

time of seed-sowing which began with our Lord's personal ministry and will end with the "harvest" (vv. 40-43). The result is the mingled tares and wheat, good fish and bad, in the sphere of Christian profession. It is Christendom (pp. 998 and 1013).

The plain meaning of the parables is that the kingdom is continuing—it has not been postponed. Only the will to believe the dispensational system necessitates a "mystery form of the kingdom."

Dispensational View of Matthew 24-25

In the SRB and NSRB the entire Olivet Discourse (Little Apocalypse) is assigned to the 70th week of Daniel 9 and the return of Jesus as King of the restored Messianic kingdom. Jesus' reference to "this generation" is an obvious hurdle, but as in the case of "at hand," the creative minds of the dispensationalists come up with another dodge:

> The word "generation" (Gk. *genea*), though commonly used in Scripture of those living at one time, could not mean those who were alive at the time of Christ, as none of "these things"—i.e. the world-wide preaching of the kingdom, the tribulation, the return of the Lord in visible glory, and the regathering of the elect—occurred then. The expression "this generation" here (1) may mean that the future generation which will endure the tribulation and see the signs will also see the consummation, the return of the Lord; or (2) it may be used in the sense of *race* or *family*, meaning that the nation or family of Israel will be preserved "till all these things be fulfilled," a promise wonderfully fulfilled to this day (NSRB, p. 1035).

How in the world would the disciples have come up with such unlikely interpretations of what Jesus said? They took him literally as the New Testament witnesses. Where have all the "literal" dispensationalists gone? Hardly anything in Matthew thus far has been taken literally. It is evident again that they are looking at Scripture from the standpoint of their own problems, largely of their own making, not those of the disciples. A number of things Jesus predicted in Matthew 24 did come true during the generation of the disciples.

Two Phases of Christ's Coming

Another distinctive feature resulting from the dispensational system is that the church will *not* go through the seven years of tribulation. This means that Christ's second coming or advent must be in two phases: (1) *for his saints* at their rapture from the earth; and (2) *with his saints* to reign on earth during the millennium. In between these two advents will be the 7-year tribulation, the 70th week of Daniel 9.

Designations of Christ's Advent

There are three Greek terms used to designate Christ's advent. Two of them occur in 2 Thess. 2:8, which we discussed earlier:

And then the lawless one will be revealed, and the Lord Jesus will slay him with the breath of his mouth and destroy him by his appearing (*epiphaneia*) and his coming (*parousia*).

A good example of the third designation is in 1 Cor. 1:7-8:

so that you are not lacking in any spiritual gift, as you wait for the revealing (*apokalypsis*) of our Lord Jesus Christ; who will sustain you to the end, guiltless in the day of our Lord Jesus Christ.

From these two passages it would seem that Paul makes no distinction between Christ's "appearing," "coming," and "revealing." But some dispensationalists attempt to associate "coming" with the rapture and "appearing" with Christ's advent for judgment.

The Day of Our Lord Jesus Christ

Another distinction they make is that between "the day of Christ" and "the day of the Lord." On the word "day" in 1 Cor. 1:8, Scofield has the note: "The 'day of Christ' relates wholly to the reward and blessing of saints at His coming, as 'day of the Lord' is connected with judgment" (SRB, p. 1212). At the same word, NSRB comments:

The expression "the day of our Lord Jesus Christ," identified with "the coming of our Lord Jesus Christ" (v. 7), is the period of blessing for the Church beginning with the rapture. This coming day is referred to as "the day of the Lord Jesus" (1 Cor. 5:5; 2 Cor. 1:14), "the day of Jesus Christ" (Phil. 1:6), and "the day of Christ" (Phil. 1:10; 2:16). . . . "The day of Christ" in all six references in the N.T. is described as relating to the reward and blessing of the church at the rapture and in contrast with the expression "the day of the Lord" . . . which is related to judgment upon unbelieving Jews and Gentiles, and blessing on millennial saints (p. 1233).

This note is based on the KJV, which translates *apokalypsis* as "coming" instead of "revealing," but it is certain that Paul understood "revealing" and "day" to refer to the same event and time point.

The Day of the Lord

In 2 Thess. 2:2 Paul is discrediting the rumor that he had claimed, "The day of the Lord has come." He assured them, you may recall, that rebellion and the son of perdition had to come first. The KJV has "Christ" here instead of "Lord," but the best Greek texts indicate that Paul used "Lord."

We noted in the Old Testament that from the time of Amos "the day of Yahweh" was considered the day of judgment for the nations and God's people. In the Septuagint this was translated "the day of the Lord," and since this Greek translation was widely used by Christians, they naturally referred to the future judgment as "the day of the Lord." At the same time, the church was teaching that God had authorized Jesus, the Christ, to act as judge on that day. Therefore, the meaning of the term "Lord" shifted from God to Jesus Christ, and thus Paul was referring to the coming of Christ on the day of judgment.

The Day of Christ

Dispensationalists note correctly that there are events or signs associated with the "day of the Lord." The real question, on the other hand, is whether Paul had a sudden "coming" in mind when he used "Christ" instead of "Lord." The NSRB note claims that "the day of Christ" refers to "the period of blessing for the Church beginning with the rapture." Moreover, it states that all six occurrences of the phrase relate to "the reward and blessing of the Church at the rapture."

The best place to begin checking these claims is 1 Cor. 1:8. Here Paul uses the full expression "the day of our Lord Jesus Christ." The fact that he uses "guiltless" in connection with that day indicates that he is thinking of the day of Christ's coming for judgment. At his advent the judge Jesus Christ will pronounce the saints "guiltless."

It is quite evident, therefore, that Paul was simply substituting "our Lord Jesus Christ" for "the Lord" in the traditional phrase "the day of the Lord." Here he is making explicit the shift from "God" to Christ," which was implicit in 2 Thess. 2:2. The expression is so long he shortens it to "the day of the Lord Jesus" in 1 Cor. 5:5 and also in 2 Cor. 1:14. In his letter to the Philippians he shifts to "the day of Jesus Christ" (1:6) and finally shortens that to "the day of Christ" (1:10; 2:16).

The reference to being "saved" in 1 Cor. 5:5 shows that "the day of the Lord Jesus" involves some verdict, and the same is true of Phil. 1:10 where "blameless" is associated with "the day of Christ." In other words, the context of three of the six occurrences negates the claim of NSRB and there is nothing explicit about a rapture in the other three. The supposed distinction between the two days is another example of dispensationalists reading their ideas into the text and then rejoicing to find them there.

The Rapture of the Saints

Paul believes in a "rapture" and he expresses it clearly in 1 Thess. 4:17: "We who are alive . . . shall be caught up . . . to meet the Lord in the air." The problem is that Paul associates this rapture with Christ's second coming and the resurrection of the righteous dead, after the tribulation.

Is there any evidence for a pretribulation advent of Christ for his raptured church? Dispensationalists think this rapture is taught in Rev. 4:1. The NSRB comments:

> Beginning with 4:1 the viewpoint of John is from heaven. As the word "church" does not appear again in The Revelation until 22:16, the catching up of John from earth to heaven has been taken to be a symbolic representation of the translation of the Church as occurring before the events of the tribulation described in chs. 6-19 (p. 1356).

This statement is an amazing expression of the logic of the dispensationalists and their will to believe. The fact that "church" does not appear between 4:1 and 22:16 is a "red-herring" argument. John *never* uses the term "church" except for the seven historical churches in Asia Minor, and since they are not involved in 4:1-22:16, there is no reason why the term should appear.

When John does refer to the church, the body of Christians, he designates it as "the Bride." In 19:6-8 there is rejoicing in heaven because Christ, the Lamb, is soon to take his Bride, the church.

If the raptured church went to heaven at the same time as John's ecstatic journey, it is mighty strange that he says nothing about the company he had! The reference to a "symbolic representation" of the rapture is grasping at straws.

It is true that from 4:1 the "viewpoint of John is from heaven." He mentions all the groups clustered around the great white throne, including the Lamb. That is where the Bride should be, but she is not mentioned until 19:7, when Christ comes for her. *It is evident that John had no idea that the raptured church was in heaven.*

The Secret Rapture

A further complication is the claim of some dispensationalists that the rapture will be "secret" and those left will not know about it until they start looking for their missing relatives and friends. The reasoning behind this claim is that the Lord will not come clear to earth at the rapture—the saints will rise to meet him in the sky.

The best prooftext for such an argument is in Matt. 24:40-41: "Then two men will be in the field; one is taken and one is left. Two women will be grinding at the mill; one is taken and one is left." But unfortunately for the dispensationalists they cannot use these verses because they have already determined that the passage describes Christ's return for judgment *after* the tribulation.

The whole argument is cogently assessed by Oswald T. Allis:

> There has been much difference of opinion among Dispensationalists regarding the question of secrecy. Darby did not commit himself on this point. Brookes accepted it. Scofield definitely rejected it. It is not an essential part of the rapture doctrine. Its significance lies rather in the fact that it illustrates the extremes to which many Dispensationalists are prepared to go to escape, or explain away, what seems to be the obvious meaning of a passage of Scripture when a strained or unnatural one is more in accord with their conception of things to come (*Prophecy and the Church*, p. 191).

The Rapture at Any Moment

We noted in the historical survey that one of the most dominant features of the Niagara and Sea Cliff Conferences was the idea that the rapture could come at any moment. The logic for this conclusion was the claim that the Bible gives no signs for the rapture as it does for Christ's coming to judge the world. Darby based his argument on 1

Thess. 4:13-18 and 2 Thess. 2:1-8, but as we have noted there is no clear-cut evidence in these passages for a rapture, let alone one at any moment.

Nathaniel West, who espoused this view for a number of years, gives the best refutation:

> We need not pursue this theory any further. It aggravates. It is built on a postulate, vicious in logic, violent in exegesis, contrary to experience, repudiated by the early Church, contradicted by the testimony of eighteen hundred years, rejected by the three schools of interpretation, and condemned by all the standard scholars of every age. . . . Kelly himself calls it an "assumption." It assumes what it professes to prove, and is refuted by every page of the Word of God. And yet, it offers itself as a matter of faith to thousands of the best and noblest Christian men and women, intelligent, devout, earnest, evangelical, brave and faithful, who, without a thorough examination, have received it as true! (*The Apostle Paul and the Any-Moment Theory*, pp. 30-31).

Unfortunately, West's closing assessment is all too true today.

What's In a Name?

We have already noted that those Christians who believe that Christ's second advent will be *after the millennium* are called "postmillennialists." It is equally logical to designate as "premillennialists" those who think that Christ will return *before the millennium*. The term "amillennialists" includes those who spiritualize the millennium, or think it is much shorter in length, or have doubts about it.

But these designations are rather general and cover a variety of views. There is a definite need for further refinement among "premillennialists" because it includes both traditional conservatives and dispensationalists. For a variety of reasons, most of them self-serving, most dispensationalists have identified themselves orally and in print solely as "premillennialists." Traditional conservatives object because their view is much earlier and they do not want to be classed with the dispensationalists. The latter think the difference between the two views is "minor," but the tribulation is hardly a minor matter.

Traditionalists believe Christ's second advent will be *after the tribulation;* therefore the church will have to go through it. Accordingly, those who hold this view are "posttribulationists." On

the other hand, the dispensationalists are "pretribulationists" because they believe the church will be raptured *before the tribulation.*
A world of trauma and horror separates the two views. The only honest approach is for each group to identify itself precisely. This will prevent any attempts to use "premillennial" as a camouflage.

English, Chairman of the NSRB Editorial Committee, sets a good example at this point: "The position held by the editorial committee of the NSRB is that the rapture of the whole Church will take place *before* the 'tribulation,' i.e. the editors are pre-tribulationists (*A Companion to the New Scofield Reference Bible*, note on p. 137). Although the "handle" is a tongue twister, dispensationalists are really "pretribulation premillennialists."

Dispensational Hermeneutics or Methods of Interpretation

We have noted time and again how the dispensationalists run through a literal approach to the prophecies about Israel and then jump through hoops trying to explain away the plain meaning of the historical context. Concerning this double standard, "Heads, I win; tail, you lose" approach to interpretation, Allis comments:

It is a singular anomaly, which cannot fail to impress the careful student of Dispensational teaching, as represented, for example, in the *Scofield Reference Bible*, that it emphasizes and carries to such extremes these two distinct and in a sense opposite principles in interpreting Scripture. In dealing with Old Testament history its treatment is highly figurative. Indeed, we sometimes receive the impression that the events of that history have little meaning for us in themselves; it is their typical meaning, a meaning which only those "deeply taught" in Scripture are able to appreciate, that is the really important thing about them. In dealing with prophecy, its treatment is marked by a literalism which refuses to recognize types and figures. Israel must mean Israel; it does not and cannot signify the Church. Canaan must mean Canaan; it does not and cannot mean heaven. Eve, Rebecca, Asenath, Zipporah, Ruth, the Shulamite, and Vashti may one and all be viewed as "types." But Israel must mean Israel and only Israel! This seems strikingly inconsistent (*Prophecy and the Church*, pp. 23-24).

After a thorough study of dispensational hermeneutics or methods of interpretation, Daniel P. Fuller concludes:

Therefore such a system, which is both internally inconsistent and unable to harmonize itself with the Biblical data, must be based on a faulty hermeneutical basis. The problem is that its adherents have proceeded non-inductively in that they have accepted the distinction between Israel and the Church before examining all the relevant data on the question (*The Hermeneutics of Dispensationalism*, p. 386).

These two evaluations are accurate and they support our findings. From an objective, inductive approach there can be only one conclusion: *as far as "truth" is concerned, dispensationalism is dead.* But as "a system" it will continue to exist, and have influence upon the unwary. It is necessary, therefore, to consider in greater detail the system's understanding of end-times. This can be done more effectively when we discuss Hal Lindsey. While he has some distinctive ideas of his own, his system and books are *essentially* jazzed-up Dallas dispensationalism.

Chapter 14
The Promise and the Promised Land

Are the promises concerning Israel to be literally fulfilled as dispensationalists and other conservatives claim? What about the concept of "the promised land"? Did Jesus and the New Testament writers teach such a doctrine? What criteria are there for determining the validity of the biblical claims? These are important questions which require careful thought.

The Covenant with Abraham

The first reference to Canaan (Palestine) as a promised land occurs in Gen. 12:7. When Abraham arrives at Shechem, an ancient holy place in the heart of Canaan, Yahweh informs him, "To your descendants I will give this land." After allowing Lot to choose the fertile plain of the Jordan Valley for himself, Abraham is told to view all the land around him. "All the land which you see," Yahweh promises, "I will give to you and to your descendants for ever" (Gen. 13:15).

The Hebrew expression behind the translation "for ever" is ^{c}ad ^{c}olam "until a long time." The period of time covered by the term was relative to the horizon of the speaker. In some places it is used referring back to the reign of David or the time of Moses. With respect to the future, it can apply to the length of a person's life (Deut. 15:17) or to the end of an age. The covenants and promises of God in the Old Testament were clearly understood to be valid for the forseeable future, but there was no clear concept of how long that would be.

In Gen. 15:18 God makes a covenant with Abraham in which he says, "To your descendants I give this land, from the river of Egypt to the great river, the river Euphrates." During the powerful 18th Dynasty, Egypt controlled the region from the river of Egypt (Wadi el-Arish) to the Euphrates and designated it as a province. The Israelites knew about this. Later on, someone took the boundaries of the old province to be the extent of the promised land and so he inserted the boundary notation after "land."

But this large area was not realistic, even in David's time. The fact is that the Israelites never had a consistent understanding of the boundaries of the promised land. These kept shifting back and forth over the various periods of Israel's history. The most commonly recognized definition was "from Dan to Beersheba." It is exceedingly doubtful that the scribal note in Gen. 15:18 is to be taken as the absolute extent of the promised land.

Scofield's View of the Covenant

Scofield's drastic separation of grace and law is highlighted by his note at Gen. 12:1:

> For Abraham and his descendants it is evident that the Abrahamic Covenant . . . made a great change. They became distinctively the heirs of *promise*. That covenant is wholly gracious and unconditional. The descendants of Abraham had but to abide in their own land to inherit every blessing. In Egypt they lost their *blessings*, but not their *covenant*. The Dispensation of Promise ended when Israel rashly accepted the law (Ex. 19:8). . . . The *dispensation* must be distinguished from the *covenant*. The former is a mode of testing; the latter is everlasting because unconditional (SRB, p. 20).

This is one of the worst notes in the SRB. It is utterly dreamy to suppose that all aspects of the covenant are unconditional because no conditions are explicitly listed. Moreover, it is magical to suggest that as long as Israel stayed in the land it would automatically receive the blessings of the covenant.

How they lived in the land must have been a concern of God even then, because he was the same righteous God who made his will known through Moses, the prophets, Jesus, and the NT writers. In fact, in Gen. 18:19 Yahweh comments concerning Abraham: "I have chosen him that he may charge his children and his household after him to keep the way of the LORD by doing righteousness and justice, so that the LORD may bring to Abraham what he has promised him."

Gen. 17:14 notes that any uncircumcised Hebrew was to be "cut off from his people" because he had broken the covenant. Had Abraham not obeyed the command to be circumcised, what would have happened to the covenant? Both as a people and as individuals, the Hebrews were under some minimal standards of conduct, and obedience was implicit in the covenant. The Abrahamic Covenant was not pure grace, therefore, and it is certainly a "rash" statement to claim that the Sinai covenant was a second-rate offer from God which Israel "rashly accepted."

Possession of the Land

The NSRB revises Scofield's note and wisely omits his "rash" claim, but it still holds that the promises in Gen. 12:1-3 are unconditional (p. 19). Accordingly, Israel will "inherit a specific territory forever."

At Gen 15:18 the NSRB comments: "The gift of the land is modified by prophecies of three dispossessions and restorations. . . . Two dispossessions and restorations have been accomplished. Israel is now in the third dispersion, from which she will be restored at the return of the Lord as King under the Davidic Covenant" (p. 24).

What are the three? One was the sojourn in Egypt noted in Gen. 15:13-14, 16. The second was the Babylonian exile and return prophesied in Jer. 25:11-12. For the third dispossession the NSRB jumps back to Deut. 28:62-65; 30:1-3. Moses warns the people that disobedience of the covenant will result in dispersion among the nations, but if there is repentance and obedience Yahweh will bring them back to the land and bless them.

According to the dispensationalists, this is the 6th or Palestinian Covenant. NSRB comments: "The Palestinian Covenant gives the conditions under which Israel entered the land of promise. It is important to see that the nation has never as yet taken the land under the unconditional Abrahamic Covenant . . . , nor has it ever possessed the whole land . . . ." (p. 251). This last claim implies that NSRB takes the editorial note in Gen. 15:18 as the standard. It is "important" because the ideal fulfillment can be pushed into the future.

It would seem that the Babylonian exile was a very fitting fulfillment of Moses' warnings, but the idealistic conditions noted in Deut. 30:3-10 did not come true after the return. Therefore the NSRB feels justified in jumping over the whole Old Testament period and making Moses' warnings apply to the Roman destruction and dispersion of A.D. 70. This means, of course, that the third restoration is due next, and so NSRB notes, "In the twentieth century initial steps toward a restoration of the exiled people to their homeland have been seen."

The Conquest

Before any further discussion of the NSRB claims, it will be helpful to survey the idea of the promised land through the rest of

Scripture. We have claimed that obedience was a factor from the very beginning of the Abrahamic Covenant. It is absolutely certain that obedience was a crucial aspect from the Sinai Covenant on.

After long, weary years in the wilderness and Transjordan, the new generation of Israelites arrive at the plains of Moab and prepare to fulfill the promise to Abraham. Moses warns them that obedience to God's commands is the way to guarantee possession of the land (Deut. 6:1-3). They are to (1) drive out all the inhabitants of Canaan; (2) destroy all their idols and places of worship; (3) occupy the country; and (4) divide the land among the tribes (Num. 33:50-54). Failure to comply with these directives would be disobedience, a breach of covenant, and therefore God would have to destroy his own people.

There are indications that the Israelites did not carry out these orders. "You are old and advanced in years," Yahweh tells Joshua, "and there remains yet very much land to be possessed" (Josh. 13:1). Judges 1:21-35 gives a list of the cities which the Israelites failed to conquer, stating again and again that the various tribes did not drive out the Canaanites and the Amorites, whose descendants still lived in the land. These descendants, together with an influx of Philistines, would continue to frustrate the hopes of the conquering Israelites.

The Monarchy

The promise of the land came closer to realization during the reign of David. He conquered the Philistines, enslaved the Canaanite and Amorite remnants, nullified the threat of neighboring countries and finally unified the northern and southern groups of Israelites. But David did not control Palestine completely. The city of Gezer belonged to the Pharaoh of Egypt.

The promise was literally fulfilled during the reign of David's son Solomon. His first and favorite wife was the daughter of Pharaoh. Her father gave her Gezer as a wedding present and in this way Solomon got control of the city (1 Kgs. 9:16). After he completed the temple, Yahweh warned him that if he and his children did not obey the commandments they would be cut off from the land (1 Kgs. 9:6-7). Ironically, however, just as the promise of the land of Canaan was being fulfilled, Solomon entered into many more treaty marriages which undercut the spiritual unity of Israel (1 Kgs. 7:8; 9:24; 11:7-8).

Solomon's son, Rehoboam, was similarly heedless of the conditions of God's promise. As a result, the northern tribes formed their own kingdom of Israel under Jeroboam (1 Kgs. 12:1-20). Without doubt, the disobedience of David's dynasty led to the division of the promised land. Consequently, for centuries the promise to Abraham was lulled to a dream.

Warnings of the Prophet

After the fall of the northern kingdom, the prophets of Judah dreamed of a reunited kingdom. But they realized that the moral condition of Jerusalem was so poor, judgment or repentance would have to occur first. Micah, the country prophet, considered Jerusalem as "Sin City" and predicted, "Zion shall be plowed as a field; Jerusalem shall become a heap of ruins" (Mic. 3:12). Isaiah, the urbanite, was not ignorant of Jerusalem's sins either. He denounced the leaders for their corruption and injustice (2:23) and claimed that the people had wounds from foot to head (1:5-6). Yet later Isaiah announced to King Hezekiah, besieged by the Assyrians, that God would defend and protect Jerusalem because of the promise made to David (37:35).

When Judah itself was later overrun, the people naively believed that God would spare Jerusalem because he was enthroned in the temple. But Jeremiah preached a sermon in the temple court in which he warned them that the temple would not save them as long as they took advantage of the aliens, orphans, and widows (7:4-6). Rather, Nebuchadnezzar would come and destroy the land (25:9).

Ezekiel shared Jeremiah's conviction that God was no prisoner in the temple. He had a vision of the glory of Yahweh leaving the temple and moving east, over the Mount of Olives (10:4, 18; 11:23). Without repentance of the people and without the presence of God, the temple and Jerusalem were both destined to destruction. Both Jeremiah and Ezekiel were convinced that there could be no holy city without God's presence, and they were equally certain that there could be no holy people without a genuine covenant with Yahweh. Jeremiah looked for a "new covenant" in which God's law could be "written on their hearts" (31:31,33). Ezekiel expected God to transplant a "heart of flesh" for their "heart of stone" (36:26).

Exilic Isaiah comforted the exiles with the assurance that they had paid for their sins and that Yahweh would lead them back home.

They were to be "a light to the nations" (49:6). Zerubbabel and Joshua tried to carry out Ezekiel's plan for a restored Jerusalem, but the Persian authorities removed Zerubbabel after Haggai's oracle predicted that he would be "a signet ring" (2:23). Not only did Ezekiel's dream fade away, but there was no evidence that God had given the Jews a new heart with a desire to live by his law. Despair settled over the Jews and we hear nothing more about them until the time of Malachi, Ezra, and Nehemiah.

Postponed Dreams

At best, the Jews were a small group surrounded by enemies. Although they managed to fortify Jerusalem, they did not occupy all the former territory of Judah, let alone all the land of Palestine. During the rest of the Persian empire and into the Greek period, a number of Jews gave up the dreams of Jeremiah, Ezekiel, and Exilic Isaiah, and went to live in other Near Eastern and Mediterranean countries. They enlarged the Diaspora (the groups of dispersed Israelites and Jews who had remained in Babylonia, Syria, and Egypt) because they doubted the necessity of returning to Palestine.

Those who remained in and around Jerusalem kept the old dreams alive and looked forward to the coming of God's new kingdom. But when Judas Maccabeus captured and rededicated the temple, aspiring to be another David ruling supremely over all of Palestine, many pious Jews (including the Hasidim) refused to follow him. They had achieved their goal of religious freedom and had no desire to establish a kingdom. Most likely the Essenes at Qumran had their roots in this segment of Judaism.

More and more, differing interpretations of the dreams of the prophets became prominent in Jewish politics. Those who took the dreams literally, as referring to a physical kingdom with a king ruling over special people within specific boundaries, became violently frustrated when the Romans incorporated Palestine into their empire. These zealots followed the example of Judas Maccabeus in numerous attempts to overthrow the government.

Other Jews, however, interpreted God's promises in figurative or spiritual terms, while many faithful Jews in the Diaspora were learning that it was possible to worship Israel's God in a foreign land, inasmuch as he was not confined to Palestine and the temple in Jerusalem. In fact, the Diaspora diffused the light by bringing God's truth to the nations where they were.

Reinterpreted Dreams

History had forced Judaism to understand the prophetic dreams figuratively. Jerusalem was still important historically because it had served for centuries as the city from which God's message emanated. But since that truth had been dispersed throughout the Greek and Roman world, it was no longer necessary for Israel to be in Jerusalem to serve as a light to the nations.

The same understanding of the prophetic dreams and the hope of a promised land is carried into the New Testament. John the Baptist, who had some dealings with the Essenes, believed in a more spiritual and universal interpretation of God's purposes. He lashed out at the Pharisees and Sadducees and warned them that they could not escape punishment simply by claiming that they were Abraham's descendants: "I tell you, God is able from these stones to raise up children to Abraham" (Matt. 3:9).

Not lineage, but true repentance was the basis for God's forgiveness. John was simply expanding on the experience of Isaiah, Jeremiah, and the other prophets who found many of Abraham's descendants hardened and calloused beyond redemption.

After John, Jesus came preaching the same message: "Repent, for the kingdom of heaven is at hand" (Matt. 4:17). Never did Jesus equate God's kingdom with Jewish rule of Palestine. He informed the Samaritan woman that the time would come when people would worship neither on Mt. Gerizim nor in Jerusalem (Jn. 4:21). Not one of the principles of his kingdom is dependent on a special sanctuary or specific territory. The risen Christ told his disciples to be witnesses "in Jerusalem and in all Judea and Samaria and to the end of the earth" (Acts 1:8). Like the Jews in the Diaspora and John the Baptist, Jesus set forth the conviction that God's purpose of redeeming the nations would not be limited to the temple in Jerusalem and the real estate of Palestine.

We have noted how Paul agonized over the disbelief of his own people, the Jews, but he believed that in time they would be grafted back into God's olive tree (Romans 9-11). In Galatians 3 he stated even more explicitly that the true children of Abraham are those who have his kind of faith: "And if you are Christ's, then you are Abraham's offspring, heirs according to promise" (3:29).

The remarkable fact about Romans 9-11 and Galatians 3 is that in spite of repeated reference to the promises to Abraham, *the concept of the promised land is ignored completely.* In reinterpreting the promises, Paul focuses on the primary factors of faith, salvation, and blessing. While he did not make an explicit statement rejecting the idea of the promised land, it certainly is strongly implied that this phase of the promise became obsolete under the new covenant.

The same can be said for the author of the letter to the Hebrews. After quoting Jer. 31:31-34 as the promise of a new covenant, he comments: "In speaking of a new covenant he treats the first as obsolete. And what is becoming obsolete and growing old is ready to vanish away" (Heb. 8:13). The Jewish Christians addressed by Hebrews are to anticipate a new city, the heavenly Jerusalem. Nowhere in the whole book does the author mention the promise of land as a valid aspect of the new covenant.

This is equally true for the apostle Peter. In John's revelation the new Jerusalem comes down from heaven and presumably it settles over the site of the old Jerusalem. But the city measures 1,500 miles square! That is large enough to cover the entire Near or Middle East (from Egypt to Iran and Asia Minor to Sudan) and then some. This vision can hardly be related in any meaningful way to the concept of the promised land.

The Great Postponement

The dispensationalists claim to be Christians, but since they believe that prophecy applies only to Israel, they have a mental and emotional affinity with those Jews who look forward to another literal fulfillment of the promise.

There is no doubt that Jeremiah, Ezekiel, and Exilic Isaiah expected Israel to be reunited and settled in the promised land, and so it is easy to understand why those who consider the Old Testament (Hebrew Bible) as the primary authority for belief are supporters of Zionism.

The issue hinges, therefore, on the definition of "fulfillment." The New Testament and Christian tradition claim that the promise of the land was fulfilled. At an early stage, God's purpose of having Israel be *a light to the nations* was best achieved by his people in their own land. Later on, however, God worked through history, some of which was the making of the Jew themselves, to disperse the light of God's truth *among the nations.* The New Testament and Christians take history as a clue to God's purpose; therefore they interpret the promises to Abraham in a spiritual sense.

According to the estimate of the NSRB, the call and promise to Abraham occurred about 1875 B.C. That is over 3,850 years ago. The fact that Moses' warning in Deut. 28:62-65 is taken to predict the Roman destruction of Jerusalem in A.D. 70, not the Babylonian exile in 587/6 B.C., is a desperate attempt to gain more time for the literal fulfillment of the promise.

As we shall see in the next chapter, Israel has a valid claim to a part of Palestine, but it is doubtful that the dispensationalists' fascination with *an idealistic, unconditional covenant* will be vindicated. The history of this dream so far has been one of continual postponement, and it is likely that the permanent feature of dispensational method will be "the great postponement."

Chapter 15
Modern Israel: Past and Future

Although the prophetic justification for Israel does not seem valid, many conservatives in Judaism and Christianity will continue to believe it. How should Christians regard Israel? It is certainly one of the thorniest problems of our time. What is the valid justification for Israel, and what are the prospects of its future?

The Justification for Israel

After the terrible Tsarist massacres of Jews in 1881, some Russian Jews went to Palestine where they formed agricultural settlements. The dream became a flicker because of illness, initial opposition from the ruling Ottoman Turks, and lack of financial support.

The French philanthropist Baron Edmond de Rothschild (1845-1934) came to the rescue. He provided financial aid and agricultural experts so that the colonists could become self-supporting. In addition he purchased thousands of acres in Galilee and Samaria. Much of this land was located in the swampy regions of the Esdraelon Valley and the Coastal Plain, and since malaria had been so prevalent, the Arabs had not settled there. They drained the swamps and made the area habitable.

This legal purchase and reclamation of land was the basis for the Jewish presence in Palestine, and *it is this secular argument which validates the Israeli claim to part of Palestine.*

Ishmael and Isaac

It is a common myth among conservative Christians to interpret the current difficulties between Arabs and Israelis as a prophetic continuation of the feud between Ishmael and Isaac. This is utter nonsense! At different periods over the last 1,200 years the two groups have lived together in Palestine and other Mediterranean countries. The differences and feelings between them have been no greater than those between neighboring nationalities elsewhere with varying customs and religious beliefs. During the Turkish rule (A.D. 1517-

1917), in fact, children of neighboring Arab and Jewish families were considered brothers and sisters of each other.

The Jews and Arabs are no more monolithic than any other groups of human beings. People on both sides range from loving, sensitive persons all the way over to angry persons with evil intent, and there are just as wide-ranging points of view in each group. The present state of the struggle is due to extremists.

Cultural Zionism

The most praiseworthy type of Zionism is that which works for the preservation and development of the spiritual and cultural aspects of Judaism. One of the great men in this movement was Asher Ginzberg (1856-1927), known commonly by his pen name *Ahad Ha*ᶜ*am*, "The One of the People." He believed that the renewal of Judaism had to occur through education and literature, and as a means to this end he was largely responsible for the revival of Hebrew as a living language. In 1889 he formed the *Bene Moshe* "Sons of Moses" Association.

In 1885, while Ginzberg was beginning his work, reform Judaism (under the leadership of Rabbi Isaac M. Wise) made its historic Pittsburgh Declaration:

> We consider ourselves no longer a nation, but a religious community, and therefore expect neither a return to Palestine, nor the restoration of a sacrificial worship under the Sons of Aaron, or of any of the laws concerning the Jewish State.

Many prominent Jews favored the spiritual, cultural type of renewal and they had the support of concerned, influential Gentiles. One of the latter was Arthur James Balfour, Foreign Secretary of the British government. On Nov. 2, 1917, he issued the Declaration which was to bear his name:

> His Majesty's Government view with favor the establishment in Palestine of a national home for the Jewish paople and will use their best endeavors to facilitate the achievement of this object, it being clearly understood that nothing shall be done to prejudice the civil and religious rights of the existing non-Jewish communities in Palestine.

Balfour himself and other government officials declared that they understood "home" to mean a "spiritual or cultural center."

Political Zionism

A far different kind of Zionism emerged in the 1890's. It yearned to form a state of Israel. The leaders of this point of view came largely from eastern Europe. During the French Revolution (1789) the ghetto walls of western Europe began to crumble. Napoleon furthered the process by forcing Jewish equality wherever his army was victorious. The story was different in eastern Europe, especially Russia and Poland. Terrible discrimination and slaughter resulted in a wave of 2,500,000 refugees coming to the United States in a few years after the 1881 massacres.

These events etched fear and hatred in the minds and hearts of many young Jews. Their experience convinced them of two things: (1) a prejudice against Jews flows in the veins of every Gentile or non-Jew, a bias which can never be eradicated; and (2) in order for Jews to find their true identity, to use a modern expression, they must live together in an independent state with freedom to determine their own future.

One can readily understand why they came to such conclusions, but that does not validate their views as universal principles. Many Jews in western Europe and the United States found that there were considerate, loving Gentiles who would allow them to be themselves and worship as they saw fit. The experiences of Jews in eastern Europe made it impossible for them to believe that such conditions were possible.

Zionists Herzl and Weizmann

The father of political Zionism was Theodor Herzl (1860-1904). In 1896 he published his book *Der Judenstaat,* "The Jewish State," a book which relied heavily on books by Hess and Pinsker, eastern European Jews. A year later at Basel, Switzerland, Herzl convened the first Zionist Congress. But difficulties within the ranks broke his health and he died in 1904. The new President, David Wolfssohn, favored "diplomatic Zionism" similar to Herzl's approach, but the Russian Jews demanded "practical Zionism," that is, the immediate colonization of Palestine. In 1911 a Zionist office was established in Jaffa and the city Tel-Aviv was founded just to the north.

The zealous Zionist Chaim Weizmann (1874-1952) saw that Great Britain was the most likely nation to accept the Zionist dream and so he left Russia in 1904 and immigrated to England. There he worked through many influential people who were sympathetic to Jewish interests.

In Dec. 1916, when the tide of World War I turned against the western Allies, Weizmann made his trump move. He offered Prime Minister Lloyd George the support of the Jews (even in Russia and the United States) on condition that the British agree to facilitate a national home in Palestine. In his original draft of the agreement Weizmann specifically referred to Palestine as "the national home for the Jewish people," and he spoke of the "reestablishment of the country."

A National Home in Palestine

But the British had already promised the Arabs that for their help Palestine would become independent after the War. Therefore, Balfour revised the draft to read "a national home for the Jewish people." Weizmann was disappointed with the "painful recession" from his proposal of "Palestine as the national home," yet he and his fellow Zionists persuaded France, Italy, and the United States to go along with the declaration.

Moreover, Balfour made explicit his understanding of "home" as "a cultural or spiritual center" by adding the strict condition, "it being clearly understood that nothing shall be done to prejudice the civil and religious rights of the existing non-Jewish communities in Palestine." The expression "non-Jewish" was a rather ironic way of referring to the Arab and Christian communities, especially since in 1917 the Jews represented only 8% of the population of Palestine.

The British Mandate

The next crucial step in the Zionist dream was in 1922 when the League of Nations, without United States participation, authorized the British Mandate of Palestine. Behind the scenes activity resulted in Article IV, which authorized the "Zionist Agency" as the appropriate "Jewish Agency" for the purpose of "advising and cooperating with the administration of Palestine" in connection with the Jewish National Home and the interests of Jews in Palestine.

At no time did the agency consider itself to be in an advisory or cooperative role. The Zionists determined, regardless of the wording

of the Balfour Declaration, to make Palestine "the national home for
the Jewish people." The British were no match for them and since
there was no Arab agency, the rights of the Arabs were jeopardized on
every hand. Inasmuch as absentee landlords in Lebanon and Syria
were cut off from their property in Palestine by the international
boundaries between the British and French Mandates, the Jewish
Agency was permitted to buy the land at bargain prices. Furthermore,
thousands of Arab tenant and farm workers were evicted from the
newly acquired land in order to make room for Jewish settlers from
Europe. Compensation for the evicted Arab families was very small,
sometimes as low as $10.00 per family.

By 1930 the British government took notice of the Arab pleas and
Mr. Ramsay MacDonald decided to control Jewish immigration to
Palestine. Weizmann, then President of the World Zionist Organization, protested and threatened to resign. The resultant political
pressure forced MacDonald to desist and again the Zionists had free
reign in Palestine. When ruthless Adolf Hitler came to power in
Germany the flow of Jewish immigrants increased drastically and by
1935 the Jewish population of Palestine had risen to 30%.

Civil War in Palestine

In 1936 war broke out between the Arabs and the Jewish
population. Three years of suffering and frustration awakened the
British government to the necessity of establishing new ground rules
for the settlement of Palestine. In 1939 a "White Paper" set forth an
equitable solution to the problem . After a ten-year interval Palestine
would become an independent binational state with Arabs and Jews
sharing the government and protecting the interests of each other.
Immigration of the Jews was to continue for 5 years at 15,000
annually, but sale of Arab lands to the Jewish Agency was to be
restricted.

Unfortunately, the forces of history conspired against the
excellent proposal. The atrocities of the Nazi gas chambers resulted in
a flood of refugees and the British, fighting for their own lives in
Britain, were too weak to cope with the situation.

While the private Jewish police force *Haganah* "Defense" carried
on its normal protective functions, more radical groups stepped up the
fighting in Palestine. In 1942, for example, Menachem Begin, a Polish
Jew, formed the *Irgun Zvai Leumi*, "National Military Organization."

One of its main activities was attacking British soldiers and officials. Inasmuch as the King David Hotel in Jerusalem was the Secretariat for the Palestinian Government, it housed a number of British officials along with some Arabs and Jews. In July, 1946, Begin and his *Irgun* blew up the south end of the hotel, killing many people.

The "hate Britain" campaign reached its peak in 1947 when the Zionists loaded 4,554 Jewish refugees on the old "President Warfield," which had been renamed "S.S. Exodus," and attempted to take them to Haifa. The British seized the vessel as a flagrant violation of regulations attempting to control the flow of immigrants, and the passengers were returned to France on three British vessels. When the refugees refused to disembark they were taken to Hamburg, Germany, and forcibly removed. The hysteria evoked by this incident brought the situation full circle to the conditions of the Jewish revolts in A.D. 66-70 and 132-135. As zealot groups became more violent, the oppressive measures of the rulers were increased. Except for the British replacing the Romans, the situations were much the same.

Displaced Persons

During the fateful years of World War II the expression "Displaced Person" (DPs) was seared on the conscience of humanity. The pathetic condition of the DPs evoked great empathy and the guilt of western civilization for having permitted Hitler to rise to power and to carry out his insane brutalities demanded that action be taken to alleviate the misery.

President Franklin D. Roosevelt tried quietly to find homes for the European refugees in the United States, Britain, Canada, Australia, and South America. Many of the DPs wanted to immigrate to these countries, especially the United States, and these nations had the room and capability of absorbing most of them. But Roosevelt found such bitter opposition to the idea he dared not push it through.

The reward for his interest in the welfare of the refugees was the label "anti-Semitic." In truth, the anti-Semites were the Zionists themselves because they did not really have the ultimate concern of the DPs at heart—they only wanted to use them as pawns to achieve the dream of a Jewish State. Although Zionist opposition to the Roosevelt idea was cloaked under the righteous indignation of humanitarianism, the real reasons were: (1) more Jews were needed to populate

Palestine; and (2) it would be exceedingly difficult to raise money for Palestine if most of the Jews were settled elsewhere.

Proof of these underlying motives came to the surface in 1947 when William G. Stratton sponsored a bill to admit DPs up to the limit of the accumulated unused immigration quotas for the war years. Passage of the bill would have permitted about 400,000 refugees to come to the United states. Here was the ultimate test of Zionist motivation. Their powerful lobby in Washington, usually so vocal, was deathly silent.

Only Gov. Herbert Lehman of New York had the courage to speak in behalf of the bill. Stratton was shocked at the lack of support, but he did not know that the President of the Zionist Organization of America had recently said, "I am happy that our movement has finally veered around to the point where we are all, or nearly all, talking about a Jewish State." The message of the Pittsburgh Declaration of 1885 was drowned out by the emotional propaganda of the Zionists and many Reform Jews were sucked into the vortex of the massive whirlpool.

Palestine and the United Nations

Conditions became so chaotic in Palestine, the British finally despaired and took the issue to the newly formed United Nations Organization. On April 28, 1947, a Special Session was called to consider the facts. In general, the Arabs favored a binational state whereas most of the Jews were yearning for a Jewish State.

An outstanding exception was Dr. Judah Magnes, President of the Hebrew University of Jerusalem. He had prayed and worked for a binational state with "understanding and cooperation between Jew and Arab." In addressing the 23rd Convocation of the University he spoke of "Zionist Totalitarianism" which was attempting to bring "the entire Jewish people under its influence by force and violence." With amazing courage he added, "I have not yet seen the dissidents called by their rightful names: Killers—brutalized men and women."

But Dr. Magnes was not permitted to express himself during the UN debate because Zionists, who were zealously at work behind the scenes, had seen to it that only the Jewish Agency would be permitted to speak for Palestinian Jews. In order for the Magnes point of view to get before the public it was necessary for Dr. Albert Einstein to issue a statement through the press.

The question whether Palestine was to be partitioned or to become a binational state turned the UN debate into "pressure-cooker politics." A 2/3 vote was required and since 12 of the smaller nations were for a unified Palestine, a telegram from 26 pro-Zionist United States Senators was sent urging them to vote for partition. General Carlos Romulo made an eloquent appeal for a binational state, but with 6 bills involving the Philippines pending before the Senate, the Philippine delegation regretfully shifted its vote. Of the 12, only Greece voted for unification. That shift of 11 votes turned the tide for partition.

A presidential election was to be held in 1948 and most of the politicians were courting the Jewish voters. President Truman was in favor of the Trusteeship Plan for Palestine, but he was warned that if he wanted to keep the Jewish vote he would have to recognize Israel. The "heat" was too much for Harry and "he got out of the kitchen" by announcing at 6:11 P.M., May 14, 1948, that the United States recognized the new State of Israel.

At that very moment the UN was in session and the United States delegation, which had *not* been informed of the recognition, was pressing for the Trusteeship Plan. Other delegations got the news first and Ambassador Austin, head of the delegation, was justly dumbfounded and outraged when he heard how the White House had double-crossed him. As one UN delegate remarked, "The representatives of the USSR and Poland were better informed on events in Washington."

The Partition of Palestine

In Palestine the Jewish militant groups had stepped up their acts of intimidation and violence. Their motivation was twofold: (1) to remove as many Arabs as possible from the area designated by the partition plan for the Jews; and (2) if possible to gain more territory than that allowed by the plan. The *Irgun's* radio unit broadcast in Arabic that typhus, cholera, and other diseases would break out among the Arabs, and the *Haganah* hinted dire consequences if the Arabs did not move.

The emigration was not fast enough, however, therefore the *Irgun* selected Deir Yassin as an example. The little Arab village, west of Jerusalem, was encircled by Jewish settlements, and on April 9, 1948, the terrorists swept in and literally butchered 254 men, women, and children. Loudspeaker vans of the *Haganah* drove through Arab settlements reporting "Arabs are fleeing in terror and fear." "The road to Jericho is open," the vans noted, "flee for your lives."

The late venerable Christian missionary Bertha Vester reported later that some of the broadcasts said, "Unless you leave your homes, the fate of Deir Yassin will be yours." In remarkable contrast to these heinous deeds, Shabetai Levi, the late Mayor of Haifa, with tears in his eyes begged the Arabs to stay. But the *Haganah* countered his plea by furnishing transportation for the fearful Arabs.

There were still large pockets of Arabs within the borders of Israel and since these were considered an internal threat, Moshe Dayan and his columns started another exodus. They roared into Lydda (Lod) with tanks and trucks and began shooting up the town. This incident and a similar one at Ramleh, south of Lod, resulted in 30,000 Arabs fleeing for the Arab-controlled sections of the hill country. Another pressure point was at Acre (Acco), north of Haifa, where an estimated 45,000 Arabs were driven out. As a result, the refugee camps near Nablus and Jericho became swollen, festering sores.

Devotion to Palestine

Various ideas were proposed to relieve the suffering of the camps, but the refugees refused to accept money for their land or to move elsewhere. The exceedingly pragmatic mentality of western culture, especially the United States, could not understand the attitude of the refugees. "Why not be sensible and accept money," so it was argued, "in order to buy land in another Arab country?" "With all the land owned by the surrounding Arab countries, why not resettle the Arabs of Palestine and thus free for the Jews the little piece of land which is rightfully theirs?"

But this line of reasoning disregarded the biblical evidence and it failed to understand the Arab point of view. To accept money for the appropriated land would, in the eyes of the refugees, amount to an admission that the Jews were right in taking the Arab land. Moreover, the western mentality failed to see that Arab devotion to a particular piece of land was as tenacious as that of the Jews.

The fundamental issue, in short, was the struggle over the same piece of land, and the basic question was "Why should the Arabs have to pay for the sins of Hitler and other Europeans?" Westerners were too involved with their guilt and sentimentality to ask this question, and to this day they have not been able to give a valid answer.

Citizens of Israel

The new State of Israel elected as Prime Minister the staunch Zionist David Ben-Gurion. He contended that all Jews should immigrate to Israel, and as the official spokesman for Zionism he made it clear that Jews who did not do so were unfaithful to the cause. Under his pressure the Israeli *Knesset* "Parliament" passed the "Nationality Bill" on July 14, 1952. The bill declared that every Jew, regardless of nationality and location, automatically could become a citizen of Israel.

But American Zionists did not rush to Israel and Ben-Gurion was quick to point up the gap between their theory and their practice. Thoughtful Jews of other countries sensed that the bill was another Zionist tactic to increase the flow of immigrants and they rejected the imposed allegiance to Israel because dual allegiance was impossible for them. Young Jews from other countries, especially the United States, took sentimental journeys to Israel for extended visits, but the glamor of the Zionist dream wore off and they returned home.

Anti-Semitism

Any open discussion of Zionist activities is usually labelled "anti-Semitism." In the first place, the designation is a misnomer. The Hebrew Bible is quite clear that the Arabs are sons of Abraham and thus Semites too. Many American Jews have observed that the Arabs look more Semitic than the European Jews. There is a good historic basis for this judgment.

Many so-called Jews are biologically the descendants of peoples who were converts to Judaism (for example, the Khazars, in what is now southwestern Russia, converted to Judaism in A.D. 740 when their leader Bulan became a proselyte). Israelis have all types of physical features and colorings, and in many instances these Jews resemble the non-Jewish peoples among whom they formerly lived. The Oriental (Arab-speaking) Jews are far more authentic racially than their European counterparts. In truth, therefore, Judaism is a religion or a point of view and it has no primary basis in race.

Far more serious than the inaccuracy of the term "anti-Semitic" is the fact that it is a vicious psychological tool. Every minority has suffered from injustice and had reason to label its misery, but somehow the racism of Europe highlighted the concept of "anti-Semitism." Herzl said, "Anti-Semitism has grown and continues to grow—and so do I." It will be recalled that the basic concept of Zionism has been the belief that the indelible prejudice of non-Jews makes it impossible for Jews to be assimilated in any Gentile nation or culture. Herzl's statement was an unintentional admission that Zionism has a stake in racism.

From the very start, Zionism has thrived on prejudice and what its advocates have never been willing to face, then or now, is that the seeds of prejudice which they claim to find in non-Jews are more often than not the projections of their own minds. People with martyr complexes invariably interpret actions of others as being inimical to their own interests and this is especially true in the case of Jews with ghetto mentalities. The tragedy of this situation is that valid criticisms are discounted and therefore all remedial measures are nullified. *When any one person or group of people puts itself beyond the reach of criticism it is committing psychological and ethical suicide.*

The late Dr. Magnes was absolutely correct when he regretfully noted that Zionism had increased anti-Semitism rather than diminished it. Without the expression "anti-Semitic" the cause of Zionism would hardly have succeeded. The British writer Ian Gilmour has stated the truth in one sentence: "Zionism aggravated the disease it professed to cure."

Anti-Zionism

But when a pro-Zionist rabbi declares, "Anti-Zionism is a new guise for anti-Semitism," one can be sure that the old psychological tool has been resharpened for use in the present situation. The fact that Semitism and Zionism are equated is proof of the obtuse Zionist mentality. The goals and methods of the Zionists are poles apart from the spirit of true Judaism. Such courageous anti-Zionist Jews as Rabbi Elmer Berger and Dr. Alfred M. Lilienthal have been saying this for years, but the reward for their labors has been the tag "traitor." *The Arabs and those who seek justice in their behalf are not anti-Jewish: they are simply anti-Zionist.*

The same can be said for other courageous Jews. Henry Morgenthau, Sr., one of the most outspoken critics, declared:

Zionism is the most stupendous fallacy in Jewish history. It is wrong in principle and impossible of realization; it is unsound in its economics, fantastical in its politics and sterile in its spiritual ideals. Where it is not pathetically visionary, it is cruel, playing with the hopes of a people blindly seeking their way out of age-long miseries.

In his book *The Decadence of Judaism in Our Time*, Moshe Menuhin (father of the violinist Yehudi Menuhin) states:

Zionist Israel is dragging an innocent and unknowledgeable world into an apocalyptic nuclear world war, which is bound to happen soon, unless a just peace is imposed in the Middle East, and all stolen and conquered Arab lands and properties are returned to their lawful owners.

Who Is Responsible?

Space does not permit a survey of events since 1952. Enough has been said to indicate the basic pattern of events. The situation of Israel and the Arabs has been much like feuding boys in a classroom. Rather than hitting his foe with his fist or a ruler, the psychologically astute school boy whispers innuendoes and makes secretive grimaces which escape the teacher. Finally in desperation the object of the psychological attack flails back only to be detected and punished.

The Israelis have pleaded innocence and managed to convince most of the world that the Arabs are the aggressors when many times, in fact, the Arabs were provoked into action by the sly, aggressive ways of the Zionists. Nasser's rhetoric in 1967 inflamed the volatile Arabs with dreams of "holy war," but *they were never really ready to fight one.* However, it gave the Israelis the perfect excuse for catching the Egyptians with their planes down.

This focus on Zionist activities is not intended to absolve the Arabs. They have done their share of cruel, harmful things, but many of these acts were brought on by festering hatred over loss of relatives and homes due to Israeli actions. The Israelis make the same claim, of course, and then inflict more than an "eye-for-an-eye" retribution in order to teach the Arabs a lesson. Sooner or later they may come to realize that "those who take the sword will perish by the sword."

The Israeli claim of innocence cannot stand up in the light of the long, aggressive history of the political Zionists working from a position of prestige, power, and financial backing. *The major responsibility for the boiling pot in the Near East rests with them.* Most certainly extremists have kept the war pot boiling, but there is no ethical justification for calling bitter Palestinian guerillas and hijackers "beasts" when Menachem Begin and his fellow butchers of Deir Yassin are praised as "heroes" and elected to high office.

Election to Responsibility

Conservative Christians never seem to tire of sentimentalizing the idea of Jews as "the chosen people." They were indeed chosen and through no merit of their own. But *their election was for service and responsibility, not favoritism.* The prophet Amos warned, "You only have I known of all the families of the earth; therefore I will punish you for all your iniquities" (3:2).

Because of their awful experience in Egypt, the Israelites were instructed that when they came into power in the land of Canaan they were to protect and treat justly the helpless groups: the orphans, widows, sojourners (aliens without voting rights). Many of the Zionists have been atheists. They gave up on the idea that the Messiah would come and deliver them from their miseries, and so they decided to take matters into their own hands. But the God of Israel did not die with their rejection and sooner or later the Zionists will have to stand before him and account for their actions.

The Peace that Could Be

There is probably more brain power per square meter in Israel than in any other country of the world. They have the advantage of centuries of education and the backing of millions of powerful, wealthy friends, both Jew and Gentile. They have rights in Palestine and the major powers should guarantee these rights. *All talk of pushing the Israelis into the Mediterranean, whether rhetoric or not, must stop.*

On the other hand, Israelis have some responsibilities. They must forget the zealot's dream, shared by the dispensationalists, that Israel has the right to all the territory between Wadi el-Arish and the Euphrates. They must quit dragging their feet and nitpicking at every issue.

Real peace will not come in the Near East until the Palestinian problem is solved. Not all those Arabs who were driven from their homes want to return to the land they used to occupy. But whether they return or not, "reparations" are due them for their material loss and years of suffering and frustration. The Israelis justly demanded and received "reparations" from Germany, and there is equally good reason why they and their friends should pay "reparations" to the Palestinians. The cost will be small compared to the millions wasted on massive defense. With peaceful borders there will be no need for 300% duty on imported items and 2/3 of the budget for military hardware.

If the Israelis seek this kind of peace "with a whole heart," the Near East can begin to blossom like Eden. With open, friendly borders they could travel and see the fantastic sites of antiquity in the area. The Arabs need their "know-how" to help reclaim land which has been abused for centuries.

In the truest sense, the Arabs and Israelis need each other, and there are many warm-hearted people on both sides who long for the day that both groups can live and work together in peace. In his book *Israel Without Zionists*, Uri Avneri, the courageous Israeli, laments that such has not been the case:

> If only we had turned Israeli Arabs into true partners in the building of the land. If only our plans for development embraced Arabs and Jews together, without discrimination. If only the Arabs were represented in all walks of natural life—in the supreme court, in the national soccer team, in our embassies and in our delegations to the United Nations.

Once when pleading for justice in Israel, Avneri was bodily removed from his seat in the *Knesset*. Many more mediating voices are needed on both sides of the dispute.

Fear has dominated the lives of most Israelis and it is crucial that this gnawing fear and insecurity be healed. Recent history, however, has shown that threats and military action will never remove it. The most secure borders are friendly borders, but to secure them, acts of justice will have to drain off the festering pools of hatred which have accumulated over the last century.

The real solution is for each side to sense and understand the physical and psychological pain of the other side. The sight of numerals tattooed on Israelis is a frightening reminder of the death they escaped. Enough sorrow has occurred already without having any more innocent blood shed. Equally touching is the sight of Palestinians in Jordan looking with tearful eyes across the Jordan Valley to the area where they used to live. There must be a just solution of this complex problem!

President Anwar Sadat's visit to Israel was a startling breakthrough, and the Israelis and Arabs conferring in Egypt on Christmas Day was an impressive symbol of the peace that could be. The dream will come closer to reality if, in the spirit of Camp *David*, President Carter can convince the Israelis to withdraw completely from the West Bank, Gaza Strip, and Sinai areas. In a real sense, the Israelis have their future in their own hands. Across the centuries, Moses still pleads: "I have set before you life and death, blessing and curse; therefore choose life, that you and your descendants may live" (Deut. 30:19).

Chapter 16
Lindseyism

The year 1977 marked the 150th anniversary of Darbyism and the 7th anniversary of Hal Lindsey's *The Late Great Planet Earth* (hereafter LGPE). During this relatively short period of Lindseyism, his six books sold over 14,000,000 copies. One of the main reasons for this phenomenon was that Lindsey was riding an apocalyptic wave of distrust of the establishment and despair of the future. Thus, about as many books were sold outside of religious circles as in them.

For this reason, Lindsey merits special treatment. As noted earlier, Lindsey has some of his own ideas about interpretation of details, but his system is essentially jazzed-up Dallas dispensationalism. Concerning his zeal for prophecy, Lindsey comments:

> For some reason, God put a great love for the prophetic message in my heart as a new believer. The urgency of history's hour as set forth in Bible prophecy was the impetus for me to attend seminary and to go into the teaching and writing of Biblical truths.
>
> From my very first faltering message on the second coming of Christ until this very day, I've been utterly amazed at the phenomenal interest and response on the part of believers and nonbelievers alike to the prophetic message. There is no comparable message for this hour in history! (*There's a New World Coming*, p. 303.)

Lindsey's Method

In his introduction to *There's a New World Coming* (hereafter TNWC), Lindsey defines his approach to Revelation as a "deductive manner." By this designation he means trying to deduce from the details of language in Revelation what God was trying to say through John's limited technical knowledge and vocabulary. The locusts with scorpion tails (9:5), for example, are possibly Cobra helicopters with some kind of nerve gas spraying from their tails (TNWC, p. 138).

Lindsey is "deductive" in a far more damaging way. He starts with his system and makes the biblical data fit it. He notes that in a number of cases in Revelation "John provides the interpretation of the symbology right in the same context. With the help of a good concordance (a book that lists Bible words and their Scripture

references) we can pretty well determine the meanings of most of the
other symbols" (TNWC, pp. 23-24).

The Valley of Jehoshaphat

This topical approach is much like Darby's in that it strings
prooftexts together from all over the Bible without using the inductive
method, in which the context determines the meaning of the words or
phrases. When different authors use the same word, there is often a
different nuance of meaning. Good interpretation, therefore, will
determine the precise meaning of terms or phrases in context before
attempting to relate them.

An excellent example of failure to do this is Lindsey's
understanding of "the valley of Jehoshaphat" found in Joel. The name
means "Yahweh has judged." The question is whether Joel was using
the name symbolically or referring to an actual valley bearing the
name of the King of Judah, who was at Samaria when the prophet
Micaiah was summoned (1 Kgs. 22:10)? Scholars disagree on this
point. Lindsey associates this valley with the Esdraelon and
Armageddon:

> Some 2,700 years ago the Prophet Joel foresaw this terrible day: "Let
> the nations be awakened, and come to the valley of Jehoshaphat (the
> place of Armageddon), for there I will sit to judge all the nations
> surrounding you. Multitudes, multitudes in the valley of decision; for
> the day of the Lord is near in the valley of decision" (Joel 3:12, 14).
> (TNWC, p. 222)

The words "the place of Armageddon" are not found in Joel.
They were inserted into the translation on the authority of the SRB
and NSRB along with regular dispensational interpreters. The same
expression occurs in 3:2 and it is that context which tells us where the
valley was located:

> For behold, in those days and at that time, when I restore the
> fortunes of Judah and Jerusalem, I will gather all the nations and bring
> them down to the valley of Jehoshaphat, and I will enter into judgment
> with them there (3:1-2).

Whether Joel used the name symbolically or with respect to a specific
valley, it is clear that he thought of Yahweh's judgment taking place
somewhere in the vicinity of Jerusalem. All of the traditional
commentators take this as certain.

Squeezing the Puzzle Pieces

What the dispensationalists have done is to take a piece from the Joel jigsaw puzzle and force it into a somewhat similar spot in John's jigsaw. Those who have had experience with jigsaw puzzles know how they can get mixed, especially if a number of puzzles are being done in the same area. In such cases there is usually some eager person who squeezes pieces into spaces not exactly fitted for them.

No matter how well-intentioned these persons may be, the pieces simply do not fit. But dispensationalists have been doing this so long it apparently doesn't bother them any more. Just smear in a little filler and it will be sufficient for the uncritical eye. It has been said earlier, but it will bear repeating: *all the jigsaw pieces in the Bible do not fit into the same puzzle*. This is one of the basic errors of the dispensational system. The references in SRB and NSRB swarm with *multiple* passages in which Ezekiel 38-39; Daniel 7, 9, 11, 12; Zechariah 12-14; Matthew 24-25; 1 Thessalonians 4; 2 Thessalonians 2; and 2 Peter 3 are interrelated with the preexilic prophets. But no amount of wishful thinking makes it true.

Lindsey Moves the Lamps

A prime example of how far Lindsey will go to make his case is one of his arguments for proving the rapture. Under the section title "Who Moved the Lamps?" he comments:

> The first of these objects is the group of seven lamps. In chapter 1 we saw these same seven lamps *on earth*, with Christ walking among them. Now these seven lamps (which, as we saw, portray the Church), are *in heaven*. This is further evidence that God will remove the Church from earth before His outpouring judgment (TNWC, p. 86).

The Greek word used in Rev. 1:20 is *luchnia* "lampstand," while that in 4:5 is *lampas* "lamp, torch." In 1:20 the lampstands are clearly identified as the churches of Asia Minor, but the lamps in heaven are the 7 spirits of God. The Greek words, the objects, the places, and the identification of the objects *are all different*. Yet Lindsey has the effrontery to equate them. By translating "lamps" in both cases, he deceives the readers and leads them down a blind alley. This is worse than fudging.

Moreover, there is no excuse on the grounds of innocence. He and his publishers note that he studied Greek at Dallas Theological

Seminary, and on the back side of the TNWC title page is the note
that the basic text is the King James Version "with clarifying
emendations from the original languages by Hal Lindsey." But what
good is technical training if it is abused in this way?

In the introduction to TNWC Lindsey comments, "I have
honestly sought to be as accurate and conservative as I know how to
be, considering the awesome scope of this subject matter." But while
the "awesome scope" of dispensationalism forces him to take such
drastic measures, honesty comes in second or is forgotten entirely. The
system has so warped his thinking he doesn't know how to be honest
in an objective manner. In the case of the "lamps," Lindsey was so
"enraptured" with his idea "he moved the lamps." The "system" made
him do it!

Lindsey and Albright

This lack of objectivity is equally evident when he quotes from
nonbiblical sources. Under the section heading "Israel, the Fuse of
Armageddon," Lindsey comments:

> Too few Biblical scholars pay any serious attention to the proven
> prophetic content of Scripture. Dr. William F. Albright, eminent
> archaeologist and professor of Semitic Languages, noted this fact after
> he had verified many historic fulfillments of Bible prophecy. He said,
> "That the prophets were not only dedicated men, but also predictors of
> the future is fully recognized in Biblical tradition but has been under-
> emphasized by modern Biblical scholars. . . ."

The context of this quotation gives the idea that Albright agreed with
Lindsey's prophecies and anticipated the battle of Armageddon. But
this was not so. He was a mediating scholar who objected to the
extreme liberal rejection of all prophecy, and yet he did not go along
with the elaborate prophetic systems such as dispensationalism.

The quotation from Albright is in his new introduction to the 2nd
edition of *From the Stone Age to Christianity*. On the very next page
he comments, "It is wholly unnecessary to reckon with 'prophecies
after the event': we have exceedingly few cases of *vaticinium ex eventu*
in the Hebrew Bible before the third or second century B.C." (p. 18).

He goes on to show that Jeremiah prophesied the 70-year exile in
605, that is, 70 was not added later. Yet Albright continues to explain
why it did not bother the ancients that things did not work out exactly

as forecast. I studied three years with Dr. Albright and kept in close touch with him until his death in 1971. He was not a literalist concerning prophetic details. While he held to the authenticity of the prophecy against the Bethel sanctuary, he believed the name "Josiah" was added later. Moreover, he held to an Exilic Isaiah and a Maccabean Daniel. Lindsey's quotation from this great scholar is prooftexting and the reader has no chance of seeing the real Albright.

Prewritten History

One of Arno Gaebelein's delights was to speak of prophecy as "prewritten history." This is essentially the presupposition back of dispensationalism even though the expression is not used much now. Revelation 2-3 will illustrate the point. Lindsey agrees with the NSRB interpretation of the 7 churches (TNWC, p. 39). The editors recognize that the letters were addressed to churches in Asia Minor, but that they have value for churches and individuals of all times.

More crucially, however, they believe that the letters are prophetic of all church history:

> It is incredible that in a prophecy covering the church period there should be no such foreview. These messages must contain that foreview if it is in the book at all, for the Church does not appear on earth after 3:22 (p. 1353).

The reason the letters "must" contain a preview is the assumption that Revelation is God's historical timetable of church events from John on Patmos to the New Jerusalem. This is what is "incredible."

Since John is involved in chapter 1 and the rapture supposedly happens in chapter 4, the letters are thought to cover the following periods:

1. Ephesus (2:1-7) is typical of the 1st-century church as a whole;
2. Smyrna (2:8-11) characterizes the church under persecution, e.g. from A.D. c. 100-316;
3. Pergamum (2:12-17) is suggestive of the church mixing with the world, e.g. in the Middle Ages;
4. Thyatira (2:18-29) reveals how evil progresses in the church and idolatry is practised;
5. Sardis (3:1-6) is representative of the church as dead, yet still having a minority of godly men and women, as during the Reformation;

6. Philadelphia (3:7-13) shows revival and a state of spiritual advance; and

7. Laodicea (3:14-19) is illustrative of the final state of apostasy which the visible church will experience (p. 1353).

The use of "suggestive, representative, illustrative" indicates how general the relation is. Only the will to believe and careful selection of data make it possible to understand the letters as consecutive church history. It takes an awful lot of filler to make the jigsaw pieces fit together.

Israel, the Infallible Sign

Lindsey notes that the Bible students who tried to fit the events of World War I and II to the prophetic signs of Christ's coming were failures and a discredit to prophecy. They overlooked the paramount prophetic sign: "Israel had to be a nation again in the land of its forefathers" (LGPE, p. 33).

He believes that prophecy was a closed book until recently because God had instructed Daniel to seal the book "until the time of the end" (12:4). "This writer doesn't believe," Lindsey confesses, "that we have prophets today who are getting direct revelations from God, but we do have prophets today who are being given special insight into the prophetic word" (LGPE, p. 78). Undoubtedly, Lindsey considers himself one of these prophets.

The infallible sign Israel is "the fig tree" of Jesus' parable, according to him, and on May 14, 1948, it put out its first leaves. Concerning Jesus' statement that "this generation" would not pass away until all had taken place, Lindsey comments:

> What generation? Obviously, in context, the generation that would see the signs—chief among them the rebirth of Israel. A generation in the Bible is something like forty years. If this is a correct deduction, then within forty years or so of 1948, all these things could take place. Many scholars who have studied Bible prophecy all their lives believe that this is so (LGPE, p. 43).

If Jesus was referring to a distant future, the least he could have done was to say "that generation" and thus give his hearers a clue that the events he was discussing would occur in some future generation, not theirs. But "this" is close to "that," and so just add a little filler. Cover things from this end and do not worry too much about how the disciples and early Christians understood things. Moreover, the batting average of prophetic "scholars" is dismally low, even those who spent their whole lives at it, therefore their combined witness is no assurance.

Reasoning from a position that the "abomination of desolation" in Daniel refers to the future, Lindsey concluded that Israel had to possess old Jerusalem and rebuild the temple:

> In March and April of 1967 I was lecturing on the subject at many college campuses on the West coast. I said that if this was the time that I thought it was, then somehow the Jews were going to have to repossess old Jerusalem. Many chuckled at that statement. Then came the war of June, 1967—the phenomenal Israeli six-day blitz (LGPE, pp. 44-45).

The Third Temple

Flushed with victory and reassured that he was reading God's timetable accurately, Lindsey went on to rival Drew Pearson with a series of "I predict" forecasts of historical events. "We must conclude," he declared, "that a third temple will be rebuilt upon its ancient site in old Jerusalem. If this is the time that this writer believes it is, there will soon begin the construction of this Temple" (LGPE, p. 46). Again, how soon is soon?

Lindsey quotes Israel Eldad, the Israeli historian: "When the Jewish people took over Jerusalem the first time, under King David, only one generation passed before they built the Temple, and so shall it be with us!" Then Lindsey comments, "When asked about the problem of the Dome of (the) Rock being on the Jewish Temple site, he replied with a wink, 'Who knows, perhaps there will be an earthquake!' What Eldad said in jest may be just the thing that will happen" (TNWC, p. 159).

The 7-Year Countdown

After the death of Christ and the destruction of Jerusalem, "God's finger once again pushed in on the divine time-clock," Lindsey comments, "and the allotted time of Israel's special outreach to the unbelieving world was stopped, *seven years short* of the promised 490 years" (TNWC, p.101). This 7-year period of tribulation is the supposedly postponed 70th week of Daniel 9. Lindsey calls this period the "countdown" (LGPE, p. 33).

It begins, of course, when the church is raptured. Some Jews will miss their Christian friends and accept Christ as Lord. Others will find Christian literature and believe. "They will be like 144,000 Jewish Billy Grahams turned loose at once!" Lindsey believes, and they "will do in only seven years what their nation has failed to do in all its history—evangelize the whole world!" (TNWC, pp. 123, 116).

The "countdown" should end about 1988, according to Lindsey, therefore the tribulation should begin about 1981. Up until now he has been cautious about precise dates and identifications. "I make no claim," he states, "of knowing exactly when the world is going to end. In fact, I have never taken to the hills with my possessions and loved ones to await Doomsday. I believe in a hope for the future" (LGPE, Introduction). Why should he take to the hills? He is going to be raptured!

But he cannot run from his predictions, and even though he has been very wary about setting dates and naming the characters of the final drama, *the noose of his own general schedule is getting tighter all the time.*

But to escape the noose, Lindsey has resorted to "the great postponement." In an interview quoted in a review of his latest book *The Terminal Generation*, he states, "I don't know how long a biblical generation is. Perhaps somewhere between sixty and eighty years" (*Christianity Today*, April 15, 1977, p. 40). Here Lindsey is trying to buy more time by shifting from his previous definition of a generation as 40 years. Jesus hardly meant to extend the time limit to the *lifetime* of infants living then. Israel really did not have all of the land until 1967, some of his faithful argue, and so the tribulation will not begin until about A.D. 2000. What a relief to feel safe for a few more years!

The First Seal

The first seal is the conqueror on the white horse. Lindsey comments: "The white apocalyptic horseman of Revelation 6 is the *European* Antichrist. I personally believe that this man is alive somewhere in the world at this very moment!" (TNWC, p. 103). Then he notes:

> During the first three and one-half years of the Tribulation the Antichrist will bring a pseudo-peace to the world. Everyone will be

singing his praises as the greatest leader in all human history (TNWC, p. 104).

European Common Market

This antichrist will arise, according to Lindsey, from the Common Market, therefore it is a crucial sign:

One of the reasons I'm convinced we're living in the closing days of the world's history is because of the emergence of the European Common Market, also known as the European Economic Community. There is no doubt in my mind that it's the forerunner of the Revived Roman Empire which the prophet Daniel spoke about with such certainty. He predicted that the number of nations in it would be limited to ten. This is the very number which the Common Market has set as its goal for inner membership! (TNWC, p.186).

When Norway turned down the invitation to join the Common Market, Lindsey had an explanation:

The European union has therefore been temporarily halted at nine members instead of ten. My personal belief is that God Himself stopped the rapid unification because the Revived Roman Empire was coming together too fast. Once the confederacy includes the ten nations of *God's choosing*, the group will begin to look for a leader powerful enough to make this new nation the nucleus of a one-world government. I believe the Roman Antichrist of Revelation 13 is going to be that leader (TNWC, pp. 187-88).

The Antichrist

This Roman antichrist is the beast with a wounded head. When it heals miraculously, the world will follow him in amazement. He "will outperform Alexander the Great," according to Lindsey. "In a matter of *weeks* he will take over the ten-nation European confederacy and eventually subjugate the whole world to himself" (TNWC, p. 189). Lindsey thinks he is alive now and will appear suddenly as the economic and political savior of the people.

Lindsey's relative restraint about identifying the antichrist contrasts with the popular game "Name the Antichrist," played by many of the prophetic "scholars" in the recent past. Villains of the Nero-type figured prominently: Kaiser Wilhelm, Mussolini, Hitler, and Stalin. Among right-wing Protestant groups, the Papacy has been one of the consistent, sure-bet candidates. Practically every Pope has been given the distinction.

Some diehards still think that Judas Iscariot, resurrected or reincarnated, will be the antichrist. After all, didn't Jesus call him a "devil" (Jn. 6:70) and "the son of perdition" (Jn. 17:12)? Since Paul called the antichrist "the son of perdition" (2 Thess. 2:3), that settles the matter, so they claim.

Men with wounded heads have been considered as well. Moshe Dayan miraculously escaped death when he lost his left eye. He became a prime candidate after his exploits in the 1967 War. The late John F. Kennedy had a double reason for being nominated. He was a Roman Catholic and his head was wounded in Dallas. Some expected him to rise from the coffin and since that didn't happen, they expect him to return in resurrected form.

The description of Antiochus Epiphanes gaining control by flatteries (Dan. 11:21) resulted in Henry Kissinger's nomination. But he did not betray Israel, nor has he continued in power.

Failures, failures, nothing but failures! But zealot predictors die hard. Most of them charged their mistakes up to experience and started looking around for a more likely candidate.

The False Prophet

Whereas the beast, the antichrist, rises from the sea, the other beast, the false prophet, rises from the land. Lindsey takes this to mean the land of Israel: "So the second Beast will come from the region of the Middle East, and I believe he will be a Jew." Inasmuch as he will try to imitate the real Lamb, Jesus Christ, Lindsey predicts:

> Millions of people will fall for his deception and honestly believe this False Prophet to be the long-awaited Jewish Messiah. Already the World Council of Churches is hard at work merging various religions together. By the time the Beast tackles the project, liberal Judaism will probably be ready to join the merger, too, since any true doctrine about Jesus Christ will have disappeared (TNWC, p. 192).

How is that for sticking your neck out?

The Roman antichrist will make "a strong covenant" with the false prophet and Israel, claims Lindsey, and he will guarantee their safety and protection. This will occur at the beginning of the 7-year tribulation period. Included in this treaty will be the right to reconstruct the temple and begin animal sacrifices (LGPE, pp. 140-41). Then Lindsey adds a most astute observation, "P.S. The Arabs are not going to like this idea of rebuilding the Temple one bit." *That prediction is infallible!*

The false prophet will set up the "image of the beast" right "in the middle of the reconstructed Temple" and all worshipers of the beast "will be compelled to receive a distinguishing mark (perhaps a tattoo visible only under ultraviolet light) on their right hand or their forehead. Everyone who refuses the mark will be cut off from economic survival. They will be forbidden to buy or sell anything." The Social Security assignment of numbers may be "the system by which this monstrous outrage will be committed" (TNWC, p. 194).

Lindsey cuts right through the complexities of trying to figure the beast's number: "Since the number 6 in the Bible stands for humanity, I believe the meaning of 666 is man trying to imitate the trinity of God (three sixes in one person)" (TNWC, p. 195).

The Second Seal and the War of Armageddon

Concerning the second seal, the red horse, Lindsey comments:

> But at the midpoint of the Tribulation the second seal is opened and, according to Ezekiel 38 and Daniel 11, Russia, the rider of the red horse, snatches peace from the earth. With her Arab allies she invades the Middle East and attacks Israel (TNWC, p.104).

The series of battles which Lindsey finds predicted in Scripture is termed the "War of Armageddon," the last one being the famous "Battle of Armageddon" (TNWC, p. 222). The first phase of the war will be the invasion of Israel by the Arab-African Confederacy. This is "the king of the south" in Dan. 11:40.

The King of the South

We noted in Daniel 11 that the king of the south was the series of Ptolemies ruling in Egypt. Of course, Lindsey postpones 11:40-45 until the tribulation. In Ezek. 38:5, on the other hand, the allies of Gog are Persia, Cush, and Put.

On the basis of some old, unreliable scholarship, Lindsey concludes that "all the black people of Africa are descended from Cush." KJV confused the issue also by translating "Cush" as "Ethiopia." Ancient

Cush was the region we call "Nubia" and the original inhabitants were "dark-skinned," but not Negroid by race. Lindsey needs the phony theory, however, because a number of the black African nations are influenced by Communism.

Ancient translations identify Put as Libya. Yet this does not include enough territory and so Lindsey comments, "Put, certainly included more than what is now Libya" (LGPE, p. 57). Thus, he adds Algeria, Tunisia, and Morocco because the descendants of Put supposedly moved west and these countries are becoming Communist. Those Arabic and Black African nations which have been influenced by Russia *must be* the new "king of the south." If this wheeling and dealing with Scriptural evidence is genuine biblical scholarship, then green is purple.

The King of the North

Lindsey has no question about "the king of the north" either. "Russia is a Gog," he informs us through one of his or Carole Carlson's catchy titles. Since Gog has allies in Ezekiel 38, Russia has to have some now. "In order to mount the large-scale invasion predicted by Ezekiel, Russia would need Iran as an ally," Lindsey comments, and so "watch the actions of Iran in relation to Russia and the United Arab Republic. This writer believes that significant things will soon be happening there" (LGPE, p. 56). We are still watching!

The Russians will have an amphibious prong to their attack. "The current build-up of Russian ships in the Mediterranean serves," Lindsey believes, "as another significant sign of the possible nearness of Armageddon" (LGPE, p. 146). The use of "significant" and "possible" indicates some wavering or inconsistency in Lindsey's thinking.

In any case, after the Arabic-African Confederacy attacks Israel from the south, Russia and its friends invade from the north and west. Somehow Russia forgets that the people attacking from the other side are its friends also, therefore it moves through Israel and takes over Egypt. In order to explain this oddity, Lindsey jumps through one more hoop: "Apparently they come into the conflict originally as allies of the Arabs but end up double-crossing them" (TNWC, p. 223). The problem is that Lindsey has double-crossed himself. It is clear in Dan. 11:40 that Ptolemy VI will attack Antiochus Epiphanes, not the Jews.

The fact that the battle involves Palestine does not mean that both of them are attacking Israel. That piece of information comes from Ezek. 38:8. Lindsey has not learned that *mixing prophets can give one a headache.*

When the Roman antichrist hears of the invasion, he prepares to come to Israel's defense according to his covenant with the false prophet. The kings of the east are assembling their army at the same time. Rumors "from the east and the north" (Dan. 11:44) reach the Russians in Egypt. They return to Israel and set up their command headquarters in the temple area on Mt. Moriah (Dan. 11:45). This is the 3rd phase of the war.

Plagues on the Earth

Before continuing predictions about the war of Armageddon, it will be instructive to see how Lindsey interprets some of the plagues which will come during the 3 1/2 years of the great tribulation. Following the red horse of the war, started by Russia and its allies, comes the black horse of economic and financial disaster. The result of these riders is the pale horse, bearing death and hades. One fourth of the earth will die by sword and famine. Lindsey takes this literally to mean that about *one billion* people will die, all of them unbelievers (TNWC, p. 106).

After the "great earthquake" of the 6th seal, the sun becomes black and the moon like blood. This data leads Lindsey "to believe that the Apostle John is describing an earthquake set off by a nuclear explosion" (TNWC, p. 109). It will have such a force, the "whole world will be literally shaken apart!" (TNWC, p. 110).

What happens to the poor inhabitants of the earth? Somehow thay live to go through more trouble. Lindsey considers the 7 trumpets to be part of the 7th seal, thus these horrors are consecutive and they increase in intensity. The "hail and fire mixed with blood" (Rev. 8:7) which John sees are really ICBM missiles (TNWC, p. 130) and the "burning mountain cast into the sea" is "probably either an enormous meteor or, more likely, a colossal H-bomb" (TNWC, p. 131).

The "great star falling from heaven" is, according to Lindsey, "another thermonuclear weapon which is a part of a series of exchanges between the nuclear powers" (TNWC, p. 132). The reduction of the light of the sun, moon, and stars by a third "will result from the tremendous pollution in the air left from nuclear explosions" (TNWC, p. 133).

The woman who gives birth to the child is given "the two wings of the great eagle" in order to flee from the dragon into the wilderness. Lindsey follows other "Bible scholars" in believing that Petra in Jordan is intended:

> Some of a massive airlift will rapidly transport these fleeing Jews across the rugged terrain to their place of protection. Since the eagle is the national symbol of the United States, it's possible that the airlift will be made available by aircraft from the U.S. Sixth fleet in the Mediterranean (TNWC, p. 179).

The Battle of Armageddon

The 4th phase of the War of Armageddon is the antichrist's annihilation of the Russian forces in Israel. The 200 million-man Oriental army at the Euphrates marks the 5th stage. The last preparatory phase is the antichrist's mobilization of the remaining world's armies on his side. Will the United States figure in this? "There's no Scriptural indication that the United States will have been wiped out before this time," Lindsey reasons, "so we can only deduce that she will be part of the Western Confederacy which unifies nations against the great Asian power" (TNWC, pp. 226-27).

"At this point," Lindsey affirms, "all the armies move into the Middle East and spread out along the entire length and breadth of Israel, with the great concentration poised for the fiercest and final battle on the Plains of Armageddon" (TNWC, p. 225). As the battle rages, judgment comes on the armies. Lindsey notes:

> Think of it: at least 200 million soldiers from the Orient, with millions more from the forces of the West headed by the Antichrist of the Revived Roman Empire (Western Europe)! Messiah Jesus will first strike those who have ravaged His city Jerusalem. Then he will strike the armies amassed in the valley of Megiddo, or Armageddon. No wonder blood will stand to the horses' bridles for a distance of two hundred miles from Jerusalem! (TNWC, pp. 205-6)

Lindsey did a little scholarly research to check out John's claim:

> It's grizzly (sic) to think about such a carnage, but just to check all this out I measured from the point where the Valley of Armageddon

slopes down to the Jordan Valley. From that point southward down the Valley through the Dead Sea to the port of Elath on the Gulf of Aqabah measures approximately two hundred miles. Apparently this whole valley will be filled with war materials, animals, bodies of men, and blood! (TNWC, p. 206)

On and on Lindsey goes, his vivid imagination and credulous mentality making a 20th-century medley of the apocalyptic themes we have studied.

Lindsey on Cloud Seven

We have covered enough of Lindsey's interpretations and predictions to get an idea of how he thinks and feels. What is equally astonishing is the "charge" he gets out of this whole outlook:

For all those who trust in Jesus Christ, it is a time of electrifying excitement (LGPE, p. 47);
Are you discovering more pieces of this stirring prophetic puzzle? (LGPE, p. 67);
As world events develop, prophecy becomes more and more exciting (LGPE, p. 77);
. . . we can scarcely contain our continuous excitement over prophetic pictures in the Bible (LGPE, p. 107).

Isn't it a remarkable coincidence that Lindsey gets his "highs" on pages which end in 7? According to his method, this *may be* a sign that Lindsey will be raptured on "Cloud Seven." Clearly, *the man is addicted to prophecy.* He has worked a number of years with west coast youth, warning them against LSD and various drugs, but he is "hooked" on a "spiritual drug" and he can't help going back to get his "kicks." What is even worse, he ties his excitement to the gospel of Jesus Christ. The "good news" of Jesus is free of Lindsey's excesses!

The Better Lindsey

When he gets off "Cloud Seven" he begins to talk sense. For example his treatment of "speaking in tongues" (*Satan is Alive and Well on Planet Earth*, pp. 136-49) is well done because he is not *addicted to tongues* like many conservatives.

In discussing the matter of spiritual gifts, Lindsey acknowledges "My spiritual gift happens to be the gift of teaching. I didn't seek it,

tarry for it, or even unnecessarily concern myself about what it was. . . .
As I grew in my knowledge of the Word and He continued to bless in a
greater way, I realized that He had given me the gift of teaching"
(SAWPE, p. 145).

James counsels against too many desiring to teach because those
"who teach shall be judged with greater strictness" (3:1). Teaching is a
dangerous business because if the content is not essentially accurate, the
minds of many students will be scrambled with error.

Lindsey and Jeane Dixon

Lindsey is convinced, of course, that he is teaching the truth: "In
this book I am attempting to step aside and let the prophets speak"
(LGPE, Introduction). He even arranged an interview with Jeane
Dixon in which he interacted with her about her use of occult
paraphernalia in making predictions. "With real regret," Lindsey
states, "I told Mrs. Dixon that I believed her prophetic ability was *not*
from God. I told her I sincerely believed that if she didn't reject this
psychic power, it would lead to her destruction. She said she was
certain her gift was from God and that she knew beyond doubt the
'feeling' of God's presence" (SAWPE, pp. 127-28).

"When our 'feelings,' no matter how right they may seem,
contradict Scripture," Lindsey declares, "we must conclude that our
feelings are wrong" (SAWPE, p. 128).

Although we have covered only a fraction of the problems in
Lindsey's views, enough has been highlighted to show that his
understanding of Scripture is as "subjective" as Dixon's "feelings."

In a conversation with Lindsey about his predictions, W. Ward
Gasque, Regent College, Vancouver, Canada, asked, "But what if
you're wrong?" Lindsey replied:

> Well, there's just a split second's difference between a hero and a bum. I
> didn't ask to be a hero, but I guess I have become one in the Christian
> community. So I accept it. But if I'm wrong about this, I guess I'll
> become a bum (*Christianity Today*, April 15, 1977, p. 40).

The indications are that he will miss by years, not seconds. A few of
his predictions may accidently hit the mark. It is very hard to be 100%
wrong. *But there isn't a chance in this world or the next that the
elaborate drama he has concocted will take place in that detail and
sequence!* I hold no brief for Jeane Dixon, but if external criteria are

any indication, in the long run she will have a better batting average than Lindsey.

Now that *The Late Great Planet Earth* has been made into a movie with Orson Welles, Lindsey's sensational nonsense is being etched even more indelibly on the minds of millions of innocents. Perhaps some day as he drives around in his automobile waiting to be raptured he will begin to realize how many words he has to eat. It is one thing for Lindsey to "become a bum," but it is quite another issue when one contemplates the cumulative frustration and disappointment his followers will experience.

Chapter 17
Seventh-day Adventism

Among the most vigorous Protestant groups is Seventh-day Adventism (hereafter SDA). The origins of this 2,500,000-member, worldwide fellowship are very interesting, and inasmuch as the distinctive views of the organization involve prophecy, both biblical and nonbiblical, it is necessary to examine its claims.

In chapter 1 we had a glimpse of the long history of broken hopes concerning the return of Jesus Christ. SDA grew out of one of these traumatic situations where prophecy failed.

William Miller

William Miller (Feb. 5, 1782-Dec. 20, 1849), born in Pittsfield, Mass., was reared in the pious faith of his mother. He was a disciplined, intelligent young man and continued in his evangelical faith until about 21 or 22, when he came in contact with some deists. They chided him about his simplistic view of Scripture and pointed out many difficulties in the biblical text. Most of them were good people and concerned citizens, and so he accepted their outlook.

In reacting against the difficulties of Scripture, he apparently rejected the essence of the biblical message and entered a period of spiritual turmoil (1804-1816), much as John N. Darby would (1820-1827). When he retired from the army in 1815 he was still haunted by the chilling thought of annihilation in the grave, and he longed for deliverance from such a prospect.

In 1816 he was suddenly impressed with the fact that there was a loving Savior who would forgive his sins. But where was the proof of such a reality? The Bible was the only source, therefore he returned to the book he had rejected. Study of it became one of his greatest joys and Jesus became his truest friend.

Miller's Method

When Miller witnessed concerning his renewed faith, his old friends turned some of his own arguments back on him. He determined to study the Bible on his own, without any commentaries, in order to harmonize the supposed contradictions. Any book which could give him such peace and assurance had to be consistent within itself. His basic premise, therefore, was that Scripture was its own best interpreter. When a passage caused him some difficulty he would consult a concordance or marginal reference for passages dealing with similar topics. There is some merit to this approach, but as we have noted a number of times, all the biblical data cannot be harmonized and made to fit into one picture.

Miller was especially intrigued with Daniel and Revelation, often spending whole nights working on the meaning of symbolism. The Bible became "a feast of reason" in which he perceived a system of revealed truths. He accepted the traditional Messianic interpretation of the 70 weeks, beginning with Artaxerxes' decree in 457 B.C. and closing with the last week, A.D. 27-34.

Time of the Second Advent

The clue to the time of the second advent he found in the 2,300 "evenings and mornings" of Dan. 8:14. These represented 2,300 years, Miller believed, but unfortunately the angel had not explained to Daniel when to begin counting. One of Miller's sources noted that "seventy weeks are determined" (Dan. 9:24) meant literally "seventy weeks are cut off." But cut off from what? The answer to this perplexity came in 1818, two years after beginning his intensive study of the Bible. The 490 years, which applied only to the Jews, were cut off from the 2,300 years; therefore both periods began in 457 B.C. This explains why Gerhard Hasel, an SDA, worked so desperately to authenticate the 457 date: *the whole SDA prophetic system hinges on it.* Thus, Miller was convinced that Christ would return in about 25 years, that is, about 1843.

He was thrilled with his findings and the delightful prospect of the Lord's return, but for fear that he might have made a mistake, he double-checked his work. For five years he considered thoroughly any difficulties he could find in his system, but "found that objections vanished before the light of God's word, as mist before the rays of the sun."

Miller's Call

With this assurance came the command, "Go and tell the world of their danger." From 1823-1831 the quiet, studious farmer witnessed privately to his friends in the Baptist Church, hoping that some minister would accept his views and become the herald of Christ's return. But such was not the case, and increasingly he felt the burden of judgment he would face if he failed to be God's alarm. All the while his friends were urging him to witness publicly about his convictions.

Finally, in 1831 Miller, almost fifty years of age, accepted God's call. He, like Elisha, would have to leave his plow and become God's messenger. Although unaccustomed to public speaking and feeling unworthy of his task, his first trembling efforts resulted in the salvation of a number of families. His influence spread and moral reformation followed his ministry. Most of his expenses were paid out of the meager profits from the farm, which his large family maintained in his absence.

Signs of the Sixth Seal

In 1833 the Baptist Church gave Miller a license to preach and this opened many more doors. Invitations to speak came in faster than he could fulfill them. The evening of Nov. 13, 1833, brought additional assurance to Miller and his followers. The fantastic meteorite shower was taken to be the last of the three signs predicted in Rev. 6:12-13:

> When he opened the sixth seal, I looked, and behold, there was a great earthquake; and the sun became black as sackcloth, the full moon became like blood, and the stars of the sky fell to the earth as the fig tree sheds its winter fruit when shaken by a gale.

The great Lisbon earthquake of 1755 was considered to be the first sign, and the astonishing "dark day" of May 19, 1780, the second. Strange atmospheric conditions over New England resulted in darkness which required candles at 11 A.M. The skies cleared for a while at sunset, but later the dark clouds returned, practically blotting out a full moon. The last of these three signs convinced Miller's hearers that he was correct; therefore they began to spread his message of urgency.

The Spread of Adventism

This concern for the unsaved was in turn taken to be the fulfillment of John's prophecy that an angel would come to earth "with an eternal gospel" and declare, "Fear God and give him glory, for the hour of his judgment has come" (Rev. 14:6-7). Some ministers became converts to Miller's prophetic views, thereby multiplying his followers. Men like Joshua V. Himes helped organize the growing mass movement. In 1840 the paper *Signs of the Times* was started and it attracted more adherents.

A general conference was held in Boston in the spring of 1842. Miller had been saying that the second advent would occur "about the year 1843," but some of the leading Millerites were uneasy about the specific date. The majority thought otherwise, however, and passed the following resolution:

> *Resolved*, that in the opinion of this conference, there are most serious and important reasons for believing that God has revealed the time of the end of the world, and that this time is 1843 (*Signs of the Times*, June 1, 1842, p. 69).

During the summer and fall of 1842, thirty camp meetings with large crowds swelled the ranks of the Millerites. Another paper *The Midnight Cry* was started in New York. As 1843 drew nearer, the people wanted a more definitive statement from Miller, but he refused to be more explicit than to claim that Christ's advent would occur "between March 21st, 1843, and March 21st, 1844, according to the Jewish mode of computation of time" (*Signs of the Times*, Jan. 25, 1843, p. 147).

Three Disappointments

Notwithstanding repeated warnings from leading Millerites, zealots began to set precise dates. One date that caught on with some of the movement was April 23, 1843. Disappointment over Christ's failure to return was short-lived, however, because they rationalized that although their zeal had been premature, they had almost a year to look for the advent.

In spite of Miller's clear-cut limitation to the Jewish year, extending into 1844, some of his followers set their hopes on the end of 1843. They too were doomed to disappointment. In a New Year's message Miller urged his followers not to give up the ship—they still had until March 21 for their hopes to be realized. Zeal increased as the day drew near. Conferences in New York, Philadelphia, and Washington were packed.

But March 21, 1844, came and went as any other day. The glee of the "scoffers" matched the despondency of the Millerites. Yet, believe it or not, the will to believe fanned the ashes of despair into a hotter flame than ever. The faithful interpreted the failure as God's test of their loyalty. He was a reality in their lives and he could not be wrong. Miller and Himes traveled extensively, as far west as Ohio, making new converts.

The Great Disillusionment

Samuel S. Snow, one of the Millerite ministers, began to publish his prediction that Christ's coming would occur on Oct. 22, 1844. The leaders opposed this new date, but it caught on with the laity and spread like wildfire. Some of the farmers refused to harvest their crops—there would be no need for the food and the time could be spent warning sinners of the wrath to come. Many followers sold all or part of their possessions. In his book *The Midnight Cry* (1944), Francis D. Nichol explains:

> First, they wished to have more money with which to support the cause. It took money to support four presses running constantly, pouring out literature on Millerism. Second, they wished to have all their dealings with their fellow men honorably concluded before the advent, including full payment of all their debts. Third, with the fervent love for others, which true religion certainly ought to generate in the hearts of men, Millerites who owed no debts themselves sought to help others pay their debts. Some Millerites, stimulated by the realization that soon earthly gold would be worthless, and warmed in their hearts with a love for their fellow men, wished to make gifts to the poor, both within and without the faith (pp. 238-39).

The fire of enthusiasm was burning so brightly the leading Millerites gave up their objections to the new date for fear they might be opposing the Holy Spirit. In order to meet the demand for more literature, four steam presses were run around the clock for weeks. As the day drew near, the faithful increased their efforts to reach the unsaved. It should be made clear that contrary to popular legends from that period, there were no groups on housetops dressed in ascension robes.

The "midnight cry" of warning continued until midnight, Oct. 22, 1844, *but the Lord did not return.* Four disappointments within 18 months were too much, even for these seemingly indomitable spirits, and devastated hopes were expressed in floods of tears until dawn and beyond. Many of them faced a bleak winter with no food in stock and no money to buy other necessities.

William Miller maintained his faith throughout the tragic aftermath and lived on for five years with the belief that Christ would return soon. But much of the Millerite movement died in convulsions of despair, disbelief, and discord.

The Adventist Remnant

One of the families supporting Miller was that of Robert and Eunice Harmon. Their last children were twin girls, Ellen and Elizabeth, born on Nov. 26, 1827. Ellen was an intelligent child with a pleasant disposition, but her world turned upside down when she was nine. A rock thrown by an older schoolmate smashed her nose and knocked her unconscious for three weeks.

Gradually she recovered and eventually returned to school. But she could not overcome the physical and psychological wounds caused by the flying rock; therefore she had to drop out of school. She prayed to die and took comfort in the hope of Christ's soon return. A period of torment followed, in which she longed to die and yet feared that she was not prepared for heaven. Assurance came in a dream where Christ placed his hand on her head and told her, "Fear not."

Ellen and her family suffered through the great disappointment, but in December, 1844, just after her 17th birthday, Ellen had her first vision. As she seemed to rise above the earth she saw Jesus leading a weary group along a narrow path. The Lord was still with the faithful adventists, in spite of their mistaken prophecy, and those who maintained faith in the second advent would not be disappointed. She related her vision to some adventists in Portland, Maine; then a second vision ordered her to continue sharing the message with others.

Accompanied by a sister, the timid semiinvalid began a tour of Millerite companies in eastern Maine, thus hoping to preserve an adventist remnant. James White, a young adventist preacher, agreed to escort the two of them. Time was too short to think about personal friendship, least of all marriage, yet rumors of impropriety followed them, and so in August 1846, Ellen Gould Harmon became the bride of James White.

Christ in the Heavenly Sanctuary

The saving feature of Ellen White's new message was the claim that Miller's prediction was correct with respect to date, but wrong as to place. He had been deceived by church tradition which understood the cleansing of the sanctuary to mean the purification of the earth at the Lord's coming. Rather, Christ as the great high priest entered the sanctuary of the heavenly tabernacle to begin a period of "investigative judgment."

This was indeed a clever argument to save the adventist movement. White "proved" her point by stringing together a number of texts. In her most comprehensive book *The Great Controversy* (1971 edition, hereafter GC) she comments, for example:

> The coming of Christ as our high priest to the most holy place, for the cleansing of the sanctuary, brought to view in Daniel 8:14; the coming of the Son of man to the Ancient of Days, as presented on Daniel 7:13; and the coming of the Lord to His temple, foretold by Malachi, are descriptions of the same event; and this is also represented by the coming of the bridegroom to the marriage, described by Christ in the parable of the ten virgins, of Matthew 25 (GC, p. 376).

Difficulties of Ellen White's View

But this argument proves nothing because White has used the same old prooftexting method which led Miller and Darby down their blind alleys. A study of the contexts of these verses indicates a variety of different situations from those imagined by White. Some of the problems involved are as follows:

1. The 2,300 "evenings and mornings" of Dan. 8:14 refer to daily sacrifices in the temple and probably mean 1,150 days;
2. At most, 2,300 days were intended, not years. It is not valid to argue that because the disbelieving Israelites suffered a year for each of the 40 days the spies were in Canaan (Num. 14:34), that a day equals a year in Dan. 8:14;
3. Daniel 8 is the most clear-cut vision of the book and interpreters of various prophetic systems recognize that 8:13-14 refers to the desecration of the temple by Antiochus Epiphanes;
4. The prophecy was fulfilled when Judas Maccabeus cleansed the temple and restored animal sacrifices;

5. Furthermore, the term "sanctuary" involved the whole temple, especially the defiled altar, not just "the most holy place";

6. The cleansing was to atone for the sins of Antiochus and his Syrian army, not "the sins of penitent believers" (GC, p. 376);

7. When the Son of Man is presented before the Ancient of Days (Dan. 7:13) he is given the authority to rule over all the nations in the Messianic kingdom. There is no reference whatsoever to judgment in the holy of holies or to a marriage of the Son to the saints;

8. In Mal. 3:1, the temple to which the Lord will suddenly come is the one in Jerusalem. First, the messenger is to prepare for the Lord's coming by judging the priests (3:1-4) who have desecrated the temple by their lives and actions (1:6-2:9);

9. Then Yahweh will come to the cleansed temple to judge his sinful people (3:5). There isn't the slightest hint of a heavenly temple;

10. Mal. 3:1 is an introductory verse covering two phases of judgment, therefore the coming of the Lord to the temple is the same event as described in 3:5, not two separate events as White claims;

11. In the parable of the ten virgins or maidens (Matt. 25:1-13) the bridegroom, in good Palestinian style, comes to claim his bride at her home, where the feast is held. The midnight cry "Behold, the bridegroom!" is addressed to the maidens here on earth, and the faithful go into the marriage feast (25:10);

12. In order to have the marriage in heaven, White has to reinterpret 25:10: "They were not to be present in person at the marriage; for it takes place in heaven, while they are upon the earth. . . . But they are to understand His work, and to follow Him by faith as He goes in before God. It is in this sense that they are said to go in to marriage" (GC, pp. 377-38).

This is a formidable cluster of difficulties. It indicates that there is *not one bit of solid biblical evidence* to support the claim that in 1844 Christ entered the holy of holies in the heavenly temple. In short, *White has read into the text what she is attempting to prove*.

The Investigative Judgment

"The work of judgment which began in 1844," according to White, "must continue until the cases of all are decided, both of the living and the dead" (GC, p. 384). Concerning this phase, White comments:

> So when Christ entered the holy of holies to perform the closing work of the atonement, He ceased His ministration in the first apartment. But when the ministration in the first apartment ended, the ministration in the second apartment began. When in the typical service the high priest left the holy (place) on the Day of Atonement, he went in before God to present the blood of the sin offering in behalf of all Israel who truly repented of their sins. So Christ had only completed one part of his work as our intercessor, to enter upon another portion of his work, and He still pleaded His blood before the Father in behalf of sinners (GC, p. 379).

White, in other words, is taking the Day of Atonement (Leviticus 16) as a literal type of Christ's atoning activity. From the time of his ascension until 1844, he was in the holy place (first apartment) "in the presence of God to plead His blood in behalf of penitent believers" (*The Story of Patriarchs and Prophets*, p. 357). In 1844 he moved on into the holy of holies (most holy place, second apartment) where he is investigating the record of every person and completing the atonement of the penitent by blotting out their sins from the records. This two-stage atonement is as follows:

> The blood of Christ, while it was to release the repentant sinner from the condemnation of the law, was not to cancel the sin; it would stand on record in the sanctuary until the final atonement; so in the type the blood of the sin offering removed the sin from the penitent, but it rested in the sanctuary until the Day of Atonement (SPP, p. 357).

The Day of Atonement

Leviticus 16 is a complicated chapter with a long history of development, but *there is no indication that the high priest "blotted out" the sins of the people when he sprinkled the blood in the sanctuary* (holy place, holy of holies). The Hebrew word translated "make atonement" (16:6, 10, 16, 18, 30, 33, 34) is *kipper*, literally "cover over." *Yom Kippur* "Day of Atonement" is based on the same verb. Hebrew had the verb "blot out," but it was not used in Leviticus 16.

The same word *(kipper)* is used in Lev. 1:4: when a sinner brings an offering, "he shall lay his hand upon the head of the burnt offering, and it shall be accepted for him to make an atonement for him." This seems to say that atonement was complete when the priests shed the blood of the sacrificial animal to which the person's sins had been transferred.

The Day of Atonement cleansed the sanctuary, tent of meeting, altar, priests, and people (16:33). Apparently it covered any sins which had been overlooked during the year, and thus began a new year with complete forgiveness. There is no indication that individual atonement during the year was partial and had to be completed on the Day of Atonement.

The Two Goats

The rituals of the two goats seem to be early methods of atoning for sins. The goat which fell by lot to Yahweh was offered as a sin offering, thus atoning for the people's sins (16:8-9). Atonement was made also by confessing the sins upon the living goat (scapegoat), which was then driven out to the evil spirit or demon Azazel in the wilderness (16:10, 21).

Notice how White spins her own theory by inserting ideas not found in the biblical text:

A substitute was accepted in the sinner's stead; but the sin was not canceled by the blood of the victim. A means was thus provided by which it was transferred to the sanctuary. By the offering of blood the sinner acknowledged the authority of the law, confessed his guilt in transgression, and expressed his desire for pardon through faith in a Redeemer to come; but he was not yet entirely released from the condemnation of the law. On the Day of Atonement the high priest, having taken an offering from the congregation, went into the most holy place with the blood of the offering, and sprinkled it upon the mercy seat, directly over the law, to make satisfaction for its claims. Then, in his character of mediator, he took the sins upon himself and bore them from the sanctuary. Placing his hands upon the head of the scapegoat, he confessed over him all these sins, thus in figure transferring them from himself to the goat. The goat then bore them away, and they were regarded as forever separated from the people (GC, p. 371).

The Bible knows nothing about transferring of sins to the sanctuary, nor of the high priest bearing them from the holy of holies. It was impossible for all the people to place their hands on the head of the scapegoat; therefore in their behalf Aaron placed his hands on the goat and confessed all the iniquities, transgressions, and sins of the people of Israel (16:21). The Hebrew language was very capable of stating explicitly what White reads into the text. The fact that the text does not say it, is proof that the Old Testament never understood the process of atonement according to White's theory.

The Heavenly Sanctuary

The author of Hebrews believed, in typical Platonic fashion, that the earthly tabernacle and furnishings were copies of the originals in heaven. He, of all the New Testament writers, was the one who, had he thought so, would have mentioned Jesus' special ministry of removing the sins of the penitent from the records in the holy of holies. He states simply, "For Christ entered, not into a sanctuary made with hands, a copy of the true one, but into heaven itself, now to appear in the presence of God on our behalf" (9:24).

White attributes this verse to Paul and quotes it as proof of her interpretation, but again she has to read her view into the text. Moreover, the writer of Hebrews implies that atonement was complete with Christ's death: "He has appeared once for all at the end of the age to put away sin by the sacrifice of himself" (9:26). *White's theory is simply not biblical.*

What White does not explain, furthermore, is why Christ should have spent over 1,800 years in God's presence pleading for penitent sinners and leaving only a few years, according to her predictions, for the truly demanding task of reviewing the records of every human being. When all the evidence is taken into account, White's theory turns out to be *a very creative reinterpretation of Scripture which served to save the faces of Miller and the faithful remnant of adventists.*

The Ten Commandments

In addition to saving adventism, Ellen White's visions gave authority to Sabbath worship. Her prooftext was Rev. 11:19: "Then God's temple in heaven was opened, and the ark of his covenant was seen within his temple." Since the ark was in the holy of holies, which was entered only on the Day of Atonement, White claims that this verse was fulfilled in 1844 when Christ opened the most holy place to begin his final ministry.

But White saw more than the ark—she claimed to see the original Ten Commandments. Highlighted "in the very bosom of the Decalogue" was the 4th commandment: "Remember the sabbath day, to keep it holy" (Exod. 20:8). She comments:

The Spirit of God impressed the hearts of those students of His word. The conviction was urged upon them that they had ignorantly transgressed this precept by disregarding the Creator's rest day. They began to examine the reasons for observing the first day of the week instead of the day which God had sanctified. They could find no evidence in the Scriptures that the fourth commandment had been abolished, or that the Sabbath had been changed; the blessing which first hallowed the seventh day had never been removed (GC, p. 383).

The "students" were White's followers. You can be sure that it was she who "impressed" their hearts and "urged upon them" the conviction about the Sabbath. The authority for this conclusion was Matt. 5:18: "For truly , I say to you, till heaven and earth pass away, not an iota, not a dot, will pass from the law until all has been accomplished." White interpreted this verse to mean, "Not one commandment has been annulled; not a jot or tittle has been changed" (GC, p. 383). But this is not exactly what Jesus meant. Rather, so long as the heavens and the earth exist, so long will the law continue to work out or accomplish its purpose. Some portions of the law would achieve their purpose (for example, the ceremonial law) and so pass away. Jesus was *not* saying that all the law would continue until the heavens and earth would be dissolved.

The Lord's Day

In general, the church recognizes the validity of devoting a day to the Lord. The essence of the 4th commandment will be valid as long as human history continues. The real question is whether one must observe Saturday as "the day" in order to meet God's demands. There is no New Testament instruction to reject the Jewish sabbath. In fact, the early Christians, especially the Jewish church members, seem to have observed both the Jewish sabbath and the Lord's day.

But gradually, as the church became predominantly Gentile, the Lord's day superseded the sabbath. In his excellent book *The Lord's Day* (1971), Paul K. Jewett outlines the biblical and theological basis for Sunday worship. "Sunday observance," he comments, "is immediately anchored in the Easter event, more particularly in the first meeting of the risen Lord with his disciples as they were gathered at the time of the evening meal on Easter Sunday" (LD, p. 66). Jewett continues:

With minds enlightened to see the full implications of Jesus' lordship over the Sabbath by his resurrection from the dead, Christians commemorated that all-important event, which occurred on the first day of the week, by gathering on that day for table fellowship, as did the original disciples who ate and drank with him both on the night in which he was betrayed and in the evening of the day on which he rose from the dead (LD, p. 67).

The shift to Sunday morning worship began about A.D. 109 because of Roman restrictions on evening meetings. It is clear from Justin Martyr, however, that by A.D. 150 worship on Sunday morning was the normal practice of the church.

Revelation 14:6-12

Probably the key passage for Ellen and James White was Rev. 14:6-12. They believed with Miller that they were living in the time of the first angel's warning, "Fear God and give him glory, for the hour of his judgment has come" (14:7). But they felt that Miller was wrong in not stressing the messages of the other two angels and the final summary: "Here is a call for the endurance of the saints, those who keep the commandments of God and the faith of Jesus" (14:12). The catchword "commandments" triggered the idea of the 4th commandment of course.

The angel's second announcement was simple: "Fallen, fallen is Babylon the great, she who made all nations drink the wine of her impure passion" (14:8). White equated Babylon with the beast, the antichrist. "This symbol," she explains, "as most Protestants have believed, represents the papacy, which succeeded to the power and seat and authority once held by the ancient Roman Empire" (GC, p. 387). Since the power of the beast was to last for 3 1/2 years = 1,260 days, the papacy would rule 1,260 years. But again, there is no basis for taking days as years. Nevertheless, taking A.D. 538 as the start of the papacy's supremacy, the end of its power would be 1798. Wouldn't you know that that was the very year when the French army took the pope captive! The catch is that other equally valid dates can be claimed for the pope's supremacy.

Message of the Third Angel

The third angel declared that eternal torment was awaiting anyone who "worships the beast and its image, and receives a mark on his forehead or on his hand" (14:9-10). The counterpart of the antichrist was the other beast, the False Prophet, who rose from the land.

This meant, according to White, that "the nation thus represented must arise in territory previously unoccupied and grow up gradually and peacefully" (GC, p. 388). It could not happen in heavily occupied Europe, and guess what country in North America was rising in 1798? You're right! "One nation," White declares, "and only one meets the specifications of this prophecy; it points unmistakably to the United States of America" (GC, p. 388). What White didn't realize, apparently, is that she supplied all the "specifications." Again, she has made the biblical text read as she wanted it to.

The fact that the false prophet made the people worship the beast indicates, so White claims, "that the authority of this nation is to be exercised in enforcing some observance which shall be an act of homage to the papacy" (GC, p. 389). That observance is Sunday worship. "Roman Catholics acknowledge," comments White, "that the change of the Sabbath was made by their church, and declare that Protestants by observing the Sunday are recognizing her power" (GC, p. 394).

Ellen White shared with many Protestants of the 19th century a paranoia about the Roman Catholic Church. This fear had some basis and the RCs delighted in exploiting it. Their boast to have changed worship from Saturday to Sunday was simply an expression of their fallacious claim to the primacy of Peter. The Roman Church did not inaugurate the change; therefore worshiping on Sunday was not a recognition of Rome's power.

The Mark of the Beast

White's fear determined her interpretation of the beast and its image and mark. "What then is the change of the Sabbath," she comments, "but the sign, or mark of the authority of the Roman Church—'the mark of the beast'?" (GC, p. 395). Back of this fear was the conviction that Protestant America was siding with the Roman Catholic Church in a conspiracy to force all worship on Sunday. She explains, for example:

The "image of the beast" represents that form of apostate Protestantism which will be developed when the Protestant Churches shall seek the aid of the civil power for the enforcement of their dogmas. The "mark of the beast" still remains to be defined (GC, p. 392).

White acknowledges that "there are now true Christians in every church, not excepting the Roman Catholic communion, who honestly believe that Sunday is the Sabbath of divine appointment. God accepts their sincerity of purpose and their integrity before Him." But then she is so bold as to predict:

> But when Sunday observance shall be enforced by law, and the world shall be enlightened concerning the obligation of the true Sabbath, then whoever shall transgress the command of God, to obey a precept which has no higher authority than that of Rome, will thereby honor popery above God. He is paying homage to Rome and to the power which enforces the institution ordained by Rome. He is worshiping the beast and his image (GC, pp. 395-96).

In this prediction she is a false prophetess on two counts: (1) enforced Sunday observance has not materialized; and (2) the world has not been enlightened concerning the obligation of the true Sabbath. The indications today are that Protestantism hardly has enough concern to keep its own Sunday, let alone trying to force all Sabbath worshipers, whether Jewish or Christian, to observe Sunday.

In discussing the impending conflict, White's paranoia overflows:

> Those who honor the Bible Sabbath will be denounced as enemies of law and order, as breaking down the moral restraints of society, causing anarchy and corruption, and calling down the judgments of God upon the earth. Their conscientious scruples will be pronounced obstinacy, stubbornness, and contempt of authority. They will be accused of disaffection toward the government. Ministers who deny the obligation of the divine law will present from the pulpit the duty of yielding obedience to the civil authorities as ordained of God. In legislative halls and courts of justice, commandment keepers will be misrepresented and condemned. A false coloring will be given to their words; the worst construction will be put upon their motives.
>
> As Protestant churches reject the clear, Scriptural arguments in defense of God's law, they will long to silence those whose faith they cannot overthrow by the Bible. . . . The dignitaries of church and state will unite to bribe, persuade, or compel all classes to honor the Sunday (GC, p. 518).

Was Ellen G. White a Prophetess?

In her introduction to *The Great Controversy*, Ellen G. White openly claims, "Through the illumination of the Holy Spirit, the scenes of the long-continued conflict between good and evil have been opened to the writer of these pages" (GC, p. 13). She comments further, "As the Spirit of God has opened to my mind the great truths of His word, and the scenes of the past and the future, I have been bidden to make known to others that which has thus been revealed" (GC, p. 14).

She certainly had the basic characteristics of a prophet: (1) susceptible to visions; (2) a compelling call; and (3) the compulsion to share insights. On the back of the 1971 edition of GC, the SDA hierarchy makes the following claims, "She is considered to have been inspired by God. Many of her prophecies about world events and the modern-day condition of man have already been dramatically fulfilled. Her insights in the fields of medicine and nutrition are being progressively substantiated by scientific research."

Are There Prophets in the Modern Church?

The July, 1977, issue of *The Ministry*, the International Journal of the SDA Ministry, has an editorial and a 24-page insert with the title "Are There Prophets in the Modern Church?" Their answer is a resounding "Yes!" The editorial reaffirms the SDA conviction "that Ellen G. White was a recipient of the true gift of prophecy" (p. 2). In one of the articles in the insert, "The Prophets Were Until John," T. H. Blincoe notes that "prophecy" is listed among the gifts of the Spirit. Then he comments, "Paul places no time limit on these gifts. He gives no hint that any of them is to terminate at the close of the first century of the Christian era" (p. 24M).

New Testament prophecy had some short-range predictions such as those given by Agabus (Acts 11:28; 21:11). In general, however, prophecy consisted of insights making relevant for those times the truths of Scripture. This kind of secondary revelation occurred throughout the Old and New Testaments, and continues to this day. The church is in trouble without the inspiration of God to help interpret biblical truths.

Both Ellen White (Nov. 26, 1827-July 16, 1915) and John Wesley (June 17, 1703-Mar. 2, 1791) qualify as prophets in this sense.

Moreover, there are some basic similarities between the two. They had concern for people and their problems; were compulsive evangelists and travelers; wrote voluminously; helped thousands find Christ and lead productive lives; founded schools and other charitable institutions; organized denominations; poured their lives and wealth back into their organizations; and finally died in their 88th year.

The Tests of Prophecy

But White had a far more prophetic temperament and made more specific claims to having revelations from God. Yet she declared, "The Spirit was not given—nor can it ever be bestowed—to supersede the Bible; for the Scriptures explicitly state that the word of God is the standard by which all teaching and experience must be tested" (GC, p. 11). Time and again she and her followers claim that all her insights lead back to, and support, the biblical witness.

There is no doubt that these claims are sincere, but the only objective means of checking them is to apply the biblical tests of prophecy. In the article noted above, Blincoe concurs in this process: "Today Seventh-day Adventists still insist that the person, writings, and total ministry of Ellen G. White be tested by the Bible" (p. 240). He lists four tests, two in the Old Testament and two in the New Testament.

The New Testament checks are too general to be of any specific help. Many people believe that "Jesus Christ has come in the flesh" (1 Jn. 4:2) and their lives bear good fruit (Matt. 7:15-20), yet they would not qualify as prophets.

The underlying principle of Is. 8:19-20 is, according to Blincoe, "that the messages given by any true prophet must be in harmony with those given by the true prophets who preceded him" (p. 24M). In line with Deut. 18:21-22, Blincoe acknowledges, "Where there is prediction, fulfillment must follow and will follow if the foreteller is truly a prophet of God" (p. 24N).

Under a section heading "Tests Applied," Blincoe notes her first vision in Dec. 1844 and comments, "Some two thousand visions and dreams were to follow during the seventy years of her ministry" (p. 24N). He observes that she proved to her followers that she was biblical, but nowhere does he really attempt to apply the two tough Old Testament tests.

Accuracy of White's Predictions

In "Looking Ahead Through Eyes of Prophecy," another article in the insert of *The Ministry*, Hedwig Jemison summarizes some of White's predictions. But most of them are simply projections on the basis of her observations, experiences, and biblical understanding. Moreover, a number of them are expressed in terms which permit Jemison to read his knowledge of our time back into the predictions.

Predictions of anarchy and riots, trend to the cities, increase of corruption and sexual perversions, pollution of the air in cities, and recourse to cults and Oriental religions indicate an observant, insightful person, but these are hardly on the level of genuine biblical prophecy.

White claimed, "At times I am carried far ahead into the future and shown what is to take place" (*Spiritual Gifts*, Vol. 2, p. 292). In warning her readers against the evils of the Roman Church she declared, "And let it be remembered, it is the boast of Rome that she never changes" (GC, p. 508). Why didn't God show her the lovable Pope John 23rd and the changes which have swept across the Roman Church since Vatican II? Had this happened, then there would be some real authentication of her prophetic claims. Moreover, it would have saved her an awful lot of rambling diatribes against the Roman Catholics.

The plain fact is that her predictions are essentially in line with her prejudices. A prime exception is that her vegetarian convictions and nutritional predictions cut across her strong habit of meat eating. In connection with her biblical and political insights, however, she misses the mark more often than she hits it. In her paranoid summary of sufferings to come on Sabbath worshipers, there are at least eleven predictions and not one of them has been fulfilled against SDA as such.

There is no external way to prove or disprove that Christ entered the heavenly holy of holies in 1844 or that the 1755 Lisbon earthquake, the 1780 "dark day," and the 1833 meteorite shower were the signs mentioned by John in Revelation. It boils down to faith or credulity.

The place where genuine checks can be made is internal biblical evidence. White claims to be true to Scripture, and undoubtedly she thought she was. There is no deception here. The real question is whether her statement is true. Some of the most sincere people have been wrong. We have noted time and again how she reads her views into the biblical text, on one hand, and denies the clear teaching of the Bible, on the other. *The distinctives of her prophetic system are built on sand.* Every step of her argument has some difficulties, and when all these are added up they become insuperable.

Identity and Credibility

Although they come out with different findings, there is a similarity in the history of SDA and Dispensationalism. Miller and Darby were intelligent, devoted, pious Christians who had a long period of spiritual turmoil. But they started with the prooftexting method and the premise that all the pieces of the Bible fit together. In order to support their basic insights they had to fudge or cheat on other biblical data. This was not done willfully. Rather, they were so enamored of their own ideas, which they attributed to the Holy Spirit, their focus was entirely on the evidence which supported their views.

The same can be said for White and Scofield. They too were intelligent people, but they were using defective presuppositions and methods. The history of prophetic interpretation shows that *there is no completely satisfactory answer to the puzzle.* Hundreds of committed Christians, assured of the Holy Spirit's guidance, have started out with the same biblical data and produced different systems with hundreds of inner variants.

Those who cut their teeth on these traditions absorb the basic arguments without realizing the difficulties involved. But when open-minded young people learn how to think and work inductively, they begin to lose their naivete. Whether the hierarchy encourages it or not, thoughtful persons in every generation go through a crisis concerning the credibility of their mother church.

It is ironic that the distinctive teachings which gave rise to SDA and Dispensationalism are among the most fallacious of their doctrines. They cannot stand the test of objective, critical scrutiny. But both groups separated from traditional Christianity because of these views; therefore they sustain them in order to justify their reason for being. No matter what the evidence, White *must* be a prophetess because she is the authority back of the church's understanding of the "seventh-day" and "adventism."

The Voice of Prophecy

Harold Marshall Sylvester Richards has been the recognized "dean of Adventist preachers." While listening to the 1924 presidential election returns, he realized the potential of radio for an evangelistic ministry. Although thirty at the time, he made plans to implement his goal. He moved to California in 1926 and began his radio ministry with occasional broadcasts over local stations. From this simple beginning H. M. S. Richards became "The Voice of Prophecy" with a world-wide outreach.

In his book *One World* (1972), Richards states his prophetic views. They are essentially those of Ellen White. The prophetic signs of 1755, 1780, and 1833 are still valid. The papacy is still the antichrist. Richards notes that one of the papal titles *Vicarius Filius Dei* adds up to 666. The same fixation about the Roman Church is there, but some of White's alarms are toned down. The messages of the three angels of Rev. 14 are crucial for our time and the sign of apostasy is still Sunday worship. Richards is cautious, but comments:

> This predicted reception of the mark of the beast is still future. Some sort of international law or agreement certainly will be required. Those who heed such a demand will dishonor God and break his command. Then it is that man will receive the mark (OW, p. 250).

The 7 plagues, which have not yet begun, will "fall upon the unrepentant after probation is closed. When they are completed, God's children will be taken from this world at the second coming of Christ" (OW, p. 285). Richards warns against the popular views of Armageddon:

> The books entirely given to the explanation of the prophecies of Daniel and Revelation should be carefully read. The popular idea of the battle of Armageddon, as it is usually called, may be far different from its true prophetic meaning in the Holy Bible (OW, p. 287).

Christ's second advent will be visible to everyone. There is no secret rapture. But since the Christians will be taken out of the world and the wicked smitten at Christ's coming, the earth will be uninhabited during the millennium (OW, p. 300). After the overthrow of Satan and the final judgment, the New Jerusalem returns to a purified earth.

Although the 7 plagues have not occurred yet, Richards believes that they will soon:

World conditions and rapidly developing political, scientific, natural, religious, and moral crises show that we must be approaching some vast and tremendous change. We should be listening to Bible prophecy with careful ears. It is our belief that the prophecies of the Bible indicate the imminent return of Christ to our world (OW, p. 287).

This brings us back to the same old question: How soon is soon or imminent? Ellen believed sincerely that Christ would return in her lifetime and although she said so for 70 years, she was wrong. Richards picked up the same theme and proclaimed it for over 50 years. Now his son is doing the same. It is the same kind of addiction which afflicts Lindsey. Although Richards has never been flamboyant like Lindsey, over the decades he has persistently proclaimed the imminent return of the Lord.

What kind of mentality is it that can keep psyched up enough to continue making proclamations when years of history witness that previous pronouncements are wrong? The will to believe keeps insisting that conditions are so bad we "must" be approaching the end. Practically every generation has had reasons to think so. One would think that with a batting average of .000, the prophetic addicts would shift over to the real "good news" of what Christ can do for us here and now, but apparently the determination to be right, drives them to continue "the great disappointment."

Chapter 18
The Blessed Hope

The scope of our study has been limited to views of persons and groups considered to be within the Christian community. A good deal of ground has been covered in the seventeen chapters thus far, but actually we have just scratched the surface of current material related to prophecy and prediction. In addition to voluminous leaflets, articles, books, and films from independent and free-lance promoters, both Christian and quasi-Christian, there are many new and revived cults. P.T. Barnum was on target when he observed that a sucker was born every minute. If anything, he was too conservative in his estimate. Millions of innocent lambs are duped and fleeced every year by theological quacks with overdoses of ego, personality, and self-confidence.

In most areas of life there are governmental standards to protect the consumer, but this is not true in religion. It is one of the most lucrative rackets today, and most certainly it is the safest. As long as the racketeers stay clean with respect to the Internal Revenue Service and financial dealings, they can commit all kinds of psychological and spiritual mayhem without a finger being laid on them.

Prophecy and the Cults

It would take two or three more books to cover all the prophetic ideas afloat in the cults today. Fortunately, William J. Petersen's excellent paperback *Those Curious New Cults* deals with some of the prophetic aspects of the more recent groups. Two thriving cults formed in the 19th century are the "Church of Jesus Christ of Latter-Day Saints" (known as Mormons) and the "Jehovah's Witnesses." Prophecy and prediction played a key role in their formation.

Mormonism and Jehovah's Witnesses

The "prophet" Joseph Smith (1805-1844) claimed to receive visions and revelations from God. The angel Moroni revealed where the "Golden Plates," written in "reformed Egyptian," had been hidden since A.D. 420. With the aid of "Urim and Thummim," provided by

Moroni, he translated the inscriptions and then returned the Plates to the angel. The result of this complex revelation was the *Book of Mormon*.

In the fall of 1948 a so-called copy of portions of the text on the Plates was sent to Dr. W. F. Albright of The Johns Hopkins University because some Mormon officials in Salt Lake City had heard that he was an expert in "reformed Egyptian." I was studying with him at the time for my Ph.D., and he hesitated for weeks to inform them that the copy was a fraudulent mishmash of letters from different alphabets known at the time Smith got his revelation. Every objective investigation of Mormon claims has shown them to be false.

"Pastor" Charles Taze Russell (1852-1916), the founder of the "Jehovah's Witnesses," boldly claimed that Jesus had him in mind specifically when he spoke of "that faithful and wise servant whom his lord hath set over his household to give them their food in due season" (Matt. 24:45). As one supposedly gifted with revelatory insight, the "Pastor" boasted that no one really understood the Book of Revelation until he came along. But sheer impudence does not have the power to convert fantasy into truth, and so his followers still have the problem of trying to authenticate their founder and his teachings.

Modern Clairvoyants

One of the most interesting and controversial of the modern prophets has been the clairvoyant Edward Cayce (1877-1945). His Association for Research and Enlightenment preserves in a data bank and on 200,000 topic cards the psychic phenomena of his claims and predictions. He had some hits and some horrendous misses. He thought, for example, that Hitler was "essentially good."

More recent clairvoyants include the late spiritualist Arthur Ford and two of his confidants, Ruth Montgomery and Jeane Dixon. Their predictions have been accurate at times, but often they were expressed in such general terms, or else mixed with qualifications, that it is difficult to prove erroneous projections. Evidently there are as few .400 hitters in modern prophecy as in modern baseball.

Armstrong's Worldwide Church of God

One of the most successful movements in our time is the Worldwide Church of God, founded in 1934 by Herbert W. Armstrong and promoted widely by his gifted son Garner Ted. The true gospel of Jesus Christ was stamped out by the Romans in A.D. 69, according to Armstrong. The church made its appearance again on the first Sunday in 1934, when Armstrong issued his publication *The Plain Truth* and began broadcasting his program "The World Tomorrow."

He claims, for example, that he has been the answer to biblical prophecy. With arrogance worthy of "Pastor" Russell, he brags:

> On the first Sunday in 1934, God's time had come. God opened a DOOR. Jesus Christ himself had foretold this event. Millions have read His prophecy. . . . What really occurred that Sunday morning, precisely at ten o'clock, was a momentous event. It was the fulfilling of a definite cornerstone prophecy of Jesus. More than that, it was the initial, start-off event of the fulfilling of some 90 percent of all the prophecies in the Bible. And approximately a third of the whole Bible is prophecy.

How is that for modesty!

British Israelism and Pyramidology

Among Armstrong's special views is his belief in British-Israelism, a view that considers Britain and the United States as the lost ten tribes of Israel. In the first place, not all of the ten tribes were lost, and in the second place, it is not true that the term "British" derives from the Hebrew words *berit* "covenant" and *ish* "man." In Herbert Armstrong's book *The United States and the British Commonwealth in Prophecy* every statement or prophecy about Ephraim and Manasseh, the Joseph tribes, is twisted to predict current events concerning Britain and the United States.

In recent years the British base for this aberration has been the Institute of Pyramidology, founded by Adam Rutherford. The belief in the prophetic dimensions of Cheops' Pyramid goes hand-in-hand with British-Israelism. The idea goes back to John Taylor's *The Great Pyramid* (1859). Oddly enough, the famous astronomer Charles Piazzi Smyth (1819-1900) was seduced by Taylor's theory. He went to Egypt to study the pyramid, and published *Our Inheritance in the Great Pyramid* (1864), which became the Bible for pyramidologists.

Sir Flinders Petrie, the father of modern archaeology was sent to Egypt by his father in order to confirm Smyth's researches. He soon noted how much the measurements of the various passages and rooms had been fudged and how contradictory the whole scheme was. While he became an avowed enemy of pyramidology, he began a long, fruitful life as an archaeologist. Cheops' predictions for 1936, 1941, and 1944 missed the mark, but the credulous faithful continue the postponement game played by all the other false prophets.

Cheops and Spaceships

Speaking of Cheops' Pyramid brings to mind the strange prophecy of the Swiss author Erich von Däniken. In his *Chariots of the Gods?* (1970), which rivals Lindsey's *The Late Great Planet Earth* in sales, he claims that sophisticated beings from outer space invaded the earth and built the great pyramid. His major "proof" is the following claim:

> Today, in the twentieth century, no architect could build a copy of the pyramid of Cheops, even if the technical resources of every continent were at his disposal (p. 78).

This completely untenable statement is indicative of von Däniken's lack of sophistication and training. Concerning a large wall painting found at Tassili, in the Sahara, he comments, "Without overstretching my imagination, I got the impression that the great God Mars is depicted in a space or diving suit" (p. 31). After reading *Chariots* and its sequel *Gods from Outer Space*, it is evident that *nothing* could "overstretch" von Däniken's imagination.

A NASA engineer Josef F. Blumrich set out to disprove von Däniken's claim that Ezekiel's visions in 1:4-28 were of spaceships which landed near him and took him for a ride (CG, pp. 37-39). In the Foreword of his *The Spaceships of Ezekiel* (1974), Blumrich confesses that he became a convert: "Seldom has a total defeat been so rewarding, so fascinating, and so delightful." But as is the case with all these so-called scientific predictions, the information and specifications are supplied by the imagination of the interpreter. *Scientific expertise and biblical naivete are sure to produce freak children.* Blumrich is simply one up on those visionaries who have found such mundane items as radios, cars, etc. in the Bible.

The Validity of Apocalyptic

We have noted the rise of such eschatological themes as God's kingdom and the return to Eden, and then observed their reinterpretation in the context of apocalyptic despair of history. We have seen that the New Testament picks up some of these same themes as well as having the expectancy of Christ's imminent return. Are all these hopes invalid because they have failed to materialize during the last 1,900 years? Extreme critical scholars answer, "Yes."

There is no doubt, as we have commented many times, that a number of the details do not fit; therefore it is unwise to be dogmatic about specifics. But what about Christ's second coming? Is this too dreamy to be taken seriously? Is it hopeless to think in terms of a world free from hunger, poverty, disease, tears, and death? This hope runs through Scripture, and although the reasons for rejecting this dream are obvious, I cannot bring myself to deny it. This exercise of faith may seem credulous, but it rests in the conviction that the biblical hope is more than Alexander Pope's "Hope springs eternal in the human breast." The God of Israel and Father of our Lord, Jesus Christ, has this goal for his creatures.

No Operation "Bootstraps"

Some optimists, both Christian and secular, share the dream of earthly bliss, but they believe that it will be achieved through a long process of human development. They point to evidence indicating that there is more maturity and justice in the world today than ever before. There is some basis for this claim and I think we do well to acknowledge it.

The reason this fact is not readily recognized is because the media bombard us with the injustices of our time while seldom comparing them with the massive injustices of previous centuries. Notwithstanding all the sorrow and misery since World War II, for example, cool heads and warm hearts have contained a hundred and one fires which previously would have spread to destructive proportions.

The evidence is decidedly mixed, however. There are indications that some human beings are more depraved and demonic than ever. Whether this is qualitatively true can be debated, but there is little doubt that the modern means of multiplying and intensifying evil make it true quantitatively.

Those optimists who think that humanity will raise itself completely by its own bootstraps have not taken seriously enough the biblical pessimism concerning human nature. The irrationality of evil was a mystery to Jeremiah, but he could not deny the fact: "The heart is deceitful above all things, and desperately corrupt" (17:9). Two thousand six hundred years of history support the ancient prophet. There will be improvement in certain areas of human activity, but the intractability of human sin witnesses against the possibility of Operation "Bootstraps." If the biblical hopes are ever realized, it will be because of God's activity in conjunction with the second coming of Jesus Christ.

"Jesus Is Coming Soon!"

The biblical theme of Christ's imminent return is commonplace today among such prophetic pushers as Salem Kirban, C. S. Lovett, Tim LaHaye, and John Wesley White. Although Billy Graham has written no book on prophecy, he has preached on the theme in practically all of his campaigns. He used to proclaim very openly "Jesus is coming soon," but when he passed the 25th anniversary of his evangelistic ministry the "soon" tended to fade out. Nevertheless, his commitment to the standard conservative eschatology is evident in his films. *His Land*, a glorification of modern Israel, set the tone for *The Return, The Rapture, A Thief in the Night, The Temple,* and *The Road to Armageddon.*

The Validity of Signs

Usually the claims of the modern prophets are supported by recourse to the biblical signs. Since these are supposedly being fulfilled, the time of the end must be near. Vernard Eller, as we have noted, is absolutely opposed to this "time-clock" or, as he puts it, "calendarizing" approach to Scripture. Yet he recognizes a biblical problem:

Here, then, is a double theme, rooted in the teaching of Jesus but permeating the New Testament as a whole. The "surprise" element, of course, accords very well with the basic counsel of perpetual readiness. However, the "time is short" element is another matter. . . .

In the first place, the "time is short" element then stands in direct conflict with its counterpart "surprise" element. How are we to handle that? In the second place, if these truly are calendar claims, then they are all *false* claims and all these writers were just plain wrong; they said something was going to happen "very soon," and it still hasn't happened almost two thousand years later (*The Most Revealing Book of the Bible*, hereafter MRBB, pp. 19-20).

The Time Is Short

Eller's answer to the calendarizers is as follows:

If we peg the idea as originating in the teaching of Jesus and then trace it through Paul, the writing of the Gospels themselves, and on down into the later epistles and writings, then we have documentary evidence that the expectation was current in the church during almost every decade from A.D. 30 on to the end of the century. Yet, through this period, writers could continue to state the expectation (and readers continue to accept it) without apparent difficulty over the fact that their predecessors had been stating the same expectation for some time—a time that was stretching out to something like seventy years. Clearly, the statement about the shortnss of the time was not being understood as a calendarizing claim—that would have forced the unavoidable conclusion that too many leaders had been too wrong too often (MRBB, p. 20).

Then Eller suggests:

It may be that these different writers were meaning to say, "*For all we know*, the time is short," or "Although we have absolutely no 'knowledge,' we ought always *to assume* that the time is short (and be ready to go on assuming that as long as necessary)." This would be a proper way of describing and fostering perpetual readiness: "Precisely because I don't know, I had better operate under the continual assumption that the time is short" (MRBB, p. 20).

In conjunction with this subjective description of "soonness," Eller thinks each biblical writer had an objective basis in God's history of redemption:

. . . he is looking *back*, there to see all that God *already has done* in the way of bringing his promise to fulfillment; . . . No matter what the dates or times which the Father has set within his own control, it is evident that the 'distance' (i.e., what needs yet to take place) between what God has done and what yet must happen is short; the end could come at any time; the time indeed is short (MRBB, p. 21).

Then Eller continues:

And note well, this is a statement Jesus could make in his day and it be entirely true and proper. Paul can make the same statement some years later; it is still just as true and proper. Seventy years after Jesus it can be made again—still true and proper. We can make it today, as the centuries stretch into millennia—still just as true and proper as it was in the mouth of Jesus. Indeed, the obligation of the church is to keep on making that statement until the end itself closes off the words. It is when the church fails to announce that the time is short that she has fallen away from the truth of the matter (MRBB, p. 21).

New Testament Expectancy

But Eller's sophisticated argument has tried to prove too much. In his concern to preserve a vital sense of expectancy he has slipped into an armchair approach, which does not do justice to some of the biblical evidence. His dialectical reasoning seems very convincing to him, but it is far too subtle for the New Testament writers. It is *not* true that from A.D. 30 to 100 the church accepted the expectation of Christ's return "without apparent difficulty." In Paul's early ministry he expected the Lord's return soon. He thought it was unwise to get married because family responsibilities would distract from the more urgent concerns of last times (1 Cor. 7:25-28). His literal belief in Christ's imminent return is even more evident in 7:29, 31:

> . . . the appointed time has grown very short; from now on, let those who have wives live as though they had none, . . . and those who deal with the world as though they had no dealings with it. For the form of this world is passing away.

Just because the New Testament writers never discuss the consequences of those early disappointments of hope is no justification for assuming that there were none. It is implicit in Paul's later letters that he had to ease the moratorium on normal human existence. The early church did not live according to Paul's "emergency ethic" from A.D. 55 until 100. There must have been a continuing series of adjustments similar to those in the Millerite-SDA tradition.

Moreover, not all the "scoffers" were outside the Christian community. Invariably, those who "have the truth" think that those countering them are "scoffers." The scribes and Pharisees were assured that they had the correct interpretation. When Jesus refuted their understanding of Scripture and came back with "But I say to you," he was considered a "scoffer." He had challenged the conservative tradition of his day. Many so-called scoffers in ancient times and ours have been persons with insight who were turned off by the hypocrisy of traditional Christianity. The issue of truth is the only criterion for determining a genuine scoffer.

One of the clearest evidences of a theological shift is the Gospel of John. This is preeminently "the gospel of deferred hope." The term "kingdom," associated so closely with Christ's rule, occurs only five times: twice in Jesus' discourse with Nicodemus (3:3, 5) and three times in his reply to Pilate (18:36). John's theme is "eternal life," a present reality in spite of Christ's failure to return (3:15-16).

The plain fact is that there is plenty of New Testament data for the calendarizers. The most straightforward and satisfactory approach is to recognize that that point of view occurs in the Bible, but that it was not valid then and therefore it is unwise to follow it now!

The Psychological Problem of Expectancy

In summarizing his argument for "eschatological expectancy," Eller declares:

> Our study has demonstrated that a sense of eschatological expectancy permeated the entire New Testament church and its literature. Further, although we have not done so, it would be easy to show that every aspect of that church's life and thought was driven by the motor of such expectancy. This eschatological expectancy was both the motivation and the content of Jesus' preaching, service ministry, and atoning work. It is the basis of the New Testament ethical teaching. It was the source of the early church's life and the explanation of her distinctive character. It was the dynamic and definition of her mission in the world (MRBB, pp. 21-22).

From this understanding Eller draws the following conclusion: "contemporary Christianity is truly Christian only insofar as it shares this eschatological expectancy" (MRBB, p. 22).

But there are serious drawbacks to this attempt to retrieve New Testament expectancy. In the first place, we have the perspective of 1,900 more years of history. There is no way we can literally repeat their experience while living in the 20th century. In the second place, Eller seems to be saying that Christians will not function meaningfully and up to par without this eschatological expectancy.

This argument, however, is somewhat analogous to the incentive of a greyhound race. The hope of Christ's soon return, like the mechanical rabbit, is always tantalizingly close, although not actualized. We have noted that some people are wired in such a way that they, like the greyhounds, can chase the rabbit day after day without any diminishing of zeal. Apparently they have the ability to blot out previous experience.

But most people cannot play this game without becoming discouraged and disillusioned: "Hope deferred makes the heart sick" (Prov. 13:12). Either they are given a more realistic goal or else they drop out in disgust. Rarely do the faithful take into account the tremendous fallout caused by their game of "let's pretend." *In evaluating the totality of life and its experiences, the minusses must be subtracted from the plusses.*

While conservatives are experts at putting notches in their theological barrels when winning converts, they suffer from amnesia when it comes to reckoning with the psychological and spiritual harm of their overzealous, proselyting techniques while anticipating the Lord's coming. It was a prophetic zealot who set the El Aksa Mosque on fire in 1969. He was convinced that he was doing God a favor by speeding up the schedule for completion of the Jerusalem temple and the resumption of animal sacrifices.

What Does "Watch" Mean?

What do we do with the biblical commands to be watchful (Matt. 25:13; Mk. 13:33, etc.)? We must interpret them in conjunction with Christ's other commands. In the parable of the talents (Matt. 25:14-30) and the parable of the pounds (Lk. 19:12-27) the emphasis is on the effective use of the money until the master returns. In Lk. 19:13, Jesus' instructions are, "Trade with these till I come." The KJV has "Occupy till I come," therefore the traditional exhortations have been "Watch" and "Occupy."

If the "watch" element takes precedence, there is the danger of growing weary and copping out of the difficult tasks, or of becoming preoccupied by looking ahead and thus ignoring more pressing issues at hand. What makes the prophetic craze so pernicious is that those hooked think they are really being pious. In many instances this infection is a case of "the Agatha Christie syndrome." Most of the prophetic addicts love to solve mysteries, but they don't dare waste time reading secular mysteries by Agatha Christie, etc. Therefore, they satisfy their inclination by working on biblical mysteries. Yet the time spent on such futile efforts is time which could be spent more effectively. Lindsey is convinced that *Satan Is Alive and Well on Planet Earth* because evil and falsehood are so prevalent. If untruth is a sign of Satan's presence, then he is hiding also in the systems of Lindsey and many other conservatives.

Mature Christianity and the Blessed Hope

The issue of one's personal eschaton is relevant to the question of the second coming of Christ. Theoretically, any given day could be our last, and because of this we should be prepared for such a possibility whether or not Christ returns. Yet the probabilities are that life will continue for a number of months or years.

The focus of a mature Christian experience is Christ's command to seek first God's kingdom and his righteousness (Matt. 6:33). This commitment is made more explicit by Christ's commission:

> Go therefore and make disciples of all nations, baptizing them in the name of the Father and of the Son and of the Holy Spirit, teaching them to observe all that I have commanded you; and lo, I am with you always, to the close of the age (Matt. 28:19-20).

Paul uses an OT analogy to make his exhortation: "I appeal to you therefore, . . . to present your bodies as a living sacrifice, holy and acceptable to God, which is your spiritual worship" (Rom. 12:1).

For this demanding call, Paul offers two refreshing assurances. When problems and temptations seem insurmountable, he declares, "No temptation has overtaken you that is not common to man. God is faithful, and he will not let you be tempted beyond your strength, but with the temptation will also provide a way of escape, that you may be able to endure it" (1 Cor. 10:13).

When evil, both human and natural, seems to wipe out our dreams and hard work, Paul consoles, "We know that in everything God works for good with those who love him and are called according to his purpose" (Rom. 8:28).

This is the kind of commitment and assurance which will never disappoint. Nor will it be fearful, because faith is anchored in him who has power over body and soul (Matt. 10:28). Thus, "whether we live or whether we die, we are the Lord's" (Rom. 14:8). *This is the blessed hope!*

This is the "good news" which insecure, frightened, suffering humanity needs to hear. It reckons with the worst this life can offer and it prepares for the life to come. The task of sharing the good news and helping the powerless is a joyful challenge which is valid as long as life exists. There is no need for rationalizations to shore up broken hopes.

Even in the first century, when "soon" was taken literally, Scripture indicates that they watched by spreading the good news. When mission, both evangelical and service, is paramount, there is the sense of watchfulness and preparedness which is ready for either the personal or the earthly eschaton.

BIBLIOGRAPHY

Allis, Oswald T. *Prophecy and the Church.* Philadelphia: Presbyterian & Reformed Publishing Co., 1945. Second Printing, 1947.

Berkouwer, G. C. *The Return of Christ.* Grand Rapids: Wm. B. Eerdmans Publishing Co., 1972.

Bruce, F. F. *Biblical Exegesis in the Qumran Texts.* Grand Rapids: Wm. B. Eerdmans Publishing Co., 1959.

Charles, Robert H. *A Critical and Exegetical Commentary on the Book of Daniel.* Oxford: Clarendon Press, 1929.

———— *A Critical and Exegetical Commentary on the Revelation of St. John.* Edinburgh: T. & T. Clark, 1920; reprinted 1950, 2 vols.

———— *Eschatology.* New York: Schocken Books, 1963.

Clouse, Robert G., Editor. *The Meaning of the Millennium: Four Views.* Downers Grove: InterVarsity Press, 1977.

Eller, Vernard. *The Most Revealing Book of the Bible.* Grand Rapids: Wm. B. Eerdmans Publishing Co., 1974.

English, E. Schuyler, Editor. *The New Scofield Reference Bible.* New York: Oxford University Press, 1967.

Fuller, Daniel P. *The Hermeneutics of Dispensationalism.* Chicago: Northern Baptist Theological Seminary, Th.D. Dissertation, 1966.

Hanson, Paul D. *The Dawn of Apocalyptic.* Philadelphia: Fortress Press, 1975.

Hasel, Gerhard F. "The Seventy Weeks of Daniel 9:24-27," supplement of *The Ministry*, May 1976.

Jewett, Paul K. *The Lord's Day.* Grand Rapids: Wm. B. Eerdmans Publishing Co., 1971.

Ladd, George Eldon. *The Last Things.* Grand Rapids: Wm. B. Eerdmans Publishing Co., 1978.

Lindblom, J. *Prophecy in Ancient Israel.* Philadelphia: Fortress Press, 1962.

Lindsey, Hal. *The Late Great Planet Earth.* Grand Rapids: Zondervan Publishing House, 1970.

———— *Satan is Alive and Well on Planet Earth.* Grand Rapids: Zondervan Publishing House, 1972.

———— *There's a New World Coming.* Santa Ana: Vision House Publishers, 1973.

Machen, J. Gresham. *The Virgin Birth of Christ.* New York: Harper & Row, 1930.

The Ministry, supplement of July, 1977. "Are There Prophets in the Modern Church?"

Montgomery, James Alan. *A Critical and Exegetical Commentary on the Book of Daniel.* Edinburgh: T. & T. Clark, 1927.

Morris, Leon. *Apocalyptic.* Grand Rapids: Wm. B. Eerdmans Publishing Co., 1972.

Nichol, Francis D. *The Midnight Cry.* Washington: Review and Herald Publishing Association, 1944.

Payne, J. Barton. *Encyclopedia of Biblical Prophecy.* New York: Harper & Row, 1973.

Richards, H. M. S. *One World.* Washington: Review and Herald Publishing Association, 1972.

Scofield, C. I. *The Scofield Reference Bible.* New York: Oxford University Press, 1917.

White, Ellen G. *The Great Controversy.* Mountain View: Pacific Press, 1971.

_____ *The Story of Patriarchs and Prophets.* Mountain View: Pacific Press, 1958.

Young, Edward J. *The Prophecy of Daniel.* Grand Rapids: Wm. B. Eerdmans Publishing Co., 1949.

GENERAL INDEX

Boldface page numbers indicate a major entry—that is, a direct and substantial discussion of a topic. Minor entries are indicated by regular type; they are brief references without detailed discussion. All biblical references, no matter how incidental, have been included.

Aaron
—and prophet's role 7
Adventism, Seventh Day
—history **224-44**
Ahab
—and Elijah 14-16
—and Micaiah 18-19
Ahad Ha^cam see Ginzberg, Asher
Ahaz
—and Isaiah **35-37**
Ahijah
—political role 13-14
Albright, W. F.
—interprets *Book of Mormon* 246
—*From Stone Age to Christianity* 210-11
Allis, Oswald T.
—*Prophecy and the Church* 179, 181
^calmah
—meaning **37-39**
Amos
—prophetic vision **20-21**
Antichrist
—in Lindsey's system **214-16**, 220-21
—in Revelation 142, 144, 150, 152
Antiochus Epiphanes
—in Daniel's prophecy 95-97, **101-2, 110, 114-15, 120-21**
antitype
—defined 167
apocalyptic
—defined **89-90**
apocalyptic prophecy
—in Daniel **100-21**
—in Ezekiel **122-23**
—in Matthew **128-33**
—in Revelation **137-56**
—in Zechariah **123-28**

Armageddon
—Lindsey's interpretation 210, **217-21**
—in Revelation 147, 150
Armstrong, Garner Ted
—Worldwide Church of God 246-47
Armstrong, Herbert W.
—Worldwide Church of God **246-47**
—*The United States and the British Commonwealth in Prophecy* 247
Association for Research and Enlightenment
—purpose 246
Atonement, Day of
—Ellen White's interpretation **232-34**
Augustine
—authority for Dispensationalists 166
—millennium, interpretation 4
Averni, Uri
—*Israel without Zionists* 205

Baal
—prophets, in Ahab's court 14-15
Babylon
—fall, in Revelation **147-49**
Balaam
—and ecstasy 10-11
Balfour, Arthur James
—and Zionist movement 193, 195
Balfour Declaration
—conditions 193, 195
beasts, in Revelation
—analysis of vision **144-45, 147-48, 150-52**
—Lindsey's interpretation 216-17
Begin, Menachem
—role in Palestine civil war 196-97

SCRIPTURAL INDEX